The Longman Companion to

America in the Era of the Two World Wars, 1910–1945

Longman Companions to History

General Editors: Chris Cook and John Stevenson

Now available

THE LONGMAN COMPANION TO THE TUDOR AGE
Rosemary O'Day

THE LONGMAN COMPANION TO NAPOLEONIC EUROPE
Clive Emsley

THE LONGMAN COMPANION TO EUROPEAN NATIONALISM, 1789–1920
Raymond Pearson

THE LONGMAN COMPANION TO AMERICA IN THE ERA OF THE TWO WORLD WARS, 1910–1945
Patrick Renshaw

THE LONGMAN COMPANION TO THE MIDDLE EAST SINCE 1914
Ritchie Ovendale

THE LONGMAN COMPANION TO BRITAIN IN THE ERA OF THE TWO WORLD WARS, 1914–45
Andrew Thorpe

THE LONGMAN COMPANION TO COLD WAR AND DETENTE, 1941–91
John W. Young

THE LONGMAN COMPANION TO NAZI GERMANY
Tim Kirk

THE LONGMAN COMPANION TO BRITAIN SINCE 1945
Chris Cook and John Stevenson

The Longman Companion to

America in the Era of the Two World Wars, 1910–1945

Patrick Renshaw

Longman
London and New York

Longman Group Limited,
Longman House, Burnt Mill,
Harlow, Essex CM20 2JE, England
and Associated Companies throughout the world.

Published in the United States of America
by Longman Publishing, New York

First published 1996

ISBN 0 582 09116 0 CSD
ISBN 0 582 09115 2 PPR

British Library Cataloguing-in-Publication Data
A catalogue record for this book is
available from the British Library

Library of Congress Cataloging-in-Publication Data
Renshaw, Patrick, 1936–
The Longman companion to America in the era of the two world wars, 1910–1945 / Patrick Renshaw.
p. cm. – (Longman companions to history)
Includes bibliographical references (p.) and index.
ISBN 0-582-09116-0. – ISBN 0-582-09115-2 (pbk.)
1. United States–History–1901–1953. I. Title. II. Series.
E741.R45 1996
973.91–dc 20 95-23386
CIP

Set by 7LL in 10/11pt New Baskerville
Produced by Longman Singapore Publishers (Pte) Ltd.
Printed in Singapore

In loving memory of my son Richard,
born 3 June 1973 died 9 June 1994

You are my sunshine,
My only sunshine,
You make me happy
When skies are gray.
You'll never know, dear,
How much I love you.
Please don't take my sunshine away

The other night, dear,
As I lay sleeping,
I dreamt that you were by my side.
Came disillusion
When I awoke, dear,
You were gone
And then I cried.

You Are My Sunshine
(*by Jimmy Davis, Governor of Louisiana 1960–64*)

Contents

Acknowledgements

This is not the kind of book which I ever expected to write, so my first obligation is to thank John Stevenson for suggesting that I do so. He also advised me how to set about it, read early drafts and made critical yet encouraging comments. The Department of History, Sheffield University, granted me study leave in autumn 1993, when I started the book, and the British Academy gave a generous award from their small grants fund. Colleagues at the department provided, as always, an excellent environment for work. Particular thanks go to: fellow Americanists Richard Carwardine, Robert Cook and Richard Thurlow; Stephen Salter and Mary Vincent, for help on European aspects of the tale told here; Mark Greengrass for crucial advice on organizing the research; and my former student Jack Hunt, for reference checking. I also owe a very great debt to my research assistant Steve Griffiths, without whom it is true to say this book would not have been written. He discussed its structure with me, did all the early library searching and wrote a substantial portion of the first chronologies, which I could then edit and expand.

The major reference works from which much of the information contained in this book was extracted are listed in the Introduction.

Finally, my deepest debt is to my wife Mary, especially for the love and courage she showed when our son Richard died as this book was being written.

Patrick Renshaw
Sheffield, 26 April 1995

We are grateful to Peermusic (UK) Ltd for permission to reproduce an extract from 'You are my Sunshine' (Davis/Mitchell) ©1941 Peer International Corporation, USA/Peermusic (UK) Ltd.

The publishers would like to thank Martin Gilbert author of *American History Atlas* and Routledge publishers for granting us permission to reproduce maps 2–5.

Introduction

Between 1910 and 1945 America moved from being a world power to holding a position of dominance in global political, economic and financial affairs without parallel in modern history. How and why this happened is a story as fascinating as it is important, and I hope readers will find this book, as it is intended to be, a useful companion to that wider theme.

Although based on a lifetime's study of twentieth-century American history, the text does not rest on original research but on many other, longer reference books. Of these, Arthur M. Schlesinger, ed., *The Almanac of American History* (New York, 1983) and Charles van Doren and Robert McHenry, eds, *Webster's Guide to American History* (Springfield, Mass., 1971) were the most useful.

The chronology in Section I covers domestic events between 1910 and 1945 in detail, combining them with diplomatic and foreign policy after 1940. Section II details US imperialism and foreign policy between 1910 and 1940. Section III treats the most significant cases involving civil liberties and major Supreme Court decisions from 1910 to 1945.

During the period covered by this book, the United States transformed itself from a nation which was still predominantly agricultural into the industrial and financial powerhouse of the capitalist world. Section IV is designed to show how this happened, mostly through the use of statistical tables. These have all been compiled from US Department of Commerce, Bureau of the Census, *Historical Statistics of the United States* (Washington DC, 1975).

In Section V, the main Cabinet officers, US Supreme Court justices and leaders of Congress between 1910 and 1945, derived from Erik W. Austin, *Political Facts of the United States since 1789* (New York, 1986) are listed. Section VI contains brief biographies of key figures in American life during this period, much of which data can be found in Allen Johnson and others, *The American Dictionary of National Biography* (New York, 1928–1980) and *Who Was Who in America*, vols I and II 1897–1942 and 1943–1950 (Chicago 1943 and 1963), including the supplements to both publications.

Maps in Section VII showing US presidential election returns between 1916 and 1944 are taken from Samuel Lubell, *The Future of American Politics* (New York, 1965). Those showing the scope of the Tennessee Valley Authority after 1933 and Allied advances in Europe

1944–45 and in the Pacific between 1941 and 1945 are based on maps in Martin Gilbert's, *American History Atlas* (London, 1968).

I had hoped to include something on two of my great loves, jazz and cinema. Jazz is a uniquely American form of music which swept the world between 1910 and 1945, while millions from other nations took their view of the US from Hollywood and the movie screen. However, I somewhat reluctantly concluded that, like sport, other aspects of popular culture and the arts, they could not be treated adequately in a book of this scope.

I am especially grateful to Peermusic (UK) Ltd, publishers of the song *You Are My Sunshine* for permission to use in the dedication a lyric my son loved while he was alive. Finally, the bibliographical essay which concludes the book provides a starting point for those who wish to go further.

Author's note on spelling

The text of this book follows standard English spelling, as in the word 'labour'. Quotations are in standard American usage, as in 'program'. US place-names and institutions retain their American spellings, for example Pearl Harbor and Defense Department.

SECTION I

Chronology, 1910–1945

1. The Climax of Progressivism, 1910–14

This domestic chronology is combined with diplomatic and foreign policy plus military events after 1940. Section II covers foreign policy in detail between 1910 and 1940.

1910

January Gifford Pinchot removed from forestry service after criticizing Richard Ballinger, secretary of the interior, for selling Alaskan coalfields under public land for private re-sale. Conservation re-emerges as a political issue between 1910 and 1945.

Consequent political scandal unites Democrats with insurgent Republicans and tempts Theodore Roosevelt back from retirement to seek presidency in 1912.

18 January United States grants Britain most favoured nation status under Payne-Aldrich tariff system.

March President William Taft, senator Nelson Aldrich of Rhode Island and House of Representatives speaker Joseph Cannon combine to try to defeat insurgent Progressives of both parties in forthcoming Spring primary elections, but popular opinion moves against them between 1910 and 1912.

19 March Coalition of Democrats and insurgent Progressive Republicans, led by the Nebraskan George Norris, oust speaker Cannon from crucial House rules committee, depriving him of power of patronage.

19 March United States grants France most favoured nation status.

20 March President Taft meets Canadian finance minister to discuss adjustment of Payne-Aldrich tariff in Canada's favour.

18 June United States Congress passes Mann-Elkins Act, which has much more Progressive content than watered-down measure originally supported by Taft. It imposes extensive regulatory conditions and enforcement on railroad companies.

25 June Creation of Postal Savings Bank system, which empowers federal post offices to receive funds and pay interest.

Congress partially restores presidential power to protect public lands from entry.

15 July Woodrow Wilson formally announces acceptance of

New Jersey gubernatorial nomination, after approaches by Democratic state bosses. Since death of New Jersey Democratic leader Leon Abbett, and the race track scandal of 1893, Republicans had controlled New Jersey.

31 August Theodore Roosevelt first publicly enunciates his 'New Nationalism' political programme, aimed at establishing genuine equality of opportunity. Methods include:

- elimination of corporate expenditures for political uses
- physical valuation of railroad properties
- regulation of industrial combines
- appointment of an expert tariff commission
- graduated income and inheritance taxes
- reorganization of national financial system
- legislative regulation of labour of women and children
- complete publicity of campaign expenditures.

15 September Meeting at Trenton, New Jersey. Democratic state convention nominates Woodrow Wilson as candidate for governorship. He immediately gains national prominence.

September–November Wilson's campaign, containing 27 speeches, marks gradual drift towards political left.

20 October Wilson resigns as president of Princeton.

8 November In Congressional and gubernatorial elections, the House of Representatives falls under Democrat control for the first time since 1892. Many traditionally Republican governorships in the east and midwest fall into Democratic hands.

Wilson elected governor of New Jersey by a *plurality* of nearly 50,000 over the next candidate (Taft had carried New Jersey in winning the White House in 1908 by a *majority* of over 80,000 over all candidates).

6 December President Taft's second annual message announces intention to complete Panama Canal 1914, and requests Congress to furnish $20 million for its defence.

Andrew Carnegie transfers $10 million to a board of trustees to promote world peace and 'to hasten the abolition of international war' through what became the Carnegie Endowment for International Peace.

1911

10 January US Navy reprimands commander John Sims for a speech in London, on 3 December 1910, saying that the US would render immediate aid to the British Empire if attacked.

17 January Woodrow Wilson beomes 43rd governor of New Jersey. His inaugural address stresses imperative need for social and economic reform.

21 January Republican insurgents form National Progressive League, publishing platform of progressive legislation.

26 January President Taft sends Congress joint resolution on reciprocal trade agreement with Canada, reducing tariffs on various manufactured goods and raw materials. Senate's refusal to act prompts Taft to call special session of Congress.

6 March Richard Ballinger resigns as secretary of the interior under pressure of public criticism following Ballinger/Pinchot affair.

10 March Governor Wilson in effect opens his campaign for the 1912 presidential election with a speech in Atlanta in his home state of Georgia. In May he is endorsed by William Jennings Bryan, Democratic candidate in 1896, 1900 and 1908.

25 March New Yorker Triangle shirtwaist fire kills 147 and injures 184 young women garment workers.

19 April Wilson signs Geran Act, stipulating direct primary nomination of all elected officials and delegates to national conventions, and outlawing various corrupt practices.

20 April Wilson signs full corrupt practices Act for New Jersey, placing limits on campaign expenditure and barring contributions by corporations or persons owning majority stock in a corporation.

21 April With Democratic support, the Canadian trade agreement approved by the House (by Senate on 22 July). Canadian voters reject agreement on 21 September.

New Jersey's Osborne-Egan Act passes, representing United States' most thorough example to date of public utilities regulation.

New Jersey's Walsh-Leavitt Act makes provision for adoption by municipalities of the commission form of government, with initiative, referendum and recall establishing greater popular accountability. Governor Wilson launches statewide fight in favour of the commission, in bid to defeat bossism. By August 1911, New Jersey's Progressive Democrats control state party machine.

15 May In an anti-trust suit, US Supreme Court upholds dissolution of Standard Oil of New Jersey. Standard, which controlled 90 per cent of the nation's oil refining industry through its New Jersey holding company, is ordered to divest itself of all subsidiaries within 30 days.

29 May Formal dissolution of the America Tobacco Company of New Jersey.

August United States Congressional bill to reduce Payne-Aldrich tariff is vetoed by president Taft.

26 October Suit filed by US attorney general George Wickersham on behalf of federal government against US Steel seeking to reverse its allegedly monopolistic purchase of Tennessee Coal and Iron in 1907.

7 November Governor Wilson suffers reverse in New Jersey state elections, with Republicans regaining majorities in both houses of the legislature. Wilson declines to provide legislative leadership.

24 November First meeting of Woodrow Wilson and colonel Edward M. House in New York. House is to become Wilson's White House chief-of-staff.

3 December John D. Rockefeller, aged 72, resigns presidency and directorship of Standard Oil, which is widely seen as another victory for anti-trust movement.

8 December Joint army and navy board conclude that the battleship *Maine*, whose sinking in Havana harbour in 1898 precipitated the Spanish–American war, was blown up by a mine placed in the water, not inside the warship by Americans.

1912

16 January United States warns Cuban government it will invade unless Cuba's presidential election is peacefully conducted.

January–June Democratic party primaries and campaign for presidential nomination. Principal contenders:

- Woodrow Wilson. Espoused almost every available Progressive tenet, with hostile oratorical flourishes directed against monopolistic practices, but usually leaving ample room for tactical withdrawal from such positions: a vague, idealistic, almost meaningless, yet popular appeal.
- Champ Clark (Missouri). Democratic party House leader 1909–11, and speaker since 1911. A loyal Bryanist, in appearance an old-fashioned country politician, he could point to a long and consistent Progressive record, backing civil service reform, free trade, anti-trust legislation and so forth. After sweeping Illinois on 9 April, he emerges as strongest candidate with a near simple majority as the convention approaches.
- Oscar W. Underwood (Alabama). First bid by a resident southerner to win Democratic party nomination since 1860, uniting disparate conservative elements in hostility against the rising tide of Progressivism in the south.

24 February Theodore Roosevelt says he will accept Republican party presidential nomination if offered, responding to a prearranged appeal from several Republican governors.

March–May Overwhelming victories for Roosevelt in the thirteen states which held primaries, including Taft's native Ohio, but Taft firmly controls Republican south and Old Guard states like New York, as well as the national committee which organize the convention in June.

7 April Floods in the Mississippi Valley make 30,000 homeless.

15 April British transatlantic liner, the *Titanic* which its owners White Star called unsinkable, strikes an iceberg on its maiden voyage and is lost with more than 1,500 lives, including millionaire J.J. Astor and journalist W.T. Stead.

12 May Socialist party convention in Indianapolis, nominates Eugene V. Debs (rail workers' leader and SP candidate in 1900, 1904 and 1908) for president with Emil Seidel, mayor of Milwaukee, as his running mate.

30 May Wilbur Wright, pioneer of powered aircraft, dies aged 45 at his home town of Dayton, Ohio.

5 June In Cuba, 450 American marines land to safeguard US property against Afro-Caribbean revolt.

18–22 June At the Republican party convention in Chicago, Taft is renominated with 561 votes, Roosevelt ordering his 344 delegates not to vote. They march out of the hall to hear Roosevelt announce his own candidacy in 'Bull Moose' campaign.

25 June–2 July At the Democratic party convention in Baltimore, Champ Clark gains overall majority, but the customary surge to the required two-thirds fails to occur as Underwood's vote stands firm. Wilson slowly gains ground, and is nominated on the 46th ballot when Underwood withdraws. Underwood declines the vice-presidential nomination, which then goes to Riley Marshall in return for his decisive delivery of Indiana's vote.

10 July–9 August Congress passes Panama Canal Act, which includes toll-free use of the canal for American coastal ships.

5–12 August Roosevelt's Progressive party convention, attended by a host of distinguished reformers, nominates him and governor Hiram W. Johnson of California.

August–November Presidential campaign. With the Republicans split, Wilson and Roosevelt are clear front-runners from the start. Wilson's *New Freedom* sought to restore free enterprise through legal destruction and prohibition of monopolies and trusts, while Roosevelt's *New Nationalism* regarded them as inescapable, efficient and even desirable if carefully regulated and controlled by law.

14 October Roosevelt shot and wounded by saloon-keeper John Nepomuk Schrank while stepping into his campaign car in Milwaukee. However, the former president goes on to address a large audience with the bullet lodged in his chest.

British foreign office protests over the exemption of US coastal shipping from payment of Panama Canal tolls.

30 October Taft's vice-president J.S. Sherman dies.

5 November Election day sees Wilson win a victory which had been in little doubt since October. Roosevelt attracts midwestern Republican Progressives, but fails to win core Republican votes, or deprive Wilson of southern support, while many conservative Republicans vote for Wilson to keep out Roosevelt. President Taft wins only 24 per cent of the popular vote, Wilson 42 per cent.

Democrats win control of House and Senate but rely on southern support, with senior conservative Democrats controlling congressional committees. In addition, southerners take more than half Wilson's cabinet posts.

31 December President-elect Wilson confers with Oscar Underwood, now chairman of crucial House Ways and Means Committee, about tariff reduction.

1913

6 January Supreme Court rules that any attempt to corner a commodity violates 1890 Sherman Anti-Trust Act.

20 January Stung by Roosevelt's taunts that, despite his electioneering rhetoric, he had done nothing to revise New Jersey's corporation laws, president-elect Wilson unveils seven anti-monopolistic bills ('the Seven Sisters') and sends them to New Jersey legislature. The key bill, forbidding formation of new industrial holding companies, becomes law on 19 February.

18 February Victoriano Huerta seizes power in Mexico.

24 February Congress passes bill empowering president-elect Wilson to create a separate department of labor.

25 February Wilson resigns his governorship of New Jersey.

26 February Colonel House assures Wall Street that forthcoming Wilson administration will not launch an onslaught on big business.

28 February Pujo committee report reveals precise details of powerful concentrations of money and credit in the hands of a small circle of bankers led by J.P. Morgan. Trusts are further exposed to public criticism.

2 March Seaman's bill, drawn up by International Seaman's Union president Andrew Furnseth to improve maritime safety and seamen's working conditions, wins Senate approval, only to be met by President Taft's pocket veto.

4 March President Wilson inaugurated.

12 March Wilson calls Congress into special session for 7 April.

15 March Wilson's first presidential press conference. Despite his awareness of the value of good public relations, Wilson's relationship with the press proves miserable. He was to abandon press conferences after June 1915.

18 March Wilson prohibits US involvement in banking consortium to fund Chinese railway construction, on grounds that the scheme would impair Chinese sovereignty.

8 April United States recognizes new Republic of China and, in attempt to distance itself from such imperialistic conspiracies as the financing of the Hukuang Railway by which western nations were exploiting China's disintegration, fails to consult other powers first.

Wilson addresses both houses of Congress in person to deliver a message recommending tariff reduction, breaking the precedent established by Thomas Jefferson of refraining from such appearances on grounds that they resembled the royal speech from the throne.

10 April A strike of streetcar workers in Buffalo leads to serious rioting and three deaths.

11 April Wilson gives tacit approval to full-scale racial segregation of United States civil service proposed in cabinet by postmaster general Albert Burleson.

22 April Underwood bill is presented to Congress, proposing significant reduction in scope and rates of existing Payne-Aldrich tariff.

8 May House approves Underwood bill: only five Democrats, alienated by its free sugar and wool provisions, vote against it.

9 May Californian legislature bars Japanese-Americans from land ownership in the state.

13 May Three American warships are ordered to the Philippines, in case of feared Japanese surprise attack.

26 May In a public statement, Wilson condemns hordes of lobbyists descending on Washington DC to win alterations to the tariff bill.

31 May The 16th and 17th Amendments to the Constitution (sent to the states by Taft on 15 May 1912) are ratified, calling for federal income tax and direct election of US senators.

2 June Wilson's attack on lobbying against tariff reduction is vindicated by heavily critical report on lobbying interests issued by Congressional select committee chaired by Albert Cummins of Ohio.

26 June Bill introduced simultaneously into both Houses to create Federal Reserve which will act as US central bank.

7 July Congressional Democrats vote to make tariff bill a party measure.

14 July Anti-American demonstrations staged in Mexico.

22 July Factory fire in Binghamton, New York, kills 25 girls.

4 August United States ambassador to Mexico resigns.

9 September Senate approves the Underwood Act, which Wilson signs on 3 October.

10 October Demolition of the Gamboa Dyke, last obstruction on the line of the Panama Canal.

23 October Senate approves a second Seaman's bill, in wake of the burning of liner *Volturno* off Newfoundland on 9 October with heavy loss of life.

4 November Tammany Hall defeated in New York city elections. Insurgent Democrat J.P. Mitchell elected mayor by largest majority ever recorded.

19 December After much debate and confusion, Senate passes much-revised version of the original Federal Reserve bill, creating machinery for more extensive central control of US banking and currency system.

1914

7 January First vessel passes through Panama Canal.

20 January President Wilson appears before joint session of Congress to announce policy of 'quiet moderation' towards big business.

31 January Post Office report urges gradual nationalization of all telephone and telegraph facilities.

3 February Wilson revokes Taft's arms embargo hoping Huerta government will lose Mexican civil war.

4 February House passes immigration restriction bill introduced by congressman John L. Burnett.

15 February House passes Keating-Owen model minimum age child labour bill by 233 votes to 43, but Wilson fails to back it and the bill later founders under Republican and conservative Democrat opposition in Senate.

31 March House approves Sims bill, repealing exemption provisions of the Panama Canal Act, by 247 votes to 162.

14 April Henry D. Clayton of Alabama, chairman of House Judiciary Committee, introduces the Clayton bill. This seeks to add teeth to 1890 Sherman Anti-Trust Act by listing and defining illegal practices in restraint of free trade.

20 April National guardsmen fire on families of coalminers striking against John D. Rockefeller at Ludlow, Colorado, and set fire to their tented camp, killing 17 women and children. The *New York Times* calls the Ludlow massacre, 'Worse than the order that sent the Light Brigade into the jaws of death, worse in its effect than the Black Hole of Calcutta.'

21 April Wilson orders US troops to occupy Veracruz, Mexico.

8 May Smith-Lever Act provides federal funds for agricultural extension work through land-grant colleges under department of agriculture.

16 May Introduction of Covington bill into the House, aimed at establishing effective interstate trade commission in place of Bureau of Commerce.

20 May–2 July US and Mexican delegates meet at Niagara Falls in attempt to mediate over American occupation of Veracruz.

1 June Josephus Daniels, secretary of the navy, prohibits officers drinking any alcoholic beverages aboard navy vessels or in navy yards and stations. This order had covered enlisted men since 1899.

1–2 June Clayton bill, designed to give legal status to trade unions, is amended in Congress, partially exempting industrial and farm workers from its scope.

11 June Senate passes Sims bill by 50 votes to 35, striking down American ships' exemption from Panama Canal tolls.

12 June Introduction of the Stevens bill, a measure ultimately incorporated into the Covington Act, establishing much-strengthened federal trade commission to oversee fair trade practices.

28 June Archduke Franz Ferdinand, heir to Austro-Hungarian throne, assassinated at Sarajevo by Gavrilo Princip, a Bosnian Serb, setting in train events which led to outbreak of First World War.

15 July President Victoriano Huerta of Mexico abdicates in favour of the constitutionalist Venustiano Carranza.

28 July Austria-Hungary declares war on Serbia.

30 July Tsar Nicholas II of Russia orders general mobilization of Russian army.

31 July New York stock exchange closes, after the imminent onset of war sends prices tumbling by an average five points the previous day.

1 August Germany declares war on Russia.

3 August Germany declares war on France.

4 August Britain declares war on Germany and Austria-Hungary, the Central Powers.

5 August Bryan-Chamorro treaty grants United States exclusive concession to build canal through Nicaragua, plus other territorial advantages.

15 August Panama Canal opened to world commerce.

Prohibition of loans to European belligerents issued by secretary of commerce William McAdoo.

18 August Wilson issues presidential declaration of US neutrality in European war.

Congress approves Act permitting foreign ships to sail under American flag, in response to Wilson's appeal of 31 July.

23 September Insurgent general 'Pancho' Villa leads rebellion in Mexico.

26 September Wilson signs the Federal Trade Commission Act.

15 October Clayton Act, in much weakened form, passes after Wilson deserts it in Senate.

3 November Mid-term Congressional elections disappoint Democrats, whose majority in House slips from 73 to 25, the Republicans regaining power in key states like Illinois, New York and Pennsylvania.

12 November Wilson tells delegation led by Boston editor and African-American leader William Monroe Trotter that segregation is wholly beneficial to blacks.

20 November Britain declares maritime blockade by order-in-council providing for capture of neutral ships on the high seas when enemy destination could be inferred 'from any sufficient evidence', and permitting capture of conditional contraband sent to a neutral port but destined for the Central Powers. This blockade caused great US–British friction between 1914 and 1917. At the same time, by reducing US trade with the Central Powers from $170 million in 1914 to $1.1 million in 1916, and increasing US trade with the Allies in the same period from $8 million to $13 billion, the blockade effectively made the US an Allied warehouse and meant America could not contemplate Allied defeat.

23 November United States evacuates Veracruz.

8 December Wilson's annual message reaffirms US neutrality in European war.

31 December Bill for complete nationalization of telephone and telegraph introduced in Congress, but with no effective presidential support it quickly dies in committee.

2. War and Peace, 1915–19

1915

2 January Senate passes Burnett immigration restriction bill, incorporating a literacy test, by 50 votes to 7.

30 January–5 June Colonel Edward M. House, Wilson's chief-of-staff, makes first voyage to Europe in attempt to broker peace.

28 January Wilson vetoes Burnett immigration bill.

4 February Germany announces retaliatory naval war zone around British Isles.

18 February United States announces Germany would be held to 'strict accountability' for loss of American property or life caused by naval blockade of Britain.

4 March Wilson signs Seaman's Act into law.

11 March Britain imposes interdiction on all neutral commerce, including that of the United States, to Germany.

28 March German submarine sinks British liner *Falaba* with death of one American citizen.

1 May German embassy formally warns American citizens against travelling on belligerent merchant vessels.

7 May German submarine torpedoes British liner *Lusitania* with loss of 1,198 lives, including 128 Americans. Bryce report suggests deliberate German atrocity campaign in Belgium.

11 May Navy demands Congress be called into session to vote $500 million for naval expansion.

28 July Wilson orders US occupation of Caribbean island of Haiti.

19 August Sinking of White Star liner *Arabic*, with loss of two American citizens.

1 September German written promise that liners would not be sunk by German submarines without prior warning.

October 1915–May 1916 Dispute over military preparedness. Wilson approves plan on 15 October to enlarge regular army and replace national guard with a continental army of 400,000, controlled by war department. Senatorial committeemen, however, have no wish to grant war department absolute command over a reserve force. Ensuing deadlock compels Wilson to accept compromise of federalizing national guard which forces Lindley Garrison to resign as secretary of war on 10 February 1916. By 13

May a compromise bill has been approved, doubling the regular army to well over 200,000 men, federally integrating national guard, and permitting war department to construct a nitrate plant.

19 October US extends *de facto* recognition of Carranza government in Mexico.

4 November Wilson announces major shipbuilding and army expansion programme, prompting strong anti-preparedness reaction.

19 November Joe Hill, Swedish immigrant migratory worker, member of the radical Industrial Workers of the World, and writer of scores of world-famous satirical songs about the labour movement, is shot after conviction for murder in an unsatisfactory trial. 'Don't waste time mourning', he writes, 'Organize!'

December Publication of reports detailing German subversive activities in Mexico and United States.

Formation of pro-intervention American Rights Committee in New York.

1916

January–November In bid to lure former Progressives into the Democratic party camp, and thus assure re-election in forthcoming presidential campaign, Wilson seeks to demonstrate beyond doubt that his party has entirely cast off former *laissez-faire* principles with a series of advanced Progressive measures.

6 January Colonel Edward House arrives in London on his second peace mission to Europe.

11 January Sixteen American citizens murdered by Pancho Villa supporters on a train at Santa Ysabel, Mexico.

14 January Wilson backs an independent tariff commission, advocated by Theodore Roosevelt and the Progressives in 1912, supposedly in order to remove the tariff issue from politics. The measure is incorporated into the Revenue Act in September 1916.

25 January Wilson threatens to sever relations with Germany unless the latter admits illegality of the *Lusitania* torpedoeing.

27 January–4 February Western tour by Wilson to stimulate popular support for military preparedness.

28 January Presidential appointment of Louis D. Brandeis to the Supreme Court. Conservatives bitterly oppose appointment because Brandeis is Jewish, a leading exponent of social and economic reform and an unreconstructed trust-buster. But Brandeis serves until the end of 1939, becoming one of the most distinguished justices in the Court's history.

31 January Introduction of administration's new shipping bill into the House, aimed at creating US Shipping Board to construct merchant ships for use as naval auxiliaries, to operate shipping lanes and regulate rates.

2 February Keating-Owen child labour bill (see 15 February 1914 above) passed by House, with a handful of dissenting southern textile votes.

10 February German government announces intention, from 29 February, to attack armed merchant ships without warning.

Secretary of war Lindley M. Garrison resigns when Wilson drops plans for continental army.

7 March House rejects McLemore resolution, warning Americans against travelling on armed belligerent ships, by 276 votes to 142.

Newton D. Baker appointed secretary of war.

9 March 'Border bandits' raid on Columbus, New Mexico, by forces of Mexican Pancho Villa kills 19 Americans.

18 March Wilson dispatches punitive expedition under general John Pershing into Mexico in response to Columbus raid.

24 March German Navy sinks unarmed French cross channel packet *Sussex* with 80 casualties.

12 April US and Mexican government troops skirmish at Parral, northern Mexico.

18 April Wilson issues stern note advising Germany to abandon its war against unarmed passenger ships.

24 April Easter Rising in Ireland. Its crushing by British forces and the execution of its leaders anger many Irish-Americans.

4 May Hollis-Bulkley rural credits bill passes Senate. Only shortage of time saved Wilson from vetoing an earlier, more radical version of the measure in February 1915. However, after a White House conference in January 1916, Wilson agrees to adopt bill as an administration measure.

Germany declares its submarines will henceforth adhere to the rules of stop and search with regard to merchant vessels.

13 May Adoption of bill doubling size of regular army and federalizing national guard.

15 May Rural credits bill is passed almost unanimously by the House.

US troops occupy Dominican Republic.

20 May House adopts shipping bill.

1 June Senate confirms Brandeis's appointment to Supreme Court.

7–10 June Republican party convention meets in Chicago. Main contenders are *Theodore Roosevelt* and *Charles Evans Hughes.* The latter bears impressive Progressive credentials. Having sprung to public attention for relentlessly leading investigations into New York utilities and insurance trusts, he had been elected New York governor in 1906 and 1908, and been part of the Progressive minority on the Supreme Court between 1910 and 1916.

Roosevelt assembles his own embattled Progressives in bid to blackmail Republican convention into nominating him, but Hughes is nominated on the third ballot with Charles W. Fairbanks of Indiana as his running mate.

In desperation, spurned Progressives who took part in 1912 Bull Moose campaign, nominate Roosevelt, who declines.

14–16 June Democratic party convention meets in St Louis. Wilson approaches convention confident of renomination. His platform openly appeals to Progressive voters, promising further social legislation, neutral foreign policy, female suffrage and US entry into a postwar League of Nations committed to peace by collective security.

Initially rather flat, the convention erupts into a series of frenzied demonstrations in favour of pacifism, crowning Wilson as the president who stood for US rights without costing a single American mother her husband or sons. Renomination by acclaim ensues.

21 June US and Mexican government troops clash at Carrizal, with 23 Americans captured.

26 June Progressive party disbanded by its national committee, on Roosevelt's instructions.

11 July Federal Highway Act authorizes federal aid to states for road construction.

July–November Presidential election campaign. Wilson's championing of social justice and bold defence of the Adamson Act (see 3 September below) contrasts favourably with Hughes's equivocation and lack of positive ideas. Independent Progressives move *en masse* into the Democratic camp, along with virtually the entire former leadership of the Progressive party. Wilson's successful coalition also includes organized labour, farm groups and most of the independent press, including the *New York Times* and the *New Republic*.

17 July Wilson signs Farm Loan Act, establishing 12 Farm Loan Banks to provide long-term credit through cooperative farm loan associations.

18 July Warned that independent Progressives regard the fate of the Keating-Owen child labor bill as a mark of his administration's true commitment to reform, Wilson urges Democratic Senate leaders to ensure the bill's safe passage. Senate adopts measure on 8 August.

19 July British government issues blacklist of US firms with which British subjects are forbidden to trade.

11 August Warehouse Act brings national licensing and inspection of agricultural warehouses with receipts acceptable to the Federal Reserve System as collateral on loans to farmers.

19 August Kern-McGillicuddy bill, drafted by American Association for Labor Legislation and offering workmen's compensation to half a million federal employees, passed by Congress.

29 August Jones Act grants Philippines what is in effect dominion status, with its own elective senate, but ultimate sovereignty is reserved by US.

1 September Wilson signs Keating-Owen Child Labor Act, banning from interstate commerce goods manufactured by child labour.

3 September Adamson Act grants eight-hour working day on interstate railways.

6 September Senate adopts revenue bill, increasing income tax and a range of other taxes.

7 September Wilson signs Workmen's Compensation Act, which gives the federal government some responsibility for accident insurance, and a Shipping Act, which effectively creates the US merchant marine.

6 September–15 January Unsuccessful attempt by US and Mexican commissioners to reach agreement over US punitive expedition in Mexico.

30 September In a speech at Shadow Lawn, Wilson first thrusts pacifism to the fore of his re-election campaign, alleging that a Hughes victory would mean involvement in the European conflict. 'He kept us out of war' becomes Democratic election slogan.

7 November Election day. After early returns show Republican sweep in the east, Wilson achieves the narrowest popular vote victory between 1912 and 1948, by gaining nearly 3 million votes more than in 1912, and uniting south and west in an appeal for peace and Progressivism. (See Map 1a.)

27 November Federal Reserve Board advises banking house J.P. Morgan not to invest in unsecured and renewable short-term bills of French and British treasuries, issued to pay for European war.

12 December Germany issues invitation to Allies, via the US, to open peace negotiations.

18 December Wilson issues note requesting that Allied powers state their war aims.

30 December Allied governments reject German peace proposals.

1917

22 January Wilson outlines vision of 'peace without victory', incorporatimg postwar League of Nations.

27 January United States agrees to withdraw troops from Mexico.

31 January Germany announces resumption of all-out submarine war.

3 February Wilson tells Congress of formal break in diplomatic relations with Germany.

25 February British secret service sends intercepted Zimmerman telegram to Washington DC, containing encoded instructions to German minister in Mexico urging Mexico to attack United States in alliance with Germany. Released to the press 1 March.

26 February Wilson asks Congress for permission to arm US merchant ships and to assert any other means of protecting US vessels and people.

1 March Congress approves armed ship bill by 403 votes to 1.

3 March Revenue Act increases direct tax burden.

13 March US grants Carranza government in Mexico *de jure* recognition.

18 March Without warning, German submarine sinks three American merchant vessels: *City of Memphis, Illinois,* and *Vigilancia.*

31 March US government buys Virgin Islands for $25 million from Dutch.

Munitions Standards Board established and shortly General Munitions Board.

2 April Wilson asks joint session of Congress to support his formal declaration of war on Germany.

6 April House approves Wilson's declaration of war with Germany by 434 votes to 1.

10–11 April By agreement with Britain and France, US navy to patrol western hemisphere.

13 April Committee on public information to whip up war fever and establish voluntary press censorship, under George Creel, is created after mayoral elections in New York and other cities reveal distinct lack of popular enthusiasm for war.

16 April Emergency Fleet Corporation chartered.

23 April First War Loan Act.

24 April Congress appropriates $7 billion for war expenditure, $3 billion earmarked for Allied governments.

18 May Selective Service Act establishes national conscription for men over 21 and authorizes president to accept up to 500,000 volunteers. More than 9.5 million men register for service by 5 June.

May Wilson establishes Food Control Program, headed by Herbert Hoover.

15 June Espionage Act allows mail censorship and harsh penalties for unpatriotic deeds or words.

July Adoption of convoy system for Atlantic crossings.

28 July General Munitions Board abolished and replaced by War Industries Board.

3 August Edward Hurley, new head of Emergency Fleet Corporation, commandeers 431 ships under private construction in private shipyards.

10 August Lever Act confers on Wilson wide-ranging presidential powers over commodities and prices.

31 August Conscription age limits expanded to cover men aged between 18 and 45.

5 September Arrest and subsequent imprisonment for long terms of more than 160 leaders of the Industrial Workers of the World (IWW), an anarcho-syndicalist labour union.

3 October War Revenue bill allows further sweeping tax increases.

6 October Passage of Trading with the Enemy Act allows censorship of all international communications and foreign language press.

2 November Lansing-Ishii agreement offers Japan nominal concessions in China and access to Open Door policy.

December Chamberlain committee investigates mobilization and reveals poor supply and transport arrangements.

28 December All railroad construction brought under control of US Railroad Administration.

1918

3 March Russia signs Treaty of Brest-Litovsk and withdraws from war. Germans launch March offensive on western front which, within a month, advances 50 miles. This is the greatest territorial gain by either the Allies or the Central Powers since September 1914.

4 March Bernard M. Baruch appointed chairman of War Industries Board, with new, more extensive powers.

20 April Sabotage Act renders sabotage of materials, utilities or transport a federal crime.

16 May Sedition Act reinforces Espionage Act of 15 June 1917.

20 May Overman Act grants president Wilson power to reorganize executive agencies without consulting Congress in each case.

31 May First US troops in action reinforcing French forces at Chateau-Tierry.

11 July Sugar Equalization Board established to control sugar supplies and prices.

10 August Independent US forces, under general John Pershing, sent to western front at the St Mihiel salient. German military high command realize they cannot win war.

25 September Bulgaria signs armistice of surrender and occupation.

26 September A force of 1.2 million US soldiers attack German line between Verdun and Sedan and reach Sedan on 7 November.

3 October Germany's new chancellor, Prince Max of Baden, appeals for armistice based on Wilson's Fourteen Points, published on 8 January, calling for an end to secret diplomacy, free trade, free institutions, national self-determination, freedom of the seas and so forth.

6 November Mid-term Congressional elections go badly for Democratic party and leave Republicans with majorities of 237 to 190 in House and 49 to 47 in Senate.

8 November Emperor Wilhelm II of Germany abdicates and flees to Holland.

11 November Armistice signed on basis of Wilson's Fourteen Points without unconditional surrender, but with mutual agreement to end hostilities in a manner which would prevent Germany restarting war.

18 November Wilson announces he will lead US delegation to Paris peace conference.

Federal government lifts ban on private operation of radio sets. General Electric and Westinghouse establish Radio Corporation of America (RCA).

1919

6 January Theodore Roosevelt dies.

12 January Peace conference opens at Versailles, bringing together representatives of 27 nations.

6 February Workers in Seattle stage general strike, bringing city to a standstill and prompting mayor Ole Hanson to warn of the start of a general workers' uprising. This gives added credibility to popular fear of revolution and 'Red Scare'.

11 February Justice department rounds up 53 west coast aliens, charges them with subversion and initiates deportation procedures.

14 February–12 March Wilson leaves the Paris conference to tour US in search of political support for his peace proposals and idea of a League of Nations.

20 February Milwaukee Socialist party congressman Victor Berger is sentenced to 20 years in prison for violating Espionage Act.

24 February Revenue Act signed, increasing total prevailing tax burden by almost 250 per cent to cope with dislocative effects of demobilization and help sustain aggregate demand.

2 March Third International (Comintern) formed in Moscow, aimed at stimulating world communist revolution.

3 March Wilson assembles 48 governors at White House to warn of likely problems stemming from postwar inflation.

Industrial Board created to coordinate purchasing agencies to contain prices; disbanded in May when Railroad Administration refuses to permit board to fix rail charges for transport of steel.

28 April Discovery of parcel bomb in mail of Seattle's mayor Ole Hanson. Subsequent investigations uncover 30 other parcel bombs, addressed to public figures such as attorney general

Mitchell Palmer, postmaster general Albert Burleson, Supreme Court justice Oliver Wendell Holmes, financier J.P. Morgan and others. California and New York enact laws criminalizing organizations which advocate use of violence, or those believed to do so.

1 May Violent attacks on socialists and communists celebrating May Day in communities all over the nation.

7 May Brockdorf-Rantzau, German foreign secretary, receives copy of Paris peace treaty which saddles Germany with sole blame for outbreak of first world war, confiscates colonies, divides the country in two and orders Germany to pay reparations to cover total cost of the war.

29 May German delegates draft reply to Paris peace treaty.

June State department absorbs War Trade Board.

4 June Congress passes 19th Amendment to the Constitution approving women's suffrage. Ratified 20 August 1920.

23 June Peace terms accepted by German national assembly.

28 June Peace agreement formally signed in the Hall of Mirrors at Versailles, five years to the day after the assassination of Franz Ferdinand which precipitated war.

1 July Hoover's resignation precipitates collapse of Food Administration.

17 July After a black teenager accidentally swims in front of a white beach on Lake Michigan, race riots break out in Chicago, lasting 13 days. Fifteen whites and 23 blacks are killed and more than 1,000 families left homeless. Similar riots occur this same month in Longview, Texas, and subsequently in Knoxville, Tennesse, Omaha, Nebraska and Elaine, Arkansas.

31 August Communist Labor party formed by left-wing socialists.

1 September Rival US Communist party formed in Chicago.

9 September Boston police strike over wage levels. Boston police commissioner rejects settlement proposed by mayor's citizens' committee, and dismisses 19 members of the AFL police trade union branch or Local. Massachusetts governor Calvin Coolidge, saying 'There is no right to strike against public safety anywhere, any time', calls out national guard and rapidly crushes strike. Strike leaders are dismissed and a new police force created.

22 September Some 343,000 US Steel employees walk out, after US Steel president Elbert H. Gary rejects union recognition, an eight-hour day and a 'living wage'.

25 September Bethlehem Steel employees walk out. Steel strike of 1919–20, now national in scope, is ruthlessly resisted by employers.

2 October President Wilson suffers stroke, leaving his left side paralysed and incapacitating him completely until 20 October.

Public is not told how ill he is, but no cabinet meetings are held until 13 April 1920, while Edward House and Wilson's wife Edith Galt exercise executive authority.

1 November Led by John L. Lewis, the United Mine Workers stop work, contravening wartime No-Strike agreement of August 1917 which remains in force until 31 March 1921.

28 October Volstead Act passed over Wilson's veto, enforcing the 18th, or Prohibition, Amendment.

8 November Attorney general Mitchell Palmer obtains injunction in Indianapolis against the striking United Mine Workers.

10 November Jailed socialist Victor Berger, released on bail pending appeal against his conviction for violating Espionage Act, is unseated in House of Representatives. After re-election by his Wisconsin district, his seat is again declared vacant in January 1920.

11 November American Legion members attack offices of miltant anarcho-syndicalist union, the Industrial Workers of the World, in Centralia, Washington, during which four of the attackers are killed. Subsequently, an IWW ex-serviceman, Wesley Everest, is lynched by local citizens. More than 1,000 IWWs arrested statewide, and 11 subsequently convicted of murder.

December Coal miners return to work after government orders a 14 per cent pay increase and establishes an arbitration commission, which eventually awards a further 17 per cent.

21 December Labor department deports 249 Russians to Finland.

3. Years of Boom and Bust, 1920–29

1920

1 January Simultaneous nationwide raids on communist headquarters by federal agents and local police, authorized by attorney-general Palmer. Of 6,000 arrested in the 'Palmer Raids' more than one-third are later released for lack of evidence, but 556 aliens are eventually deported.

5 January After months of brutal struggle, AFL calls off national steel strike, marking the start of organized labour's 15 years of steady and steep decline in membership and influence. Steel remains an open shop industry until 1937.

16 January Volstead Act (Prohibition enforcement law) goes into effect making manufacture, sale or transportation of intoxicating liquor illegal.

1 February President Wilson asks secretary of state Robert Lansing to resign, in belief that Lansing had not adequately pressed the League of Nations fight. His successor is Bainbridge Colby, New York lawyer on the Shipping Board.

28 February Congress approves Transportation Act, sponsored by midwestern Progressive Republicans. Contrary to nationalization proposals of railroad labour brotherhoods, this act returns railroads to private ownership under federal supervision. The ICC is empowered to draw up consolidation plans to organize railroads into systems exempt from antitrust legislation, set minimum and maximum rates, and supervise sale of railroad securities and expenditure of proceeds.

1 March Railroads return to private owners and wartime Railroad Administration folds.

19 March Senate rejects League of Nations treaty 49–35.

April Mexico's president Venuztiano Carranza is ousted and replaced by Alvaro Obregon, who refuses to uphold US concessions in Mexico until courted by secretary of state Charles Evans Hughes in 1921.

May 1920–August 1927 Sacco-Vanzetti case: two anarchists, Nicola Sacco and Bartolomeo Vanzetti, are arrested for murder on 5 May 1920 in South Braintree, Massachusetts. Convicted in 1921 on very unsatisfactory evidence before a deeply prejudiced judge, they are executed on 23 August 1927 after prolonged public debate and worldwide protests.

31 May Government withdraws price support on wheat. Agricultural prices decline steadily in 1920s.

5 June Approval by Congress of Jones Merchant Marine Act empowers Shipping Board to sell as many vessels as possible to predominantly US-owned corporations at very attractive prices. Private shipping is further encouraged by offer of government loans, mail contracts and monopolies on shipping between colonial territories and the US. A federally owned Merchant Fleet Corporation is authorized to open new shipping lines and operate surplus vessels.

8 June Republican party convention opens in Chicago. Main contenders are:

- General Leonard Wood. Inherited Theodore Roosevelt's following, advocating compulsory, universal military training.
- Frank O. Lowden. Strong midwestern following.
- Herbert Hoover. Enormous success feeding and reconstructing war-torn Europe after 1918 had made him a popular hero courted by both major parties.

Favourite sons include the gregarious mediocrity Warren G. Harding of Ohio.

Votes of Wood and Lowden delegates cancel each other out, prompting an adjournment on 14 June after nine ballots. A cabal dominating the national committee, including chairman Henry Cabot Lodge, senator Boies Penrose and Republican national chairman Will Hays, conspires to foist Harding on the convention, which expresses independence only by rejecting Harding's choice of senator Elmer Lenroot of Wisconsin in favour of Massachusetts governor Calvin Coolidge (who had crushed 1919 Boston police strike) for second spot on the ticket.

The platform explicitly rejects all forms of Wilsonian liberalism, advocating higher tariffs, lower taxes, far fewer immigrants, more farm aid and a firm rejection of Wilson's proposed League of Nations.

10 June Water Power Act creates Federal Power Commission, consisting of secretaries of war, interior and agriculture, to license and regulate dams and hydro-electric power plants in the public domain. Leases to run for 50 years, after which federal government might purchase at net cost.

28 June Democratic party convention meets in San Francisco. Main contenders are:

- William G. McAdoo. A senior southern Democrat, senator from Georgia and Wilson's son-in-law.
- A. Mitchell Palmer. Wilson's attorney-general who organized the Palmer Raids and deportation of left-wing revolutionaries.
- James M. Cox. Governor of Ohio with a strong Progressive record.

Delegates supporting McAdoo and Palmer slug it out for 37 ballots; on the 38th Palmer releases his delegates to Cox, who wins on the 44th ballot on 5 July. His running mate, Franklin D. Roosevelt, is assistant secretary of the navy and Wilsonian supporter of the League of Nations.

The platform, while sidestepping Prohibition and independence for the Philippines, supports the League but is very vague over form of US participation. Wilson describes the party's choice of Cox as 'a joke'.

July–November 1920 Election campaign: Harding remains on his front porch and, between 31 July and 25 September, 600,000 people flock to Marion, Ohio, to hear his bland speeches. Then he does make a short series of speaking tours.

For the Democrats, Roosevelt makes non-intervention abroad an issue by boasting not only that the US would control 12 Latin American votes in the League assembly, but also, and most notoriously, that he had personally written the Haitian constitution.

22 July Harding's acceptance speech at Marion is non-controversial, adopting a middle position on all issues, irrespective of how many positions there actually were.

7 August Cox's acceptance speech at Dayton, Ohio, takes up, under pressure from Wilson, the challenge of the election as a 'great and solemn referendum' on the League of Nations.

16 September A bomb explodes outside the offices of J.P. Morgan, on Wall Street, killing 38 and injuring over 100.

15 October Appearance in the press of full-page endorsement of Harding by 31 prominent pro-League Republicans.

2 November Election day. Normal Republican majority is restored and joined by various dissidents, harbouring grudges from eight years of Democratic government. Industrialists, civil libertarians, independent Progressives, Irish- and German-Americans vote Republican to give Harding a massive victory:

- Harding with 16,152,000 popular votes, and an electoral vote of 404, takes every state outside the south. Harding's 60.3 per cent share of the popular vote is also the largest in history.
- Cox with 9,147,000 popular votes, has an electoral vote of 127.
- Eugene V. Debs Socialist party candidate for the fifth time, wins 919,799 votes while campaigning from Atlanta jail where he had been sent in 1918 for opposing the war.

In the House, Republicans win 303 seats and Democrats 131, while in the Senate the Republican majority is 22. (See Map 1b.)

Election day also sees radio broadcasting station KDKA in east Pittsburgh start daily transmissions to become America's first regular radio station.

5 November Harding announces his intention to depart on vacation to Texas and Panama and promises on returning to consult the nation's 'best minds' about his cabinet and future policies.

1921

March British government unveils plans to resume large-scale naval construction.

3 March Woodrow Wilson, in last act before leaving the White House, vetoes emergency tariff bill imposing high duties on imported farm products.

4 March Warren Harding inaugurated as president.

6 April W.J. Bryan, in a speech at the liberal Univerisity of Wisconsin, calls for atheistic teachers of Darwin's theory of evolution to be purged from public schools. Eager response by such southern fundamentalists as J. Frank Norris of Fort Worth, Texas, who publishes the weekly journal *The Searchlight.*

11 April Congress re-enacts emergency tariff bill, signed by Harding on 27 May.

May 1920–1922 Severe economic recession causes prices to drop after May 1920, worsening in 1921. Almost 5 million unemployed.

May Congress passes Budget and Accounting Act, establishing the offices of director of the budget, in the executive branch, and comptroller-general, in Congress, to oversee expenditure.

19 May President Harding approves bill limiting immigration to 3 per cent of population of respective ethnic groups resident in US in 1910.

21 May German government is presented with war reparations bill for $33 billion.

25 May Senate approves senator William Borah's resolution to open disarmament negotiations with Britain and Japan.

10 June Budget Act approved, establishing Bureau of the Budget and requiring the president to submit an estimate of receipts and expenditures to every regular session of Congress.

29 June House also approves senator Borah's disarmament resolution.

8 July British foreign office expresses its desire for disarmament negotiations.

11 August Secretary of state Charles Evans Hughes issues invitations to Britain, China, Italy, France, Netherlands, Portugal and Belgium to join the United States in a disarmament conference in Washington DC in November.

Franklin Roosevelt is stricken with polio and crippled for life.

15 August Packers and Stockyards Act forbids price discrimination and other monopolistic practices in restraint of trade in livestock, poultry and dairy products.

Other agricultural matters dealt with during this session of Congress include extension of War Finance Corporation for three years; empowering it to lend up to $1 billion to stimulate agricultural exports; and increasing the capital of land banks.

24 August Grain Futures Act forbids monopoly in grain markets. When declared unconstitutional by Supreme Court, a second act is passed by Congress on 21 September 1922.

12 November–6 February 1922 Washington conference on disarmament and Pacific Ocean affairs, chaired by secretary of state Hughes. He startles opening session with sweeping proposal for naval arms limitations.

23 November Revenue Act which, as the first step in treasury secretary Andrew Mellon's tax reduction programme, wipes out wartime excess profits tax and reduces maximum surtax rate on personal incomes to 50 per cent. By 1926, maximum surtax will have been slashed to 20 per cent.

13 December United States, Japan, Great Britain and France sign the Four-Power Pact, agreeing mutual respect for island possessions in the Pacific Ocean and promising to meet jointly if disputes arise among themselves or with outsiders.

1922

January Mill owners' attempt to raise hours and cut wages defeated by textile workers' strikes.

February First assembly of conference for Progressive political action convened by (predominantly African-American) railroad labour brotherhoods in Chicago.

4–6 February Nine Power treaty signed by Big Four and by Italy, Belgium, Portugal, China and the Netherlands. Guarantees Chinese territorial integrity, China's right to establish stable government, and the Open-Door policy.

The Five Power treaty (the Big Four plus Italy) sets tonnage quotas for battleships after replacements: GB and US 525,000 tons each; Japan 315,000 tons; France and Italy 175,000 tons each.

In addition, quotas for aircraft carriers are established. United States, Great Britain and Japan agree not to enlarge existing naval bases or create new ones. Japan also agrees to evacuate Siberia, return Kiaochow Bay and the Shantung Peninsula to China and to confirm US cable rights on Yap Island.

9 February Congress creates Foreign Debt Commission to negotiate first world war debts amounting to over $10 billion, which the US insists must be repaid.

18 February Co-operative Marketing Act (Capper-Volstead Act) exempts agricultural cooperatives from anti-trust laws.

April–September In protest against wage reductions, 500,000 coalminers strike.

7 April Secretary of interior Albert B. Fall secretly leases Teapot Dome naval oil reserves to the Mammoth Oil Company. This is later proved in court to be part of huge financial scandal.

21 June Violence erupts when the Southern Illinois Coal Company attempts to resume production using strikebreakers. Two strikers killed by company guards, prompting response by striking miners at Herrin which leads to the death of 19 strikebreakers in the 'Herrin massacre'.

July–November Four-term Wilsonian Democrat senator Charles Culberson of Texas is defeated in primary election by Earle B. Mayfield, one of four Ku Klux Klan candidates. The Klan also wins many local contests in Dallas and state-wide. In Oregon, Walter M. Pierce strongly defeats anti-Klan incumbent governor Ben Olcott and a legislature dominated by Klansmen passes the only compulsory state education law in US history, outlawing parochial Roman Catholic, Jewish and other schools. The Klan also controls the Indiana legislature.

1 July Railway shopmen's strike begins in response to 12 per cent pay cut. Ends on 1 September when federal judge James H. Wilkerson issues injunction forbidding union from undertaking virtually any form of strike activity.

19 September Congress approves Fordney-McCumber Tariff Act, raising duties on farm products, chemicals, textiles, chinaware, cutlery, guns and other industrial goods. Tariff Commission instructed to examine production costs, and make recommendations to president, on the basis of which he might make upward or downward tariff revisions by as much as 50 per cent.

Harding vetoes revised bonus bill offering payment of 20-year endowment policies to war veterans.

4 November In mid-term Congressional elections, Republican majorities in House and Senate are cut to 18 and 8 respectively.

December Secretary of interior Albert Fall leases oil reserves at Elk Hills to Pan-American Petroleum Company.

1923

11 January France and Begium occupy Rhineland when Germany fails to make reparations payment on due date to the Allies.

15 February Charles R. Forbes, head of Veterans' Bureau, is forced to resign as corruption allegations come to light.

2 March Congress launches investigation of Veterans' Bureau.

4 March Agricultural Credits Act establishes 12 intermediate credit banks, financed by the treasury, for farm loans of six months to three years. It also authorizes creation of National Credit Corporations as private banks for livestock farmers.

14 March Charles F. Cramer, legal adviser to Veterans' Bureau, commits suicide.

2 August President Harding dies of a stroke in San Francisco. Calvin Coolidge sworn in at his small Vermont home at 2 a.m. on 3 August.

23 September Oklahoma governor J. C. Walton pronounces martial law in bid to defeat Ku Klux Klan. In retaliation, the Klan secures his impeachment and expulsion from office on 18 November.

October Sub-committee of Senate public lands committee launches investigation into activities of Albert Fall, secretary of interior.

1924

16 January Two Republicans, senator Charles L. McNary, of Oregon, and congressman Gilbert N. Haugen, of Iowa, introduce Farm Relief Bill requiring federal government to control farm surplus and raise prices by purchasing annual surplus stocks at agreed prices and selling them abroad at world prices.

3 February Woodrow Wilson dies.

February–June The Harding scandals emerge:

- Former director of the Veterans' Bureau Charles R. Forbes indicted for defrauding the government by corrupt contracts, convicted 4 February 1925 and jailed for two years. Forbes had managed to pilfer or squander some $250 million.
- After Senate investigation headed by Thomas J. Walsh of Montana, secretary of interior Albert B. Fall and oil executives Harry Sinclair and Edward Doheny indicted for conspiracy to lease federal oil reserves at Teapot Dome, Wyoming, and Elk Hills, California. Fall received a 'loan' of $100,000 from Doheny and $223,000 in government bonds, $85,000 in cash and a herd of cattle from Sinclair. Fall and Sinclair are convicted, Doheny acquitted.

March President Coolidge forces attorney general Harry M. Daugherty to resign when it is proved he had received bribes.

9 April US commission, headed by Charles G. Dawes, produces Dawes Plan, advocating a private loan totalling $200 million to enable Germany to meet reparation payments and stabilize German currency on the gold standard, while avoiding repetition of the nightmare inflation which destroyed the German mark in 1922–23.

10 April Japanese ambassador Hanihara warns of 'grave consequences' should Congress put Japanese immigration on quota basis, which in effect would restrict Japan to 246 immigrants annually.

19 May Congress passes Soldiers' Bonus Act over Coolidge's veto, providing all veterans of the rank of captain or below with endowment policies on the basis of $1–$1.25 for every day of wartime service.

26 May Immigration quota act (National Origins Act) sets more severe limits, restricting annual immigration to 2 per cent of the total number of a nationality resident in the US by 1890 census. Maximum total quota of immigrants is reduced to 164,000 favouring north and west Europe.

Title II of the Act, due to come into force on 1 July 1929, reduces quotas as a percentage to maximum 150,000.

2 June Revenue Act cuts maximum surtax from 50 to 40 per cent and halves taxes on middle and small incomes. Maximum estate tax is increased from 25 to 40 per cent, and a new gift tax is imposed.

3 June McNary-Haugen bill to control farm surpluses rejected by the House.

10 June Dominated by conservatives, Republican party convention, meeting at Cleveland, nominates incumbent president, Calvin Coolidge, on first ballot: only Wisconsin and South Dakota delegates dissent. Earlier, futility of pressing the Progressive cause within Republican party had caused Robert M. La Follette to withdraw from primaries in Wisconsin, North Dakota and Michigan.

Republican platform promises economy, tax reduction and limited aid to American farmers.

24 June–10 July Democratic party convention meets in New York City. Main contenders are:

- William G. McAdoo. Woodrow Wilson's son-in-law is strongly supported in the south and west, and endorsed by the Ku Klux Klan, but fatally linked to the Teapot Dome scandal as Edward Doheny's lawyer.
- Alfred E. Smith. Roman Catholic reform governor of New York, opposed to Prohibition, supported by Irish- and Catholic-dominated eastern and midwestern political machines.

Needing a two-thirds majority for nomination, the convention drags on rancorously for three weeks. Facing stalemate, both men withdraw by mutual consent on 96th ballot, and on the 103rd ballot convention nominates John W. Davis, a dull corporation lawyer, with governor Charles W. Bryson of Nebraska as his running-mate.

Democratic platform makes party disunity explicit, as a resolution condemning the Klan as un-American (sponsored by the Smith camp) fails by a vote of 543–542. Unable to compromise northern and southern differences, the platform fudges Prohibition too. In addition, it calls for public referendum on the League of Nations, denounces Fordney McCumber tariff and promises independence to the Philippines.

4 July Conference for Progressive political action meets in Cleveland, comprising insurgent Republicans, representatives of organized labour and western farmers, socialists and independent Progressives. Condemning reactionary policies of the two major parties, delegates organize the Progressive party, nominating Robert M. La Follette as presidential candidate and adopting a platform which advocates nationalization of railroads, public ownership of hydro-electric power, development of a new public utilities system, abolition of injunctions in labour disputes, the right of Congress to overrule Supreme Court decisions and direct nomination and election of presidents.

12 July Inauguration of Santo Domingo's president Horatio Vasquez after American-supervised elections. US occupation forces gradually withdraw.

August–November Presidential election campaign: disdainfully ignoring Democrats Davis and Bryson, Republicans turn full fire on Progressive La Follette, alleging he is a Communist front man. The latter is hampered by lack of funds, ebbing trade union support and an untimely rise in farm prices only a month before the election. Davis's attempts to make an issue of Coolidge's big business connections drown in anti-Red commotion raised by the Republicans.

October Liberal Carlos Solorzano elected president of Nicaragua.

4 November After presidential election with low turnout of 52 per cent:

- Coolidge wins with 15.7 million popular votes and 382 electoral votes from 35 states.
- Davis wins 8.4 million votes and 136 electoral votes from 12 states, all in the south. His 28.8 per cent share of the popular votes is worst showing by major party candidate since the Civil War (apart from Taft in 1912).
- La Follette wins 4.8 million votes and 13 electoral votes from his own state Wisconsin. His 16 per cent share of the popular votes is creditable. (See Map 1c.)

December Congress empowers president to undertake, before 1 July 1927, construction of eight 10,000-ton cruisers, following lead of Britain and Japan in abrogating naval Five Power Treaty of 1922.

3 December Senator George W. Norris of Nebraska presents Senate with his plan for public operation of hydro-electric and nitrate fertilizer plant at Muscle Shoals.

1925

January Appointment of William E. Humphrey, formerly a Washington congressman, as chairman of Federal Trade Commission gives conservatives decisive control of vital commission at a crucial time.

14 January Senate approval of Underwood bill, which provides for private enterprise to operate hydro-electric and nitrate generation at Muscle Shoals, nullifies proposal of senator Norris.

12 February Congress adopts Revenue Act which reduces basic tax, cuts maximum surtax from 40 to 20 per cent, abolishes gift tax and halves estate tax.

26 February Senator Norris succeeds in blocking Underwood bill by filibuster.

3 March House passes resolution urging US participation in League of Nations' World Court.

5 May After Tennesse legislature forbids teaching in state schools and colleges of any theory contrary to the Bibical version of creation, the American Civil Liberties Union offers to sponsor defence of biology teacher John Scopes to test the constitutionality of the statute. W. J. Bryan accepts the state's offer to join the prosecution team; Clarence Darrow joins the defence.

14 July Scopes trial opens at Dayton, Tennessee, rapidly degenerating into a verbal duel between Darrow and Bryan. Scopes is quickly convicted, prompting brief revival of anti-evolutionist crusade. Anti-evolution bills also pass in Mississippi (1926) and Arkansas (1928).

22 July Bryan dies suddenly of a heart attack at the end of the Scopes trial.

August US marine guard withdrawn from Managua, Nicaragua, after election in October the previous year of Carlos Solorzano as president, but when defeated conservative Emiliano Chamorro ousts Solorzano, US withholds recognition.

September Mill owners attempt to impose 10 per cent pay cut in Passaic, New Jersey, leading eventually to textile strike in January 1926 which spreads throughout state and ends in victory for the strikers in May 1926.

1926

January Textile strike, which began in Passaic when mill owners tried to impose 10 per cent pay cuts, spreads throughout New Jersey.

27 January Senate approves US membership of Permanent Court of International Justice, but attaches reservations unacceptable to Court itself. So though it had urged establishment of the World Court at the two Hague conferences in 1899 and 1907, US does not join an institution established by the League of Nations in 1920. Presidents Coolidge, Hoover and Franklin Roosevelt make continuing efforts to enrol the US on the Court, but isolationist sentiment and propaganda, spread largely by Hearst press and broadcasts of the 'radio priest' Father Charles Coughlin, result in all efforts failing in 1935.

26 February Congress adopts Revenue Act, which reduces basic rate of tax, cuts maximum surtax from 40 per cent to 20 per cent, abolishes gift tax and halves estate duty.

7 March Radio Corporation of America, American Telephone and Telegraph Company and British General Post Office transmit first successful transatlantic radio-telephone conversation between London and New York.

Passaic textile strike, which had spread throughout New Jersey in January, ends in victory for the strikers.

5 May Novelist Sinclair Lewis turns down Pulitzer prize for his novel *Arrowsmith* on the grounds that such awards make writers 'safe, polite, obedient and sterile'.

2 July Congress establishes Army Air Corps in the same year that colonel 'Billy' Mitchell, who has advocated a separate air force for many years, resigns from the army after being court-martialled for disobeying orders to demonstrate potential of air bombard- ment. US is now committed to the idea of air power.

October Faced by US refusal to recognize Chamorro's August 1925 coup, Nicaraguan Congress elects Adolfo Diaz, long-time conservative friend of US, and wins immediate recognition.

Air Commerce Act vests control of commercial aviation in Commerce Department, not private enterprise.

25 October US Supreme Court holds that president has power to remove cabinet officers without consent of Senate, thus voiding 1867 Tenure of Office Act, defiance of which led to impeachment proceedings against president Andrew Johnson in 1868.

November In mid-term Congressional elections Republicans lose seats in both House and Senate, while Progressives gain.

1927

January–May In response to hasty US October recognition of Diaz regime, exiled liberal vice-president Juan B. Sacasa returns to Nicaragua to raise revolt. Calvin Coolidge is forced to send 5,000 US marines to support Diaz and restore order.

1 January Mexican government passes law limiting foreign concessions to a maximum 50 years. With US oil rights under threat banker Dwight D. Morrow is sent to negotiate in September. Secretary of state Frank B. Kellogg alleges Mexico's government is working in collusion with Soviet agents towards a 'Mexican-fostered Bolshevik hegemony intervening between the United States and the Panama Canal'.

10 February President Coolidge calls for Five Power naval disarmament conference to be staged at Geneva. France and Italy decline to attend.

25 February Coolidge vetoes revised McNary Haugen farm bill, denouncing the measure as unacceptable special interest legislation.

April–May Coolidge's attempt to crush liberal revolt against president Adolfo Diaz in January by sending 5,000 US marines to restore order provokes heavy protest in US. Later Coolidge sends

Henry L. Stimson as president's personal representative. Stimson persuades liberals to disarm and take part in free elections, which they win. Between 1927 and 1932 state department abandons unpopular pro-US conservatives and supports liberals. By 1933 all US troops are withdrawn from Nicaragua.

6 April French foreign minister Aristide Briand proposes bilateral treaty with US aimed at 'outlawry of war'. Briand's idea had been suggested by visit of James Shotwell, supporter of Salmon Levinson's American committee for the outlawry of war, formed in 1921. Coolidge's secretary of state Frank B. Kellogg responds on 28 December with multilateral treaty which outlaws war as an instrument of national policy but permits defensive war – the Kellogg-Briand pact.

21 May Charles A. Lindbergh completes first non-stop solo trans-Atlantic flight New York–Paris in his plane *The Spirit of St Louis.*

20 June Geneva conference, aimed at naval arms limitations, opens but is singularly unsuccessful.

23 August Sacco and Vanzetti, two anarchists arrested in May 1920 and sentenced to death for murder in the course of armed robbery in July 1921, are executed (see May 1920).

November–December Mexican Supreme Court and Congress guarantee that US companies active in Mexico prior to 1917 will enjoy uninterrupted ownership.

1928

January At Pan-American conference in Havana, Coolidge's representative Hughes refuses to offer US decree of non-intervention in domestic affairs of other American nations.

13 March Senate approves George Norris's bill for public operation of Muscle Shoals hydro-electric power.

May Coolidge vetoes McNary-Haugen farm bill a second time.

25 May Congress approves senator George Norris's bill for public operation of hyrdro-electric and nitrate generation at Muscle Shoals, where a dam had been built in 1918 on the Tennessee River. Federal corporation is to be established to administer public ownership and construct a new dam at Cove Creek, Tennessee, for flood control. Vetoed by Coolidge in 1926, and again by president Hoover on 3 March 1931, this idea finally bears fruit with Tennessee Valley Authority during New Deal.

12 June Republican party convention meets at Kansas City, nominating secretary of commerce Herbert Hoover of California for president and senator Charles Curtis of Kansas for vice-president.

Republican platform generally offers more of the same. Prohibition and protective tariff approved, farm relief promised without artificial price supports.

26 June Democratic party convention meets at Houston, Texas. Southern delegates fight stubbornly to prevent nomination of New York governor Alfred E. Smith, finally yielding when Smith camp agrees to jettison Prohibition amendment repeal from Democratic programme. Smith, unbowed, agrees to enforce Prohibition laws, but reserves right to work for repeal of 1920 Volstead Act which had orginally enforced Prohibition.

Democratic platform favours farm relief, collective bargaining in industry, an act ending injunctions in labour disputes, strict public control of hydro-electric power and independence for the Philippines.

July–November Election campaign: Hoover repeatedly presses for continuation of policies in the Harding-Coolidge vein, telling voters that individualism can secure permanent prosperity. Despite his outstanding reform credentials, Smith launches a fundamentally conservative campaign, seeking to reassure voters that Democratic victory will not rock the boat of Republican prosperity, going so far as to appoint GM executive John J. Raskob, an avowed Republican only a year before, national party chairman.

Smith's Roman Catholic faith, opposition to Prohibition, association with New York's Tammany Hall (the nation's oldest political machine), and his humble east-side origins make him deeply unpopular, particularly in the south where anti-Smith resentment runs strongly among traditional Democratic voters.

27 August Fifteen nations sign treaty of Paris, and later another 47, all denouncing war as an instrumemt of national policy.

6 November Election day: Hoover captures North Carolina, Tennessee, Florida, Kentucky, Oklahoma and Texas in the 'solid south'. Outside the south Smith carries only Massachusetts and Rhode Island.

- Hoover with 21,391,993 popular votes wins 444 electoral votes.
- Smith with 15,016,169 popular votes wins 87 electoral votes.

Immediate lesson drawn is that a Roman Catholic could not become president. However, more significantly for the future, Smith gives the Democrats for the first time a narrow majority in the nation's 12 largest cities and captures 122 northern counties from Republicans. What destroys him in the south and in rural small-town America is his making elsewhere.

Smith narrowly loses his home state New York, where Franklin D. Roosevelt is elected governor by a plurality of 25,000. (See Map 1d.)

19 November President-elect Hoover embarks upon goodwill tour of Latin America, returning on 6 January 1930.

17 December J. Reuben Clark of the state department drafts a memorandum which questions intervention in the affairs of other American nations as a legitimate Monroe doctrine option. The memo- randum is later published in March 1930.

1929

March After United Textile Workers launch an organizing drive in the south, violence breaks out as vigilantes, company guards and state troops battle with 5,000 striking rayon workers at Elizabethton, Tennessee.

15 April President Hoover calls Congress into special session to deal with falling farm prices and farm relief.

25 April–13 June Senate passes export debenture plan, offering farmers federal funding for exporting surplus crops in the form of debentures to be used by importers to pay customs duties. Legislation later fails in the House.

15 June Agricultural Marketing Act establishes Federal Farm Board. It is furnished with $500 million to offer loans to farm cooperatives, and empowered to create stabilization corporations to buy up surplus crops.

1 July New restrictive immigration quotas go into effect: during 1930s total net immigration was to amount to less than 70,000.

6 July US and Britain agree parity in naval combat strength.

26 September Bank of England raises bank interest rate to 6.5 per cent to prevent outflow of gold.

October Seven Communist leaders of textile strike at Gastonia, North Carolina, convicted of murdering Gastonia police chief.

7 October Prime minister Ramsay MacDonald addresses Congress and reaffirms British commitment to naval arms limitation.

15 October Wall Street stock market prices begin to fall steadily.

24 October 'Black Thursday': while nearly 13 million shares change hands as prices collapse, J.P. Morgan & Co and a group of other banks attempt to rally the market by purchasing stocks from hastily formed $240 million pool.

25 October President Hoover announces that the economy is on 'a sound and prosperous basis'.

29 October Some 16.5 million shares change hands, as average stock market prices fall an unprecedented 40 points.

19 November Hoover meets railroad presidents, extracting promises to continue planned railroad construction and so sustain employment.

21 November Facing most serious financial crisis in history, and fearing it might trigger economic depression, Hoover secures pledges from business leaders to maintain production and wage levels, and from labour leaders to offer full cooperation.

23 November Hoover calls upon mayors and governors to increase public works expenditure.

4. The Great Depression, 1930–33

1930

21 January London naval conference opens. Representatives of US, Britain and Japan agree to construction 'holiday' on capital ships for five years, and to scrap nine battleships.

- United States agrees to restrict itself to 325,000 tons in cruisers, 150,000 tons in destroyers and 52,700 tons in submarines.
- Britain to 339,000 tons in cruisers, 150,000 tons in destroyers and 52,700 tons in submarines.
- Japan to 208,850 tons in cruisers, 105,500 tons in destroyers and 52,700 tons in submarines.

22 April Main principles of the London naval conference are completed, with France and Italy agreeing to comply. Britain secures inclusion of 'escalation' clause permitting nations to expand fleets if national security is threatened by naval construction of another nation.

17 June Hawley-Smoot tariff hoists rates higher in face of economists' protests. Seventy-five increases are imposed on agricultural products and 925 for manufactured goods.

4 November In mid-term Congressional elections, Democrats gain eight seats in Senate and 53 in the House, securing a majority in the latter.

20 December Congress authorizes expenditure of more than $100 million for public works at the request of president Hoover.

1931

February–June American economy appears to rally slightly.

March French bankers demand immediate repayment of all their loans.

11 May Failure of the *Kreditanstalt* of Vienna (Austria's largest bank), prompts heavy withdrawals of gold from Germany.

3 March Hoover vetoes senator George Norris's bill for federal public works project at Muscle Shoals dam.

18 June Unable to meet reparations payments, Germany's president Hindenburg appeals to Hoover for assistance.

21 June Hoover announces one-year moratorium on all reparations payments. Britain and Germany agree at once, but France continues to make Germany pay for a further two weeks.

1 August As French bankers withdraw gold from Britain, the Bank of England arranges a short-term gold loan.

21 September Bank of England defaults on gold payments. Britain comes off the gold standard.

4 October Hoover calls secret meeting of leading bankers and insurance executives, compelling them under threat of Congressional action to form a credit pool of $500 million and to refrain from mortgage foreclosures where borrowers are in honest distress.

6 October Hoover secures support of Congressional leaders for measures to tackle what is now seen as a devastating economic depression, with unemployment at 8 million and rising fast.

1932

22 January Reconstruction Finance Corporation (RFC) established, with Charles Dawes as head, to offer federal loans to banks, insurance and railroad companies, with capital of $500 million and authority to borrow up to $1.5 billion more. Loans of $1.2 billion made in its first six months.

23 January Additional cash provided for federal land banks.

27 February Glass-Steagall Act facilitates rediscount of commercial paper by Federal Reserve banks and makes $750 million of government gold available for business loans.

23 March Norris-La Guardia Act ends use of injunctions in labour disputes and outlaws 'yellow-dog' contracts which forbid workers to join unions.

29 May 15,000 ex-servicemen (army veterans) descend on Washington DC seeking to secure passage of a bill sponsored by senator Wright Patman of Texas to pay balance of veterans' bonus in $2.4 billion of paper money.

14 June Republican party meets in Chicago, renominating Hoover president and Curtis vice-president on the first ballot in a subdued atmosphere.

The platform: emergency relief loans to states, maintenance of gold standard, banking reform.

15 June The House passes Patman's veterans' bonus bill, which is rejected by Senate on 19 June in face of certain presidential veto by Hoover.

27 June Democratic party meets in Chicago. Leading candidates are: *Franklin D Roosevelt*, governor of New York, and *Al Smith*, backed by Tammany Hall. Roosevelt has built strength in west and south, but lacks necessary two-thirds majority. By swinging Roosevelt's votes into action gradually on second and third ballots, his campaign managers create illusion of a landslide, and decisively take Texas and California on the fourth ballot in exchange for the vice-presidential nomination of John Nance Garner of Texas. Roosevelt breaks precedent by travelling to

Chicago (by plane) to deliver acceptance speech in which he pledges 'a new deal' for the American people.

The platform: repeal of 18th (Prohibition) Amendment, balanced budget, reduction of federal expenditure by 25 per cent, government withdrawal from private enterprise, sound currency and banking reform, unemployment and old age insurance under state law, lower tariffs and control of crop surpluses.

July–November Election campaign: Hoover is ineffectively defensive. Roosevelt, more confident in the knowledge that simply being a Democrat will almost certainly secure victory, surrounds himself with 'brains trust' of advisers. He vaguely outlines future programmes, but insists on condemning Hoover's 'reckless spending' in a speech on 19 October.

11 July Hoover vetoes Garner-Wagner relief bill, which would have vastly expanded public works and offered direct relief to individuals.

16 July Relief and Construction Act instructs RFC to loan $300 million to states lacking resources, and a further $1.5 billion for public works.

22 July Federal Home Loan Bank Act creates home loan banks with capital of $125 million to enable finance companies to obtain funds without foreclosing on home owners.

28 July Riot occurs in Washington DC when police try to clear army veteran Bonus Marchers out of abandoned buildings, with resulting death of two veterans. Subsequently, general Douglas MacArthur uses tanks, cavalry and bayonets to evict remaining veterans and their families from shanties at Anacostia Flats.

August Farm strikers attempt forcibly to prevent food from entering Sioux City and Des Moines in Iowa for fear agricultural prices will be further depressed.

31 October In the midst of a heavy run of bank withdrawals, the state of Nevada declares 12–day bank holiday.

8 November Election day:

- Roosevelt with 22.8 million popular votes wins 472 electoral votes in a huge landslide.
- Hoover with 15.6 million popular votes wins 59 electoral votes.
- Norman Thomas the Socialist party candidate wins 881,951 popular votes.
- William Z. Foster the Communist party candidate wins 102,785 popular votes. (See Map 1e.)

1933

30 January Adolf Hitler inaugurated as chancellor of Germany.

4 February Governor Huey P. Long of Louisiana declares 10–day bank moratorium.

6 February 20th Amendment goes into effect, providing that in 1937 and after Congress would convene each year on 3 January and the president take office on 20 January after election of previous year.

14 February Week-long bank moratorium announced in Michigan.

15 February Attempted assassination of president-elect Franklin D. Roosevelt by Giusseppe Zangara, who misses Roosevelt but shoots dead mayor Anton Cermak of Chicago.

20 February Passage of 21st Amendment repealing Prohibition is ratified on 5 December 1933.

March American manufacturing output is now half what it had been in 1929, farm prices 40 per cent lower than the already depressed level of that year, corporate deficit has risen to $5.7 billion, national income has halved, one quarter of the workforce is jobless, 37 per cent of the non-agricultural workforce is unemployed. Agriculture, banking, business, industry are at the point of collapse.

3 March Banks either closed or working under highly restricted conditions in 47 states.

4 March Franklin D. Roosevelt inaugurated. In his address, FDR tells the American people that 'the only thing we have to fear is fear itself' and promises, if necessary, to wield 'broad executive power' to solve the economic crisis. He also announces 'good neighbour' policy towards Latin America.

5 March FDR declares national four–day bank holiday, and halts all gold and silver transactions. Congress called into special session to deal with banking crisis.

9 March Emergency Banking Act passes Congress in less than seven hours. Sound banks to reopen under treasury department licence and to issue currency against their assets. President granted wide powers over money and banking.

11 March Economy Act imposes federal salary and pension cuts to help balance the budget, further deflating the economy.

12–13 March National convention of Farm Holiday Association meets in Des Moines, Iowa, demanding action to raise farm prices.

12 March Roosevelt's first radio 'fireside chat', explaining what government has done to render the banking system secure.

22 March Beer and Wine Revenue Act amends Volstead Act to permit sale of beers and wines with up to 3.2 per cent alcohol by volume.

27 March All federal agricultural credit agencies consolidated into Farm Credit Administration.

31 March Unemployment Relief Act creates Civilian Conservation Corps (CCC) to provide work in special camps for men aged 18–25 for $30 per month wages.

5 April CCC goes into operation, and in its seven-year life becomes the most popular New Deal agency.

6 April Senator Hugo Black's bill, aimed at establishing 30–hour week in industry, is passed by Congress but not welcomed by FDR's administration which is sceptical about shorter hours and seeks its own alternative.

19 April Roosevelt officially takes US off the gold standard.

23 April US signs Antiwar Treaty of Non-aggression and Conciliation of the American States.

27 April In Le Mars, Iowa, 600 angry farmers attack a judge sent to foreclose on their land.

3 May Raymond Moley and Hugh Johnson present draft recovery bill to US chamber of commerce, which approves it.

12 May Creation of Federal Emergency Relief Administration (FERA) under Harry Hopkins to provide grants to states and cities.

Agricultural Adjustment Act establishes Agricultural Adjustment Administration (under George Peek) to make subsidies to farmers in return for reducing crop acreages, and offers refinancing of farm mortgages. The Thomas amendment empowers president to reflate the economy by coining silver, issuing paper money and devaluing the dollar.

15 May National Industrial Recovery Act (NIRA) presented to Congress to plan industrial sector of the economy.

18 May Creation of Tennessee Valley Authority (TVA) to construct dams and hydro-electric power plants in Tennessee valley, to produce and sell electricity, to produce nitrate fertilizer and plan development of the whole Tennessee valley area, which covers parts of Tennessee, North Carolina, Kentucky, Virginia, Mississippi, Alabama and Georgia. It transformed the ecology of the whole river basin and led to a string of similar dams elsewhere by the 1940s. (See Map 2.)

27 May Federal Securities Act requires corporations to register all new security issues with Federal Trade Commission.

5 June Gold Repeal. Joint resolution of Congress cancels gold payment clause in all federal and private contracts.

12 June International economic monetary and financial conference opens in London.

13 June Home Owners' Refinancing Act creates Home Owners' Loan Corporation to borrow up to $2 billion for refinancing home mortgages.

16 June Glass-Steagall Banking Act legally separates commercial from investment banking and establishes the Federal Deposit Insurance Corporation (FDIC) to insure all bank deposits below $5,000. Bank failures, which averaged 600 a year in the 1920s, total less than this in the next decade.

Farm Credit Act authorises the Farm Credit Administration to refinance farm mortgages.

Emergency Railroad Transportation Act puts railroad holding companies under supervision of Interstate Commerce Commission and appoints Joseph Eastman coordinator of transportation.

National Industrial Recovery Act establishes National Recovery Administration under general Hugh Johnson. The NRA permits industry to draw up competition codes immune from antitrust legislation, covering wages and hours and incorporating Section 7a to guarantee workers' right to collective bargaining. It also creates the Public Works Administration under Harold Ickes with $3.3 billion to spend on job creation.

30 June Congress adjourns after passing 16 major pieces of legislation covering all aspects of the economy in three months – the Hundred Days.

5 July President Roosevelt kills London international economic conference by refusing to stabilize the dollar, which he had previously taken off gold and devalued to reflate the domestic economy. From now on New Deal financial policy becomes national, not international. By December all wartime debts are effectively cancelled.

5 August Roosevelt appoints National Labor Board to mediate disputes prompted by labour's organizing efforts in the wake of Section 7a of NIRA, under chairmanship of senator Robert F. Wagner of New York.

October 1933–February 1934 NRA industrial codes drawn up amid massive publicity and public fervour campaign engineered by Johnson under slogan 'we do our part'.

25 October FDR begins gold buying programme, hoping to reduce value of the dollar to help reflate economy and ultimately stabilize the dollar. Policy, announced in fireside chat of 22 October, is soon seen to be mistaken and abandoned in January.

8 November Civil Works Administration is established under Harry Hopkins to reduce unemployment.

16 November Roosevelt extends diplomatic recognition to Soviet Union.

3 December At Montevideo, secretary of state Cordell Hull formally renounces United States' claimed right of intervention in domestic affairs of other nations in the western hemisphere.

5. Recovery and Reform, 1934–40

1934

30 January Gold Reserve Act ends gold buying, nationalizes all gold held in Federal Reserve Banks and further stimulates economy by reducing gold content of the dollar by between 50 and 60 per cent. FDR calls it 'the nicest birthday present I ever had'.

31 January Roosevelt fixes price of gold, which had been $20 at $35 an ounce, where it stays until 1971.

15 February Civil Works Emergency Relief Act provides $500 million for civil works and relief.

Spring FDR abolishes National Labor Board, replacing it by tripartite National Labor Relations Board to stage elections to determine workers' choice of collective bargaining representatives.

13 April Johnson Debt Default Act forbids loans to any nation which has reneged on debts owed to US.

19 April Senate appoints Nye Committee to investigate arms market. Under chairmanship of isolationist senator Gerald P. Nye it concludes that munitions manufacturers were responsible for US entry into first world war.

29 May United States abrogates 1901 Platt amendment, which had left Cuba little independence, satisfied that current Fulgencio Batista dictatorship will safeguard US, if not Cuban, interests.

6 June Securities Exchange Act creates regulatory Securities and Exchange Commission under 'poacher turned gamekeeper' Joseph P. Kennedy.

12 June Reciprocal Trade Agreements Act authorizes president to negotiate agreements with other nations for purpose of raising or lowering tariffs by up to 50 per cent.

19 June Communications Act creates Federal Communications Commission (FCC) to regulate interstate and foreign radio and telegraph communication networks.

Silver Purchase Act makes concession to silver bloc by empowering president to increase treasury's silver holdings up to one-quarter of its total monetary reserve.

28 June Congress adopts Frazier-Lemke Farm Bankruptcy Act enabling farmers to recover property on easy credit terms.

National Housing Act establishes Federal Housing Administration (FHA) to insure loans for house repair or construction.

August Formation of right-wing American Liberty League, consisting of Republicans and conservative Democrats like Al Smith, John Davis and the Du Ponts in sworn enmity to the New Deal and all its works. 'At no point,' historian Arthur M. Schlesinger writes, 'did [it] construe "liberty" as meaning anything else but the folding stuff.'

15 August US marines leave Caribbean island of Haiti.

24 August Secretary of state Cordell Hull concludes reciprocal trade agreement with Cuba integrating it even more fully into US economy.

27 September Having already secured Hugh Johnson's resignation, Roosevelt appoints National Industrial Recovery Board consisting of managerial, labour and public representatives.

6 November Novelist Upton Sinclair, who had surprisingly won the 1934 Democratic party primary in California with his 'production for use' plan to End Poverty in California' (EPIC), is defeated for governor by Republican Red-baiting campaign backed by conservative Democrats. Roosevelt is persuaded to withhold endorsement of Sinclair.

Mid-term elections give Democrats unprecedented majority of 45 in Senate and 219 in the House.

Father Charles Coughlin, gifted and popular radio broadcaster and Roman Catholic priest from Detroit, forms National Union for Social Justice, calling for nationalized banking, credit and currency, but private control of public utilities and natural resources, and fairer system of taxation.

1935

4 January In his annual message to Congress, Roosevelt announces a new broad programme of reforming legislation, later known as the second New Deal.

7 January In the 'hot oil' cases, the Supreme Court invalidates Section 9c of NIRA on grounds that it unconstitutionally confers regulatory powers over petroleum industry to the president.

2 March US renounces right of intervention in Panama.

16 March Hitler re-establishes compulsory military training in Germany.

8 April Emergency Relief Appropriation Act (ERA) authorizes expenditure of $5 billion on works programmmes. Works Progress Administration, established under Harry Hopkins, employs $3 million within one year and launches such programmes as the Federal Theatre Project, Federal Writers' Project and Federal Art Project.

1 May Resettlement Administration is established under auspices of ERA, headed by Rexford G. Tugwell, for purpose of resettling impoverished urban and rural families. Creates model communities at Greenbelt, near Washington DC, and Greendale, near Milwaukee.

11 May Establishment of Rural Electrification Administration under ERA Act to finance construction of electrical plants and power lines in rural areas.

16 May Senate approves National Labour Relations Act introduced by senator Robert F. Wagner.

27 May 'Black Monday': the Supreme Court invalidates Frazier-Lemke Farm Mortgage Act (*Louisville Joint Stock Bank v Radford*) on grounds that it unconstitutionally deprives mortgagees of property, and NIRA (*Schechter Corporation v United States*) on grounds that the statute wrongfully confers effective legislative authority to the president, and that the kosher chicken company in question is technically engaged in intrastate commerce only.

31 May In a press conference Roosevelt complains of the Court's potentially disastrous 'horse and buggy' definition of interstate commerce.

Summer Seventh Comintern meeting in Moscow launches Popular Front strategy against Nazis and fascists.

19 June Roosevelt requests Congress act to reverse growing concentration of economic power, and promote fairer distribution of wealth.

26 June National Youth Administration is established to employ high school, college and graduate students.

5 July National Labor Relations Act, popularly known as the Wagner Act, requires employers to bargain collectively with elected representatives of workers, legitimizes the closed shop and sets up National Labour Relations Board to deal with unfair labour practices. Industrial relations transformed.

August Formation of United Automobile Workers (UAW).

14 August Social Security Act gives old-age pensions to those over 65 up to maximum $85 a month, to start in 1942 and be funded jointly by employer and employee contributions, with special provision for those unable to participate in programme. In addition, a federal-state plan of unemployment insurance is created, and federal funds granted to states for dependent mothers, the physically handicapped, blind and other categories of medical handicap.

23 August Banking Act replaces the Federal Reserve Board with seven-man board of governors, to exercise greater control over regional banks, remaking discount rates and reserve requirements. The reflationist Marriner Eccles becomes head the following year.

26 August Public Utility Holding Company Act empowers Federal Power Commission to regulate interstate commerce in electrical power and the Securities and Exchange Commission to exercise control over financial operations of holding companies. They compel giant utility companies, such as Commonwealth and Southern, to self-destruct within five years, but permit smaller organizations to operate within consolidated geographical areas.

29 August Alcohol Control Act revives NRA liquor code, vesting enforcement in treasury department.

30 August Revenue Act raises maximum surtax to 75 per cent, and increases taxes on estates and excess profits.

Guffey-Snyder Bituminous Coal Stabilization Act establishes commission to lay down competitive rules for soft coal industry, based closely on former NRA code.

Roosevelt signs Walsh-Healey Act, an attempt to create fair labour standards in manufacturing and construction, covering wages, hours and safety.

31 August Neutrality Act authorizes president to proclaim a state of war, ban all arms exports to belligerents, and warn US citizens against travelling on belligerent vessels.

8 September Assassination of Louisiana senator Huey Long, creator and leader of Share-Our-Wealth clubs.

3 October Italy invades Ethiopia: Roosevelt imposes an arms embargo, but exports of oil and other items to Italy continue.

16 October At American Federation of Labor convention in Atlantic City, delegates reject proposal by John L. Lewis of the mineworkers to organize skilled, semi-skilled and unskilled workers in single unions along industrial lines.

10 November John L. Lewis and leaders of eight other AFL unions form Committee (later Congress) of Industrial Organizations in Atlantic City. The CIO's aim is to organize industrial workers into industrial unions.

December Father Coughlin explicitly condemns the New Deal and president Roosevelt. His anti-Semitic rhetoric is now more noticeable.

1936

6 January Supreme Court strikes down the Agricultural Adjustment Act (*US v Butler*), arguing that agriculture was technically not interstate commerce and that Congress could not use taxation to regulate agriculture.

27 January Congress enacts immediate payment of veterans' bonus over Roosevelt's veto.

17 February In *Ashwander* v *Tennessee Valley Authority*, Supreme Court upholds TVA's right to dispose of surplus power, but only in specific case of the Ashwander Dam.

26 February Junior officers of Japanese imperial army mutiny to bring pressure on emperor Hirohito to promote social reform and pursue an aggressive foreign policy to find resources to finance it.

29 February Soil Conservation and Domestic Allotment Act passed to reintroduce policy of planned crop restriction embodied in 1933 Agricultural Adjustment Act struck down on 6 January by Supreme Court in the *Butler* case. Subsidies to farmers, encouraging them not to plant, and to raise farm prices are disguised as policy of soil conservation.

Neutrality Act extended a further six months; loans embargo added. Later, Act is extended to prevent aid to Loyalist government in Spanish Civil War, and stop US acting against Hitler or Japan.

2 March Carnegie-Illinois Steel Co., a subsidiary of US Steel, signs recognition agreement with the CIO Steel Workers' Organizing Committee (SWOC). All US Steel subsidiary companies quickly follow suit.

7 March Hitler occupies the Rhineland.

April Labour unions form non-partisan league to coordinate political activity for 1936 presidential election.

18 May US Supreme Court declares Guffey-Snyder Coal Stabilisation Act unconstitutional (in *Carter* v *Carter Coal Company*) on grounds that coal mining is not interstate commerce.

1 June In *Morehead v New York*, US Supreme Court strikes down New York state minimum wage law for women and children.

9 June Republican party nominating convention assembles at Cleveland, Ohio. Principal candidates are Herbert Hoover, senator Arthur Vandenberg of Michigan, senator William Borah of Idaho and governor Alfred M. Landon of Texas. Backed by the Hearst newspaper chain, Landon is nominated on the first ballot on 11 June with *Chicago Daily News* publisher Frank Knox as his running-mate.

The platform denounces New Deal but in effect acknowledges public support for it by promising not only to maintain most existing legislation, but also to furnish more effective relief, farm subsidies and labour programmes.

23 June Democratic party nominating convention assembles in Philadelphia, Pennsylvania, where Roosevelt and Garner are renominated by acclaim.

The platform advocates enlargement of existing New Deal programmes, with special emphasis on enforcement of antitrust legislation. Nothing is said about reforming the US Supreme Court.

11 July Sheriff's deputies kill two strikers at Republic Steel plant in Massillon, Ohio.

17 July Spanish Civil War begins.

14 August The new Union party convention meets in Cleveland and nominates radical North Dakota farm leader William Lemke for president and Thomas O'Brien of Massachusetts for vice-president. Ticket is backed by Father

Coughlin, Dr Francis E. Townsend and Rev. Gerald L.K. Smith, Huey Long's successor as leader of the Share-Our-Wealth Clubs and one of the most influential demagogues of his generation.

August–November The presidential campaign: Landon fails to inspire, while Roosevelt mounts a powerful, confident and increasingly demagogic attack on inequality, injustice and vested interests, roundly condemning trusts and 'economic royalists'. With the support of the farm belt, the industrial working class, blacks, organized labour, the intelligentsia and others, by mid-October Roosevelt's coalition appears invincible.

25 October Formation of the Rome–Berlin axis.

3 November Election day:

- Roosevelt with 27.8 million popular votes (60.8 per cent, the largest share in history) and 523 electoral votes wins a stunning endorsement.
- Landon with 16.7 million popular votes and 8 electoral votes loses in his home state of Kansas and carries only Maine and Vermont.
- Lemke wins 882,479 popular votes.

Democratic party majority in the House is 229 and in the Senate 56. Many state legislatures and governorships are won by Democrats for the first time in living memory. (See Map 1f.)

25 November Germany signs anti-Comintern pact with Japan.

23 December Buenos Aires declaration: all sovereign states in the western hemisphere agree never to intervene in each others' internal affairs.

29 December United Autoworkers members begin momentous sit-down strike at General Motors Fisher Body plant at Flint, Michigan, to win right to organize and bargain collectively conferred by 1935 National Labor Relations Act.

1937

8 January Congress extends Neutrality Act to include civil wars, such as that in Spain.

11 January Clashes occur between police and pickets in Flint, Michigan, as police attempt to block food deliveries to UAW sit-down strikers occupying GM plant.

20 January In his second inaugural address Roosevelt draws attention to America's central problem: 'one third of a nation ill-housed, ill-clad, ill-nourished'.

30 January Circuit judge Paul Godola issues an injunction ordering all UAW sit-down strikers to quit GM property in Flint. Strikers refuse to comply, and the sheriff of Flint refuses to arrest them.

3 February Michigan governor Frank Murphy refuses to instruct national guard to enforce the court injunction ordering sit-down strikers to quit GM property and joins Roosevelt in putting pressure on GM management to negotiate with their striking employees.

John L. Lewis, leader of the CIO, begins talks with GM vice-president William S. Knudsen to end strike.

3 February Roosevelt submits to Congress judiciary reorganisation bill, empowering the president to appoint additional Supreme Court justices (up to six), whenever a member of the Court fails to retire within six months of attaining the age of seventy. The same rule would also apply to all federal circuit judges, the maximum number of new appointees being 50.

11 February GM capitulates and agrees, without a certification election supervised by NLRB, to recognize UAW as sole bargaining agent under terms of the National Labor Relations Act.

March American Federation of Labor expels ten unions, including the UAW and Steel Workers' Organizing Committee, belonging to the CIO, which renamed the Congress of Industrial Organizations becomes a rival national labour federation.

1 March Congress passes Supreme Court Retirement Act, permitting justices to retire on full pay at or after the age of seventy.

2 March US Steel recognizes SWOC as sole union and signs contract giving 10 per cent pay rise, eight-hour day and forty-hour week.

21 March Chief justice Charles Evans Hughes writes an open letter denying Roosevelt's allegation that the Supreme Court is too slow in reaching judgements, arguing that a larger court would work more slowly.

24 March After negotiations between John L. Lewis and Chrysler, UAW ends its two-week occupation of the Chrysler plants.

29 March In *West Coast Hotel* v *Parrish*, the Supreme Court approves a Washington minimum wage law.

8 April Chrysler agrees to recognize the UAW as sole bargaining agent in its plants.

12 April Supreme Court upholds the National Labor Relations Act in *NLRB* v *Jones* and *Laughlin Steel Corporation*, dramatically reversing precedent of its earlier strict definition of interstate commerce, as in *Butler*, *Schechter* and *Carter* v *Carter* cases.

1 May Congress passes a stronger Neutrality Act. Whenever the president declares that a state of war exists anywhere in the world, US will make no arms sales or loans to belligerents, and forbid US citizens to travel on belligerent vessels.

6 May German airship *Hindenburg* explodes on landing at Lakehurst, New Jersey, igniting in a split second. Remarkably 65 survive. US monopoly of helium meant Germany had to use highly inflammable hydrogen, but this marks the end of airship passenger travel.

18 May Conservative justice Van Devanter announces intention to retire from the United States Supreme Court on 1 June.

24 May Supreme Court approves 1935 Social Security Act in *Steward Machine Co.* v *Davis*.

Roosevelt urges Congress to enact minimum wage and maximum hours legislation.

30 May Chicago police attack pickets and kill ten strikers at Republic Steel plant in 'Memorial Day massacre'.

June The 'Roosevelt recession': encouraged by economic recovery since 1935, Roosevelt responds to conservative critics, and seeks to redeem his 1932 pledge to cut government spending by a quarter. This he does by halving WPA rolls and lowering PWA and other spending. As a result, substantial economic gains since 1935 are wiped out: unemployment rises, GNP tumbles, and industrial production is reduced to 1934 levels.

3 June Roosevelt urges Congress to create six additional public power generating authorities like TVA.

12 July Roosevelt asks Congress to recreate the AAA programme by more careful, piecemeal legislation.

14 July Democratic Senate majority leader Joseph Robinson dies suddenly of a heart attack while working to keep the Supreme Court reform bill from foundering. His successor is senator Alben Barkley, of Kentucky.

22 July Senate sends Judiciary reorganization bill to committee.

Approval of Bankhead-Jones Farm Tenancy Act which establishes Farm Security Administration in place of the Resettlement Administration. It makes loans to tenant farmers, regulates working conditions of migrant labourers and sets up camps where workers can live.

31 July Senate approval of the Fair Labor Standards Act blocked by the House in committee.

17 August Hugo Black appointed to Supreme Court vacancy.

26 August Roosevelt signs Judicial Procedure Reform Act, a product of much compromise, which empowers the US attorney general to participate in lower federal court cases affecting the constitutionality of federal law and permits such cases to be switched direct to the Supreme Court. But it makes no changes to the structure of the Court itself.

1 September Approval of Wagner-Steagall Housing Act establishes the United States Housing Authority, with capital of $1 million and borrowing capacity of $500 million, later raised $1.6 billion, to make loans to local agencies for slum clearance and construction of affordable public housing.

October Roosevelt delivers his 'quarantine the aggressors' speech, indicating US desire to join with democratic Western nations to isolate Germany, Italy and Japan if they continue policies of military aggression against other sovereign states.

12 October Roosevelt calls Congress into special session to attempt to halt severe economic slump.

6 November Italy joins Germany and Japan in the anti-Comintern pact.

15 November In a 'fireside chat', Roosevelt presents an anti-recessionary programme to the American people to include new agricultural legislation, abolition of child labour, wages and hours legislation, reorganization of the executive department and an anti-trust crusade.

1938

10 January Influenced by FDR's plea on 6 January, the House rejects Ludlow amendment to Neutrality Act calling for national referenda before Congressional declarations of war. The vote is 209–188, but western and midwestern isolationist Democrats combine with Republicans to vote in favour.

16 February Approval of second Agricultural Adjustment Act, which empowers secretary of agriculture to set marketing quotas for export crops, creates Commodity Credit Corporation to store crop surpluses and make loans in order to achieve parity with 1909–14 agricultural purchasing power. Federal Crop Insurance Corporation launched to underwrite minimum crop prices.

12–13 March The *Anschluss*: Germany annexes Austria.

14 April In a special message to Congress Roosevelt announces looser credit restrictions and argues that these be used to stimulate more private spending to fill the gap left by reduced public spending.

30 April President makes public appeal for passage of Fair Labor Standards Act.

23 May House approves Fair Labor Standards Act. Though it excludes all farm workers and domestic servants, and many non-farm workers, its significance stems from establishing for the first time a national minimum wage (25 cents an hour) with a maximum working week (44 hours), and forbidding interstate commerce in goods manufactured, even in part, by children under 16.

27 May Conservatives in Congress push through a Revenue Act, cutting corporation tax in a bid to stimulate investment and thus economic growth.

16 June Creation of Temporary National Economic Committee (TNEC) by joint Congressional resolution under chairmanship of senator Joseph O'Mahoney of Wyoming to investigate monopoly and honour FDR's commitment to 'trust busting'.

24 June Congress passes Food Drug and Cosmetic Act requiring manufacturers to list product ingredients on labels and forbidding misleading advertising.

Roosevelt declares his intention to take part in forthcoming Democratic primaries in order to purge reactionary southern politicians.

25 June Congress passes Fair Labor Standards Act.

12 August Publication of independent *Report on Economic Conditions in the South* highlights the region's chronic economic problems.

29–30 September At Munich conference Britain and France capitulate to Hitler's demand for German occupation of the Sudetenland in Czechoslovakia.

8 November Mid-term Congressional election results reveal failure of FDR's campaign to purge southern conservatives from Democratic party ranks. Among others, senators Walter F. George of Alabama and Millard Tydings of Maryland survive defiantly. Democrats lose 7 seats in Senate and 70 in the House.

24 December Lima declaration, by which the US and 20 other nations in the western hemisphere agree to uphold republican institutions and to consult when their mutual security is threatened.

1939

January In *Tennessee Electric Power Co.* v *TVA*, US Supreme Court rules that government competition against private power companies is legitimate, thus enhancing 1936 *Ashwander* decision on constitutionality of TVA.

4 January For the first time in one of his annual messages, Roosevelt steers public attention towards foreign affairs and the danger of war.

15 March Hitler annexes rest of Czechoslovakia.

3 April Administrative Reorganization Act promotes greater efficiency for the executive branch of government by regrouping administrative agencies. On 1 July FDR establishes several umbrella offices: the Federal Security Agency, the Federal Works Agency, the Federal Loan Agency, and, by executive order 8248, the executive office of the president, which expands the size of the president's staff. This last measure will soon greatly enhance the power of the executive branch.

15 April Roosevelt asks Hitler and Mussolini for assurances that they do not intend to change European frontiers by force. Hitler responds in a speech which combines scorn with derision.

10 July Senate foreign relations committee refuses to amend 1937 Neutrality Act to allow US to send military aid to Britain and France.

August President of Commonwealth and Southern Corporation Wendell Willkie sells Tennessee Electric Power Co. to the TVA for $79 million. TVA's David Lilienthal personally hands Willkie the cheque in public.

2 August Hatch Act forbids participation of federal officers in political campaigns.

23 August Joachim von Ribbentrop and V.M. Molotov, foreign ministers of Germany and the Soviet Union, sign Nazi–Soviet non-aggression pact.

1 September Germany invades Poland.

3 September Britain and France declare war on Germany.

5 September US declares its neutrality in European war.

28 September Germany and Soviet Union partition Poland.

3 October US declaration of Panama defines entire western hemisphere south of Canada a 'safety zone', reaffirming the Monroe doctrine.

4 November Neutrality Act of 1939 is amended to allow export of arms to belligerents on cash and carry basis. President further empowered to declare combat zones from which US vessels are prohibited.

30 November Soviet Union invades Finland.

1940

26 January US allows 1911 trade treaty with Japan to lapse.

9 April–22 June German *Blitzkrieg* overwhelms Norway, Denmark, the Netherlands, Belgium and France.

18 April Roosevelt extends protection of Monroe doctrine to Greenland.

10 May Following German defeat of British expeditionary landing at Narvik in Norway, Neville Chamberlain resigns as prime minister. Winston Churchill forms war coalition. Churchill begins personal correspondence with Roosevelt which continues throughout war until FDR's death in April 1945.

16 May In special message to Congress, Roosevelt stresses need for US preparedness, and proposes construction of 50,000 aircraft per year.

17 May Organization of the national committee to Defend America by Aiding the Allies promotes new concept of US as Arsenal of Democracy.

26 May–3 June Evacuation of British (and some French) troops, completely routed by German blitzkrieg, from Dunkirk. More than 330,000 fighting men are saved, but arms, equipment and tanks are lost.

28 May Advisory commission re-established to Council of National Defense, under GM chairman William S. Knudsen, president of General Motors.

31 May Roosevelt asks Congress to vote a further billion dollars for defence.

10 June Fascist Italy joins Nazi Germany in dismemberment of France.

12 June German army enters Paris. Victory parade follows through French Arc de Triomphe.

25 June Congress authorizes RFC to finance construction of new defence plants.

27 June Roosevelt revives Espionage Act of 1917.

28 June Republican party presidential convention meets at Philadelphia.

Candidates: Robert A. Taft (Ohio), Thomas E. Dewey (New York) and Arthur Vandenberg (Michigan) are all strong contenders, with Vandenberg the leading isolationist force in the party. When their votes cancel each other out, delegates revolt and nominate Wendell L. Willkie on the sixth ballot.

Willkie is the last real 'dark horse' to be nominated for president, and was actually a registered Democrat when the Republicans chose him. But his record fighting for Commonwealth and Southern against TVA and the whole New Deal throughout the 1930s has impressed both rank-and-file Republicans and FDR.

Senator Charles L. McNary (Iowa), his running mate, favours tariffs and subsidies for farmers. Willkie and McNary campaign on a platform which, although highly critical, implicitly accepts much New Deal legislation. Internationalists persuade party to accept principle of prompt defence and aid to nations falling victim to military aggression.

7 July Congressional amendment to naval appropriations bill forbids president to transfer to a foreign power equipment deemed essential to national defence.

29 June Alien Registration Act requires all aliens to register, tightens deportation laws and makes it illegal to advocate or teach overthrow of any US government by force or to organize a group for such purposes.

15 July Democratic party convention opens in Chicago.

Roosevelt announces he will not break the 'George Washington precedent' and actively seek presidential renomination for a third term. After his campaign staff engineer delegate acclaim, FDR is nominated on first ballot. His running-mate, secretary of agriculture Henry A. Wallace, is accepted as Garner's successor only after vigorous arm-twisting.

16 July Fall of moderate Yonai cabinet in Japan signals more active military policy to break perceived economic encirclement by democratic Western powers.

26 July US enforced embargo on export of aviation fuel, scrap metal and lubricants to Japan is expanded to include steel, iron ore and pig iron in September and December 1940.

September Formation of isolationist America First Committee stimulates further debate about US involvement in global military and political conflict.

2 September US agrees to give 50 used destroyers to British government, in return for pledge that Britain will never surrender its fleet, and 99–year leases on British naval bases in the Caribbean and Newfoundland.

September–November In Battle of Britain German airforce fails to win command of the skies over London and Britain as a whole. With British fleet still in command of the waters between the continent of Europe and the British Isles, Hitler's embryonic invasion plans are abandoned. Badly bombed, Britain fights on alone, aided briefly by Greece, until June 1941.

22 September Japan occupies northern French Indo-China.

27 September Axis-Japanese military pact signed in Berlin, pledging mutual assistance if attacked by a nation not already at war.

October Prompted by apparent failure of his initial campaign to woo voters, Wendell Willkie starts to brand Roosevelt a war-monger.

8 October Britain reopens Burma Road, vital to the British Empire and chief supply route to Nationalist China and its government in Chungking.

Revenue Act encourages further US defence construction by permitting businessmen to write off costs through tax deductions.

28 October In campaign speech at Madison Square Garden, Roosevelt stresses that US can only keep out of war by helping Britain defeat European aggressors.

30 October Roosevelt makes pledge to Boston campaign audience that 'Your boys are not going to be sent to fight in any foreign wars'.

5 November Election day.

- Franklin Roosevelt. With 27.2 million votes, and 449 electoral votes, he wins impressive endorsement for an unprecedented third term as president with 54.3 per cent of the popular vote.
- Wendell Willkie. With 22.3 million popular votes (more than any previous Republican) and 82 electoral votes, he adds the grain-belt states, Colorado, Iowa, Michigan and his home state Indiana to Maine and Vermont, which Landon had carried in 1936.
- Norman Thomas. Wins only 100,264 votes for the Socialist party.
- Earl Browder. Wins a derisory 48,579 votes for the Communist party. (See Map 1g.)

16 December FDR tells reporters of principles behind new policy of lend-lease, announcing it to the nation in a radio 'fireside chat' on 29 December.

6. The Second World War, 1941–45

1941

6 January President's annual message contains first public announcement of the Four Freedoms, which envisage a postwar world based upon freedom of speech and religion, and freedom from want and fear.

7 January Office of Production Mangement (OPM) created by executive fiat under William S. Knudsen, of General Motors, and Sidney Hillman of the CIO.

10 January–11 March Congress approves Lend-Lease bill. When Roosevelt signs Act he asks Congress for a $7 billion appropriation, which Congress grants.

25 March Germany extends war zone to Iceland and Denmark Strait, off Greenland sending submarines and aircraft into north Atlantic to attack Allied shipping. FDR authorizes US naval yards to repair British vessels.

31 March US coast guard seizes 30 Axis (German and Italian) merchant ships in US ports.

10 April American neutrality patrol extended to longtitude 25 degrees west, off the coast of Iceland but including the Azores in the central north Atlantic.

11 April FDR's adviser Leon Henderson appointed to head Office of Price Administration and Civilian Supply (OPA) to protect consumer interests in wartime by controlling inflation.

14 April Secret discussions open between US secretary of state Cordell Hull and Japan's Amercan ambassador admiral Kichisaburo Nomura.

15 May German submarine torpedoes US freighter, the *Robin Moor*, in South Atlantic.

22 June Germany renounces Nazi–Soviet pact of 23 August 1939 and invades Soviet Union with scores of armoured divisions.

25 June Prompted by threatened protest march on Washington, Roosevelt issues executive order 8802, requiring blacks to be admitted to federal job training programmes, outlawing discrimination in defence contract work and establishing Fair Employment Practice Committee.

7 July Because of its strategic importance to naval control of the north Atlantic, US occupies Iceland with agreement of Winston Churchill and consent of Icelandic prime minister.

14 July Japan demands surrender of French land, air and naval bases in southern Indo-China.

28 July US retaliates against Japanese occupation of southern Indo-China by seizing all Japan's assets in US and barring Panama Canal to Japanese shipping.

1 August More raw materials, including oil, added to list of exports banned to Japan.

9 August Roosevelt and Churchill meet aboard US cruiser *Augusta* off Newfoundland. On 15 August they sign the Atlantic Charter, setting out various common principles for the future: no territorial aggrandisement, no territorial changes without consent of those affected, the right of all persons to choose the form of goverment under which they live, economic collaboration and the right of the world's people to enjoy FDR's Four Freedoms.

28 August President suspends Office of Production Management, leaving an OPM council and setting up supplies priorities and allocation board under Donald M. Nelson of Sears Roebuck.

4 September German submarine attacks US destroyer *Greer* south of Iceland, after it had joined a British aeroplane in trailing the U-boat.

11 September Claiming attack on *Greer* is part of German plan to control the Atlantic, prior to an assault upon the western hemisphere, Roosevelt announces that all friendly vessels will be protected in waters between US and Iceland, and that all German and Italian vessels of war will be attacked on sight.

2 October America's final refusal to hold peace conference with Japan until both governments can reach agreement over ending Japan's war with China.

9 October Roosevelt asks Congress to amend Neutrality Law to permit arming of American merchant ships.

16–17 October US destroyer *Kearny* torpedoed by German submarine with eleven American sailors' lives lost.

18 October Following US refusal to talk about peace in China, Prince Fumimaro Konoye's Japanese government falls.

31 October German submarine torpedoes US destroyer *Reuben James*, with 115 Americans killed.

7 November On anniversary of Bolshevik revolution, US declares Soviet Union is eligible for Lend-Lease.

Senate sanctions arming of American merchant marine.

13 November House approves arming of merchant vessels, and their passage through war zone to British ports such as Liverpool and London.

6 December Japan breaks diplomatic relations with US.

7 December Before Japanese embassy staff can communicate message about breaking diplomatic relations, two waves of

Japanese aircraft attack main US Pacific Ocean naval base at Pearl Harbor in Hawaii. More than 2,000 men of the US marines and navy are killed, five of eight battleships are sunk or disabled. Aircraft carriers are at sea and so are spared. This proves decisive in the US winning the Battle of Midway the following summer. (See Map 3.)

Simultaneous military attacks are launched in the Philippines, Hong Kong, Wake and Midway islands, Siam and Malaya, while Japan declares war on US and Britain.

8 December In special address to Congress, Roosevelt calls 7 December 1941 'a date that will live in infamy'. Congress declares war against Japan.

AFL and CIO agree to a no-strike pledge for duration of war.

11 December Germany declares war on US, followed by Italy, and America reacts by declaring war on both. Congress quickly orders all men aged 20–44 to register for military service.

Japan captures strategically important Pacific island base at Guam.

British battleships *King George V* and *Repulse* sunk off Hong Kong by Japanese aircraft, giving Japanese imperial navy capital ships command of the Pacific Ocean.

22 December Winston Churchill arrives in Washington DC for Arcadia conference to devise war strategies and establish Combined Chiefs of Staff. Conference concedes Churchill's key demand that defeat of Germany in Europe be given priority over defeat of Japan in Asia and the Pacific, despite strong US lobby urging contrary view.

23–25 December Japan captures American base at Wake Island in the Pacific and key British naval base and colony of Hong Kong, just off the mainland of southern China.

1942

January Emergency Price Control Act empowers price administrator to set maximum prices and rents in key areas of the war economy.

Albert Einstein, a German physicist who published the theory of relativity in 1905 but had been forced to leave Nazi Germany for the US in 1933 because he was Jewish, writes to Roosevelt warning that German scientists could develop an atomic bomb. He urges the president to make sure US gets there first. Manhattan Project is born.

1 January United States, the Soviet Union, Britain and 23 other Allied nations sign the United Nations declaration, supporting principles of the Atlantic Charter.

5 January In his annual budget message, Roosevelt proposes $7 billion dollars in new taxes to win the war.

12 January War Labor Board created to prevent strikes and reconcile wages with control over inflation and the war economy.

Composed of representatives of management, unions and public, the board offers unions maintenance of membership, by which existing membership levels and bargaining rights remain effectively intact for the duration of the war, but new workers are not compelled to join unions.

15–28 January At Rio de Janeiro conference, republics in western hemisphere agree to sever relations with Axis powers, although Chile and Argentina do not comply until January 1943 and January 1944 respectively.

16 January Creation of War Production Board under Donald Nelson with overall command of domestic war economy.

26 January First US troops for European theatre of war arrive in Northern Ireland.

15 February Japanese army captures key British naval base at Singapore in Malaya by inland invasion cutting the route north to Burma.

19 February California and the whole west coast is deemed a theatre of war. By executive order 9066, Roosevelt commands general John L. De Witt to remove all 118,000 Japanese-Americans living on the west coast, many of them second generation American citizens born in the United States.

By April more than 100,000 had been sent to concentration camps. The victims – 47,000 *Issei,* or Japanese ineligible for naturalization under the 1924 Act, and 80,000 *Nesei,* or Japanese-Americans born in the United States – are forced to leave everything behind. After screening, 18,000 are interned in camps at Tule Lake, California, while 36,000 are given option of resettlement in midwest and east, often starting on farm camps. They lose their jobs, businesses, property, but at the end of 1944 the US Supreme Court upholds the action in *Korematsu* v *United States.* In his lone dissent, justice Frank Murphy describes the decision as 'the legalization of racism'. Later all victims of internment receive compensation from federal government.

April War Manpower Commission is established under general Paul V. McNutt, to channel and control flow of workers into war industries.

28 April Office of Price Administration (OPA) issues first general maximum price regulation, fixing many prices and rents at level of March 1942.

6 May Japanese troops complete conquest of Philippines. General Douglas MacArthur vows 'I shall return'.

7–8 May US conduct of Battle of the Coral Sea deters large Japanese naval force from attacking Port Moresby in New Guinea, checking Japanese advance in southwestern Pacific.

26 May Soviet foreign minister Molotov signs 20-year treaty of alliance with Britain, with no references to postwar Soviet frontiers.

General Erwin Rommel launches Germany's north African advance towards the Suez Canal with the Libya campaign.

29 May V. M. Molotov arrives in Washington DC for military conferences. He demands Allies open a second front in Europe to take pressure off the Soviet Union.

30 May Britain's RAF launches first 1,000-bomber raid against Germany on Cologne (Koln).

3–6 June US naval and air forces win Battle of Midway, preventing Japanese naval and land forces capturing Midway Island. Within seven months of Pearl Harbor America has gone on the offensive, and this was to prove a decisive turning point in the Pacific war. (See Maps 4 and 5.)

24 June General Dwight D. Eisenhower is appointed commander US forces in Europe.

16 July War Labor Board announces 'little steel' formula. This gives most American workers a 15 per cent pay increase to offset wartime inflation, but later bedevils pay bargaining and helps stimulate industrial unrest.

8 August Eight German saboteurs, sent to US in May but captured almost immediately in Long Island and Florida, are executed.

At Battle of Savo Island, Japanese sink four Allied cruisers, but fail to press home advantage.

17 August US Army Air Corps joins air war against Germany.

16 August Appointment of special committee under Bernard M. Baruch starts to investigate wartime rubber shortage. Urges petrol rationing and national 30 mph speed limit for road vehicles.

19 August British and Canadian surprise raid on Dieppe ends in disaster.

2 October Anti-Inflation Act empowers Roosevelt to limit pay and prices (but not profits) at level current on 15 September for remainder of war.

3 October Supreme Court justice James F. Byrnes is made head of Office of Economic Stabilization. Byrnes rapidly assumes complete control of allocation of steel, aluminium and copper, and freezes agricultural prices.

21 October Revenue Act brings unprecedented range of tax increases: combined corporate income tax is raised to 40 per cent, excess profits tax to 90 per cent, with 50 million Americans now paying federal income tax.

24 October British 8th Army launches decisive north African counter-attack at El Alamein.

3 November Mid-term Congressional elections bring large gains to Republicans, including election of Thomas E. Dewey as first Republican governor of New York since 1920.

8 November First landings by Anglo-American forces under Eisenhower in strength in north Africa at Morocco, Casablanca, Oran and Algiers. General Erwin Rommel's German army faces war on two fronts. (See Map 3.)

18 November Military draft age lowered from 21 to 18.

19 November Soviet counter-offensive begins at Stalingrad.

December Leon Henderson, influential economic adviser to FDR, resigns as administrator of OPA.

2 December Since E.O. Lawrence built first cyclotron in 1930 to smash atoms, race has been on to release atomic power. Enrico Fermi, an Italian physicist who came to the US in 1939, and others in America and Europe, carry out a series of experiments to produce atomic energy by splitting uranium-235 atoms. Now A.H. Crompton and others achieve first controlled atomic chain reaction in disused racket court at Stagg Field, University of Chicago. Top secret plan, codenamed the Manhattan Project, to develop an atomic bomb is now well in train.

1943

January Coalition of southern Democrats and conservative Republicans dominates new 78th Congress.

2 January US forces capture Buna in New Guinea from Japanese imperial army.

14 January Roosevelt arrives in Casablanca for conference with Churchill. Both sides agree to invade Sicily and defer full-scale invasion of France until 1944. Allies to insist on unconditional surrender of Axis powers.

30 January German armies under field marshall Friedrich von Paulus surrender at Stalingrad on FDR's birthday and tenth anniversary of Hitler becoming chancellor. More than 330,000 German soldiers are killed or captured.

7–8 February Japanese withdraw from Guadalcanal in the Solomon Islands.

11–12 February Allies launch counter-offensive in north Africa. Montgomery's 8th Army and Anglo-French–American forces inflict heavy losses on Axis armies, reopening Mediterranean to Allied shipping.

22 February Roosevelt delivers stinging veto to revenue bill amended by conservative Congress to raise less than one quarter of the $16 billion requested in his budget message to win the war.

2–4 March Battle of Bismarck Sea brings Solomon Islands/New Britain area of Pacific under US control.

2 April FDR vetoes bill to exclude subsidy and parity payments from calculation of agricultural parity levels.

22 April Occupation of Hollondia completes US conquest of New Guinea.

1 May John L. Lewis of United Mine Workers calls general coal strike in pursuit of wage increase. President seizes coal mines, orders miners back to work. Unrest in coal industry continues throughout 1943.

Roosevelt gives general Leslie R. Groves and army corps of engineers control of top-secret Manhattan Project, to develop atomic bomb. Work is moved to Los Alamos, New Mexico, where professor J. Robert Oppenheimer supervises greatest array of scientific talent ever assembled in one place. Though Germany is defeated before bomb is produced, it is exploded under test conditions in New Mexican desert at Alamogordo on 16 July 1945 and dropped on Hiroshima and Nagasaki in Japan on 6 and 9 August 1945, forcing Japanese surrender.

11 May Churchill arrives in Washington for talks codenamed Trident, which approve plans for intensified aerial bombardment of Germany, invasion of Italy and invasion of France with Operation Overlord in May 1944.

11 June Miners renew strike action, but return to work when Roosevelt threatens to draft them.

20 June Rioting in Detroit sparked off by fight between a white man and an African-American lasts several days, during which 25 blacks and 9 whites are killed.

26 June War Labor Disputes Act, passed over Roosevelt's veto, empowers president to seize any strike-bound plant, and makes 30-day cooling off period and secret strike ballots compulsory.

July At Kursk in the Ukraine, German army launches huge counter-attack against Soviet forces in attempt to win back initiative lost after catastrophic defeat at Stalingrad. After the greatest tank battle in history, and at a cost of some 750,000 casualties on both sides, German army is beaten again. Thereafter it is always in retreat on the eastern front.

10 July 160,000 Allied troops land in Sicily from north Africa, bringing war closer to the south German frontier.

25 July Benito Mussolini, Italian fascist dictator since 1922, is deposed and arrested. German troops later free him. New government under marshal Badoglio opens negotiations with Allies.

3 August Allied forces under admiral Mountbatten and US general Stillwell take Myitkyina from Japanese in Burma.

11–24 August At Quebec conference foreign secretaries Hull, Molotov and Eden establish European Advisory Commission to determine postwar policy on Germany.

17 August German and Italian forces in Sicily surrender.

3 September British 8th Army crosses Straits of Messina to launch invasion of Italian mainland.

8 September Italy signs armistice with Allies. German troops surround Rome and secure airfields to prevent Allied landings.

10 September US 5th Army lands in Gulf of Naples and occupies the city on 7 October.

14 October Heavy losses in raid on ballbearings factories in Schweinfurt convince US air commanders to suspend daylight raids on German cities.

18–30 October Foreign secretaries Hull, Molotov and Eden confer in Moscow. Much agreement on immediate and postwar aims, including reconstitution of Austria as independent and liberated state, although Poland remains a sticking-point. Stalin signs Four Power Declaration.

1 November Announcement of Three Power (America, Britain and France) declaration on war crimes, promising swift and severe punishment of all found guilty of war crimes.

20–24 November Allied capture of Tarawa and Makin Islands from Japanese in central Pacific.

22–26 November At Cairo conference, Roosevelt, Churchill and Chiang Kai-shek of China agree to:

- wage war until Japan surrenders unconditionally
- return to China all possessions taken by Japan since 1931
- strip Japan of Pacific islands, including those granted by League of Nations mandate in 1919
- restore independence to Korea, which had been absorbed into Japan in 1905.

23–27 November First wartime Big Three conference of Roosevelt, Churchill and Stalin held at Teheran. Stalin eager to commit US and Britain to precise time and place for invasion of France; all agree to partition postwar Germany so forestalling future German resurgence; Roosevelt outlines plan for creation of United Nations; Stalin agrees to enter war against Japan after capitulation of Germany. Prevailing spirit of cordiality convinces FDR that he has laid the basis for peaceful postwar cooperation with Soviet Union.

4–6 December At second Cairo conference, Roosevelt and Churchill agree to make general Dwight D. Eisenhower supreme commander of invasion of France.

1944

15 January General Eisenhower arrives in London to plan and organize Operation Overlord for the invasion of France.

22 January Allied landings at Anzio and Nettuno on west coast of Italy.

23 February With resumption of daylight air-raids, US air command begins campaign to destroy German aircraft industry.

24–25 February Senate and House override Roosevelt's veto of 1944 Revenue Act so that tax taken to win war is greatly reduced.

29 February Allied troops occupy Admiralty Islands, north of New Guinea, completing encirclement and isolation of Japanese naval and air base at Rabaul.

4 June Rome, which had been declared an Open City to avoid war damage, is liberated.

6 June After 24-hour delay caused by bad weather, Eisenhower launches the greatest combined, amphibious military operation in history by invading France, joining William the Conqueror and Julius Caesar as the only military commanders to lead successful invasions across the English Channel. Some 4,000 invasion craft land 176,000 troops, with 6,000 warships and 11,000 planes in support. US troops take heaviest casualties at Utah and Omaha beaches on the Cotentin Peninsular of Normandy. By July Allied armies have control of Caen and Germans cannot throw invaders back into the sea. By September, 2 million men and 3 million tons of supplies have been landed. (See Map 3.)

15 June US launches sustained air war against Japan, where anti-aircraft defences are much weaker than in Germany.

19–20 June Japanese suffer heavy air and naval losses in first Battle of the Philippine Sea.

23 June Launch of huge Soviet offensive, entering Poland and the Baltic states, which finally arrives at the Oder river, 45 miles from Berlin by the end of the year. Combined with the advance of Allied powers on the western front, German strategic military situation now appears terminal. (See Map 3.)

26 June Republican nominating convention opens in Chicago. Thomas E. Dewey, governor of New York, is nominated on the first ballot by an overwhelming 1,056 votes to 1. Governor John W. Bricker of Ohio receives vice-presidential nomination. An internationalist, liberal platform is adopted, with no talk of undoing the New Deal.

1–22 July Key international monetary and financial conference at Bretton Woods, New Hampshire, establishes International Monetary Fund to stabilize national currencies, and the Interantional Bank for Reconstrucion and Development to lend money for postwar reconstruction and investment in under-developed regions. All currency values will be linked to American dollar, but main aim is to avoid the problems of debt and trade which poisoned world politics between 1918 and 1939.

11 July Franklin Roosevelt announces he will accept Democratic presidential nomination, frustrating his conservative critics and effectively ending the nomination contest.

17 July Labour leader Sidney Hillman withdraws support of CIO's influential political action committee from FDR's choice for vice president, senator James Byrnes of South Carolina. Byrnes withdraws his candidacy.

18 July Moderates oust admiral Tojo and form new Japanese government under navy minister Mitsumasa, seeking rapid end to war.

19 July Democratic convention opens in Chicago. As FDR planned, Harry S. Truman wins vice presidential nomination on the 3rd ballot, with support of Hillman and the CIO, defeating incumbent Henry Wallace. Roosevelt is renominated on first ballot. Convention adopts platform of continued New Deal policies at home, and US leadership in postwar world.

20 July Well-planned attempt to assassinate Hitler by German officers and anti-Nazi groups led by colonel Claus von Stauffenburg fails. All conspirators are summarily executed.

25 July Allies commence campaign to break out of bridgehead in Normandy. Patton's 3rd Army advances west into Brittany.

August–November Presidential campaign. Dewey is hampered by good war news and his general concurrence with FDR's policies, but benefits from president's visibly declining health. Roosevelt campaigns vigorously from Washington DC, assisted by CIO-PAC's effective work on the ground.

15 August US 7th Army lands in southern France, catching German forces in France in a pincer movement.

16 August US government freezes Argentina's assets held in US after pro-Nazi, anti-American demonstrations in Buenos Aires.

21 August–7 October Dumbarton Oaks conference in Washington DC establishes structure for postwar United Nations organization to replace the League, but British, Soviet and US delegates cannot agree on voting procedure for the UN.

25 August To spare the city damage, the German commander of occupying troops in Paris surrenders to Free French soldiers supported in strength by Americans.

20 October US combined air, ground and naval forces start to liberate US dominion of the Philippine islands.

24–25 October Most of remaining Japanese fleet destroyed in Battle for Leyte Gulf, as Japan fails to halt US assault upon Philippines.

28 October In his economic Bill of Rights speech at Soldier Field, Chicago, Roosevelt calls for large-scale public spending to sustain American prosperity after the war and ward off the threat of socialism.

7 November Election day:

- Franklin Roosevelt with 25.6 million popular votes and 432 electoral votes wins a fourth overwhelming victory.
- Thomas E. Dewey wins 22 million popular votes and 99 electoral votes.
- Norman Thomas of the Socialist party, wins 81,000 popular votes.
- Democrats gain 20 seats in House, mostly in large cities, and 5 governorships. (See Map 1h.)

11–16 September Second Quebec conference produces agreement between Roosevelt and Churchill on American and British occupation zones in Germany.

9–18 October At the second Moscow conference Churchill and Stalin agree to partition Balkans into British and Soviet spheres of influence, and bind Poland by Curzon line in east and Oder river in west.

23 October US finally recognizes French government-in-exile under generals Charles de Gaulle and Henri Giraud, who form provisional government in liberated France.

21 November Aachen becomes first German city to fall to Allies. Unlike in 1918, Germany now suffers invasion.

December In *Korematsu* v *United States,* Supreme Court rules that forced evacuation of Japanes–Americans into concentration camps in 1941–42 was constitutional on grounds of clear and present danger of war and overriding demands of national security.

16 December German counter-offensive led by general Gerd von Rundstedt in Ardennes achieves impressive success, but is halted on 26 December. German army retreats, though V-1 and V-2 terror weapons are still raining death on British civilian targets in and around London. (See Map 3.)

1945

4–11 February Crucial Big Three conference at Yalta. Agreement on partition of Germany, future government of Poland, organization of United Nations (including voting procedures), and future Russian control of Outer Mongolia.

19 February–16 March US marine corps, at great cost in casualties, invades and captures Iwo Jima in the Philippines.

6 March Cologne (Koln) is first major German city to fall to US 1st Army.

7 March US troops capture Ludendorff bridge across the Rhine at Remagen.

9 March US airforce launches heavy firebombing raid on Tokyo, killing and wounding 185,000 Japanese civilians and totally destroying 16 square miles of the city.

20 March Allies capture Mandalay and regain initiative in Burma from Japan.

24 March Anglo-American armies cross the Rhine in strength.

28 March General Eisenhower, supreme commander Allied powers in Europe, informs Soviet dictator Joseph Stalin of his decision not to press on to capture Berlin, instead concentrating upon the areas of Bavaria and western Austria selected by Hitler for Nazi Germany's last stand.

1–21 April US marines capture Okinawa, major island in chain leading to Japan itself. Japanese lose 111,000 dead and 4,000 aircraft, while US forces take 50,000 casualties.

8 April Japanese emperor Hirohito appoints baron Kantaro Suzuki as prime minister, charging him with bringing an end to the war.

11 April US troops reach river Elbe, 53 miles from Berlin.

12 April Franklin D. Roosevelt dies at 4.35 p.m. of cerebral haemorrhage. His last words are 'I have a terrific headache'. Harry S. Truman is sworn in as president.

15 April Marshal Grigori Zhukov launches Soviet offensive across river Oder.

24 April–2 May Soviet troops enter and capture Berlin.

27 April US and Soviet troops meet on the river Elbe near Torgau.

28 April Italian Communist partisans capture and shoot fascist dictator Mussolini, hanging his dead body from a Milan lamp post.

30 April Hitler appoints admiral Karl Doenitz his successor as *Führer*, then marries his mistress Eva Braun, forces her to take poison and shoots himself. His dead body is burned by Nazis outside his Berlin bunker. Goebbels and Himmler also commit suicide. Goering tries to escape but is captured.

3 May Capture of Rangoon by British completes reconquest of Burma.

7 May Colonel-general Alfred Jodl surrenders unconditionally the remnants of all German land, air and sea forces at Rheims. All hostilities to cease at midnight on 8 May: V-E Day.

9 May Soviet Army occupies Prague in Czechoslovakia.

5 July US completes liberation of Philippines. General Douglas MacArthur honours his May 1942 vow to return.

12 July After more than three years of top secret work by an international group of scientists, like Fermi from Italy and Teller from Hungary, in an elite team headed by the American physicist J. Robert Oppenheimer, construction of first atomic bomb begins at Los Alamos, New Mexico. The Manhattan Project comes to fruition.

16 July First successful detonation of atomic bomb at Alamagordo air base, New Mexico.

17 July–2 August Crucial Potsdam conference in Berlin, attended by Truman, Stalin, Churchill and Churchill's successor as prime minister, Clement Attlee. Conference agrees that:

- Council of foreign ministers of the Big Five – America, Britain, France, Kuomintang (Nationalist) China and the Soviet Union – to prepare peace treaties and deal with central German government as and when it comes into being.
- Polish-German borders to be settled by final peace treaties.
- Germany to be democratized and de-Nazified.

- Occupied Germany to be single economic unit.
- Soviet Union to remove capital equipment from Germany in lieu of reparations.

26 July Truman tells Stalin US has atomic bomb.

Potsdam declaration calls upon Japan to surrender or face 'the utter devastation of the Japanese homeland'. Suzuki government unable to persuade army leaders to surrender.

6 August First atomic bomb dropped on Hiroshima, killing an estimated 115,000 mostly civilian Japanese.

8 August Soviet Union enters war against Japan, occupying Kurile islands.

9 August Second atomic bomb, of slightly different design, dropped on Nagasaki with similar loss of life.

10 August Japan offers to surrender. (See Map 5.)

14 August Japanese government accepts Allied peace terms, which keep emperor Hirohito in place. US troops start to occupy Japan.

2 September General MacArthur takes Japan's surrender aboard US battleship *Missouri* in Tokyo Bay. MacArthur further humiliates Japanese delegation by dressing in casual uniform.

6 September In his domestic message to Congress, president Harry S. Truman calls for relaunching of New Deal reform, including expansion of social security, increased minimum wages, renewal of slum clearance, national health insurance, full employment legislation and extension of wartime economic controls.

8 October In radio broadcast, Harry Truman tells US voters that higher wages are imperative to fill drop in purchasing power after the war, and argues that FDR's economic Bill of Rights (announced the year before and based on public spending to stimulate demand) be the nation's target.

November Republican-dominated Congress responds negatively to this by making $6 billion in tax cuts.

5 November National labour-management conference convened in Washington DC at Truman's request. Fails to avert series of very costly postwar strikes.

19 November General Eisenhower replaces general Marshall as US army chief of staff.

President Truman urges Congress to adopt a national, federally funded health insurance programme.

21 November More than 180,000 auto workers begin 113-day UAW strike against General Motors plants for 30 per cent pay rise.

15 December General Marshall appointed special ambassador to China to make peace between Mao Tse-tung's Communist and Chiang Kai-shek's Nationalist forces struggling for control of world's largest nation.

20 December All limited wartime rationing of meat, butter, shoes, tyres and petrol ends.

31 December Truman dismantles War Labor Board and replaces it with Wage Stabilization Board in attempt to control postwar pay, prices, profits and inflation.

SECTION II

Foreign Policy, 1910–1940

1. US Imperialism in the Caribbean

American foreign policy has been covered in general between 1910 and 1940, and in detail between 1940 and 1945, in the first chronological section. This section is designed to tell separately the detailed story of US imperialism and foreign policy from 1910 until 1940.

Cuba

1898–1902 US military government occupies Cuba after Spanish–American war, repairs civil war damage and adopts new framework of government.

2 March 1902 Platt amendment to Congressional appropriations bill requires Cuba to make no treaties with foreign powers which might impair independence. US would enjoy right to intervene 'for the preservation of Cuban independence, the maintenance of a government adequate for the protection of life, property and individual liberty'. Embodied in treaty of 22 May 1903 and Cuban constitution.

1904 President Roosevelt enunciates his corollary to the Monroe doctrine, signalling that US would exercise police power but tolerate no futher European intervention in the Caribbean. As Britain withdraws large portions of her naval squadron in 1904–5 the US seeks maritime supremacy in the Caribbean.

December 1905 Second national elections in Cuba see anti-US rioting. President Tomás Estrada Palma requests American intervention.

1906–09 Further US occupation establishes provisional government under Charles E. Magoon, governor of the Canal Zone. New elections held and a government formed.

1911 Marine detatchments sent in and stationed at the naval base of Guantanamo in response to another popular revolt.

1917 Further US intervention.

Puerto Rico

29 August 1916 Jones Act accords measure of self-government and US citizenship to all inhabitants.

The Virgin Islands

31 March 1917 Purchased from Dutch government for $25 million. A purchase treaty had been previously rejected by the upper chamber of the Dutch parliament in 1902.

The Dominican Republic

7 February 1905 Customs receivership gives US agents right to collect and administer the Republic's customs revenues.

1916–24 In response to revolutionary disturbances chronic since 1911, US troops occupy the Republic on 26 November 1916 and establish military government which lasts until 1924.

Haiti

28 July 1915 President Wilson issues an occupation order after disturbances in which a Port-au-Prince mob kills president Guillaume.

By 9 August US Navy has taken control and compelled Haitian national assembly to elect the pro-American Sudre Dartiguenaue president. A 20-year treaty establishes US receivership and forbids Haiti to enter into any treaty which might impair independence.

2. Dollar Diplomacy and Wilson's New Freedom in Central America

2 August 1912 Senator Henry Cabot Lodge persuades Congress to adopt his corollary to the Monroe doctrine, which warns that US would not tolerate transfer of strategic sites in the Americas to companies that might be acting for a European power.

27 October 1913 In his Mobile address president Wilson states that US would 'never again seek one additional foot of territory by conquest'.

Panama

18 November 1903 After US troops prevent Colombian forces from suppressing separatist revolution in Panama, Panamanian plenipotentiary conveys to the United States *in perpetuity* a zone 10 miles wide across the isthmus, known as the Panama Canal Zone, for $10 million cash and rental of $250,000 per year. Panama's independence, in reality, could only be guaranteed by US military power.

7 January 1914 First ship passes through Panama Canal.

15 August 1914 Panama Canal opened to world commerce, having cost the United States $375 million to construct.

6 April 1914 Secretary of state W.J. Bryan signs treaty with Colombia which expressed America's 'sincere regret' regarding any incidents which might have marred its relationship with Colombia in the past, when it took Colombian territory to build Panama Canal. US pays $25 million indemnity and allows Colombian citizens same rights as Americans in using canal.

Nicaragua

1909 Nicaraguan dictator José Zelaya conducts virulently anti-US campaign against the Nicaragua Concession, a Pittsburgh-owned mining company. Thereafter United States helps engineer a revolution by dispatching marines to the Nicaraguan city of Bluefields to protect foreign nationals and property.

1911 Adolfo Diaz, former secretary of the Nicaragua Concession, installed as president.

6 June 1911 Knox-Castrillo convention, by which Nicaragua's debts funded by two New York banks, and US receivership of customs established. US Senate refuses to ratify the treaty, but nevertheless bankers make a series of short-term loans totalling $1.5 billion to Nicaragua, in return for control of state railways, national bank and appointment of receiver-general from bankers' nominees.

1912 President Taft sends 2,700 marines to prop up the Diaz regime during anti-Diaz, anti-US outbursts. Token guard of 100 remains until 1925.

5 August 1914 By Bryan-Chamorro treaty US agrees to pay Nicaragua $3 million to reduce its foreign debt under US supervision. In return, US receives exclusive concession to build any canal through Nicaragua, lease of two islands off east coast of likely canal route and 99–year lease of a naval base (never established) under US sovereign authority in the Gulf of Forseca. Senate approves 18 February 1916.

Mexico

1910–13 Democratic revolt by Francisco Madero, fighting for constitutional liberties suspended by dictator Porfirio Diaz. Madero seizes power in 1911.

18 February 1913 When Madero threatens upper-class privileges, army chief Victoriano Huerta seizes power, murdering the deposed Madero and vice-president Suarez on 23 February. On 11 March newly inaugurated president Wilson announces that US would not recognize Huerta government, contrary to traditional US pragmatic policy of recognizing a government actually in power.

27 August 1913 Having failed to prod Mexico towards constitutional government by sending emissary John Lind (former governor of Minnesota), Wilson announces a 'watchful waiting policy' in Mexico: no arms were to be supplied to either side in the civil war.

October 1913 Huerta launches full-scale dictatorship, to which Wilson responds by facing Britain with the choice between US or Mexican friendship, thus cutting off Huerta's foreign support.

3 February 1914 Wilson revokes Taft's arms embargo when it becomes clear that unaided Venustiano Carranza's revolutionaries could not overthrow Huerta.

21 April 1914 Arrest and release of a party of US soldiers by Huertist forces, and news of the impending arrival of a German merchant ship the *Ypiranga* at Veracruz, with arms for the Huerta government, gives Wilson sufficient pretext to order US occupation of Veracruz. Carranza, however, denounces this action as unwarranted US aggression.

15 July 1914 After American–Mexican mediation conference at Niagara Falls (20 May–2 July) fails, Huerta abdicates and Carranza enters Mexico City on 20 August.

23 September 1914 Breakaway general 'Pancho' Villa declares war on chief of the revolution Carranza.

23 November 1914 US forces evacuate Veracruz.

14–16 April 1915 Carranza decisively defeats Pancho Villa, who flees to Chihuahua.

19 October 1915 US recognizes Carranza government *de facto.*

11 January 1916 A band of Villa supporters stops a train at Santa Ysabel, removes 17 American engineers travelling to operate mines at Carranza's invitation, and shoots 16 of them, in a bid to provoke the US into war.

9 March 1916 Villa's 'border bandits' cross US border to raid Columbus, New Mexico, setting fire to the town and killing 19.

18 March–September 1916 In response, Wilson sends general John J. Pershing and punitive expedition of 1,500 men into Mexico, ordering him to pursue Villa deep into the Mexican interior. Pershing makes no significant contact, and dispatch of an additional 8,000 troops, and mobilization of 150,000 militiamen on the US southern border, prompts fears of full-scale US invasion of northern Mexico. On 12 April Pershing's men clash with Mexican government troops at Parral, killing 40. Carranza reacts on 22 May by instructing his military commanders to resist US forces if they show an inclination to move in any direction except towards the US border. In a further clash at Carrizal, 23 Americans are captured; Wilson demands their immediate release. War fever, however, cools on 26 June when a newspaper account, written by an eyewitness, reveals that the clash at Carrizal had been prompted by American aggression.

6 September 1916–15 January 1917 US and Mexican commissioners meet without reaching agreement.

24 November 1916 Agreement reached for the withdrawal of the US punitive expedition within 40 days, provided conditions in Mexico are deemed suitable. Carranza, however, responds negatively.

22 January 1917 With the US being drawn inexorably closer to war in Europe, Wilson agrees to begin withdrawal of American troops.

13 March 1917 US grants *de facto* recognition of Carranza's new constitutional government. This constitution remains intact until 1945 (and indeed until 1995). Yet Carranza himself, Emiliano Zapata and Pancho Villa are all assassinated in the next few years, victims of the unstable nature of Mexican politics and its whole political and social economy.

3. The Far East

1899 Secretary of state John Hay declares US policy in China to be preservation of its commercial Open Door policy and maintenance of its territorial integrity.

1904–5 Russo-Japanese war: Treaty of Portsmouth (5 September 1905) establishes Japan as a major presence in the Far East, as a counterbalance to Russia.

18 February 1908 'Gentleman's agreement' with Japan: Japanese government agrees not to issue passports to labourers bound for US.

30 November 1908 Root-Takahira agreement: both US and Japan committed to maintenance of Pacific status quo, mutual respect for territorial possessions and preservation of the Open Door, with territorial integrity, in China.

14 December 1909 Secretary of state Frank Knox proposes internationalization of Manchurian railways, to offset Japanese expansion in the area and maintain the Open Door. Proposal merely serves to embitter the Japanese, who had believed their position in Manchuria secure and recognized by the Root-Takahira agreement. Japan had been engaged in the construction of feeder lines into south Manchuria, along which her political and military jurisdiction advanced.

May 1911 After state department prompting, a US banking syndicate is formed by J. P. Morgan and Co and admitted to an international banking consortium to fund the building of a rail network in central and southern China. On 13 March 1913 president Wilson announces that the US will not participate in the consortium, representing as it does the prospect of lengthy outside interference in Chinese affairs.

8 April 1913 Wilson recognizes new Republic of China, created on 12 February after Sun Yat-sen's successful revolution overthrew the Manchu dynasty.

Japanese Immigration

6 April 1913 California's assembly, with president Wilson's advice, passes an alien bill prohibiting Japanese from owning land in California, in a manner sufficiently indirect to avoid violating

1911 Japanese–American treaty which extended free entry, residence, and the privilege of owning or leasing shops and land for the purpose of residence and trade. Despite Wilson's pleading and the hasty dispatch of secretary of state W.J. Bryan to Sacramento, the Californian legislature insists upon enacting on 9 May a much stronger measure denying landownership to persons 'ineligible to citizenship'. Japanese ambassador lodges official protest.

13 May 1913 Fearful of Japanese surprise attack, US naval chiefs order three warships anchored in the Yangtse river to protect the Philippines.

June 1914 After the fall of the Yamamoto ministry, the new Japanese foreign minister baron Kato terminates negotiations over mutual landownership rights.

Japan and the First World War

Since her defeat of Russia in 1905, Europe and the US had feared that Japan would use upset in balance of power caused by war to further her ambitions in the Far East.

7 November 1914 Japanese forces march across Shantung province and force surrender of the German garrison at Tsingtao naval base.

7 May 1915 Japan sends China an ultimatum consisting of 21 demands, divided into five groups. In its entirety, this represents a Japanese protectorate over China, to be accepted within 24 hours. However, US and British joint pressure succeeds in reining in Japanese ambitions by excluding Article V, the most injurious section to Chinese sovereignty. Thereafter Japan concentrates upon tightening its economic grip upon China by offering capital no longer forthcoming from European sources, and preparing for recognition of its gains in the postwar world. Great Britain (17 February 1917), France (1 March), Russia (5 March) and later Italy all pledge to support Japanese claims, in return for wartime support.

2 November 1917 Lansing-Ishii agreement: culmination of a visit by viscount Ishii to the US (between 6 September and 2 November) to obtain recognition of Japan's 'special influence' in China. Each make nominal concessions on the basis of easily retractable language: US recognizes Japan's special interest in provinces contiguous to Japanese possessions, while Japan reaffirms support for the Open Door and Chinese independence.

4. Europe and the First World War

Britain and the Panama Canal

August 1912 Senate approval of exemption of US coastal shipping from payment of Panama Canal tolls.

14 October 1912 British foreign office protests, arguing that US action violates the 1901 Hay–Pauncefote treaty promising equal rates for all.

26 January 1914 With tariff reductions and the Federal Reserve Act in the bag, Wilson meets Senate foreign relations committee to urge repeal of August 1912 exemption clause. After Wilson's address to a joint session on 5 March House and Senate approval of repeal rapidly follows, making US coastal shipping liable to Panama Canal tolls.

The Road to War, 1914–17

Establishing Neutrality

18 August 1914 After making an official declaration of neutrality, Wilson appeals to the US people to remain 'impartial in thought and deed'.

August 1914–December 1916. With war two weeks old, secretary of state Bryan issues a statement prohibiting loans to belligerents. However, since France and Great Britain represent America's principal possible wartime overseas customers, this prohibition is relaxed in March 1915 when Bryan extends state department approval to a $50 million commercial credit to the French government, and in September 1915 offers no objections to an Anglo-French loan of $500 million. Over the next 18 months, US bankers advance a further $1.8 billion.

The Submarine War

3 November 1914 Britain declares North Sea a 'military area', into which neutrals would enter at their peril except in accordance with admiralty instructions. A range of contraband is defined in order to deny Germany access to copper, oil, cotton and other raw materials, a list to which food was subsequently added. On 26 January 1915 the *Wilhemina*, bound from St Louis via the Mississippi River to Germany with a cargo of food, is stopped and seized.

Despite several notes of objection (for example the note of 26 December 1915), the US in effect broadly accepts and participates in the British blockade of Germany. As a result the US becomes the prime source of Allied war goods.

4 February 1915 In retaliation, Germany announces that all vessels entering its unilaterally declared war zone around the British Isles would incur the risk of being torpedoed by German submarines. In response, US announces it will hold Germany to 'strict accountability' for any US property or lives lost.

Against the background of colonel Edward House's wholly unsuccessful peace mission to Europe (between 30 January and 5 June 1915), a series of incidents challenge US neutrality:

(1) *28 March 1915* Sinking of British liner *Falaba* without warning by a German submarine; one US citizen Leon C. Thrasher, is killed. Not wishing to compromise House's mission, Wilson holds his peace, wavering between condemnation and passivity.

(2) *7 May 1915* British liner *Lusitania* torpedoed off south coast of Ireland, with loss of 1,198 lives, including 128 Americans. The Bryce report, published on the same day, lends credence to the notion that Germany has pursued a deliberate policy of cruelty in Belgium.

Wilson's response to the *Lusitania* sinking, framed in a series of notes to the German government, is conciliatory, suggesting rather unrealistically that submarine war be conducted under traditional rules of visit and search, but also warning that further sinkings will be regarded as 'deliberately unfriendly'. Secretary of state Bryan resigns over Wilson's *Lusitania* notes, believing Britain should be held equally accountable.

(3) *19 August 1915* The *Arabic*, a White Star liner, is sunk with the loss of one American life. On 25 August the German chancellor Theobald von Bethmann-Holweg announces that the submarine commander responsible must have exceeded his orders, since instructions forbidding torpedoeing of passenger ships were issued on 6 June.

(4) *August 1915* US secret service agents retrieve suitcase of papers left on a train in New York by Heinrich Albert, head of German propaganda, bearing details of German propaganda effort in America. The revelations are subsequently published in US newspapers.

(5) *December 1915* Newspaper publication of reports made by US secret service agents concerning activities of Franz Rintelen von Kleist (head of German secret service organization in US) and military attachés Franz von Papen and Karl Boy-Ed, who have

intrigued with and funded Huertist and Villa forces in Mexico and attempted to delay Allied war orders in the US. This is subsequently crucial in bringing America into war.

(6) *18 January 1916* Secretary of state Robert Lansing issues proposed amendment to rules of marine warfare to the effect that armed merchant vessels will be deemed auxiliary cruisers and hence must either disarm or expect legitimate submarine attack. Once the German government announces on 10 February its intention to attack armed merchant ships without warning, Lansing avoids likely rupture with Britain by declaring on 15 February that the US will not warn its citizens against travelling on armed merchant ships. Panic results in Congress, as it seems to some that Wilson is dragging US into war with Germany. A resolution proposed by Republican congressman Jeff McLemore of Texas, warning US citizens aginst travelling on armed merchant ships, is defeated in both houses.

(7) *24 March 1916* Sinking of unarmed French cross-Channel passenger packet *Sussex* with 80 casualties prompts Wilson's strongly worded note to German government, threatening severence of diplomatic relations. Kaiser Wilhelm II finally relents on 14 May and declares German submarines will henceforth adhere to rules of stop and search.

Friction with Britain

24 April 1916 Savage British repression of Dublin Easter uprising evokes revulsion in the US.

August 1916 Doubting US commitment to the war, should Germany scuttle the peace conference, British foreign secretary Sir Edward Grey informs Commons that British government could not yet countenance a peace conference.

19 July British government issues blacklist of American and Latin-American firms with whom British subjects will be forbidden to deal. Despite US appeals, Britain refuses to withdraw it. In retaliation, the Shipping Act of 7 September empowers president to refuse clearance to any ships refusing to carry the freight of a blacklisted American.

The US as Peace Broker

30 January–5 June 1915 Colonel House's first peace mission to Europe meets singular lack of success.

January–February 1916 Colonel House's second peace mission to Europe, with the aim of establishing a peace conference under US auspices, under prior agreement with the Allies, and incorporating a postwar peace of nations. Its course is as follows:

26–29 January In Germany: German leaders adamantly refuse to cede Belgium.

2–8 February In Paris: little progress.

17 February In London: Lord Grey and colonel House draft memo agreeing that Wilson will preside over a peace conference, at a signal from the Allies. If Germans insist on unreasonable terms, US will throw its weight behind the Allies.

12 December 1916 Germany issues invitation to the Allies, via the US, to open direct negotiations with ultimate aim of avoiding a righteous US-supervised peace.

18 December 1916 Wilson issues note requesting that belligerents state their war aims.

30 December 1916 Peace efforts break down publicly, when Allied governments reject German peace conference proposal and on 10 January Germans accuse Allies of prolonging war for territorial gain.

22 January 1917 Wilson, addressing US Senate, laments recalcitrance of belligerents and lays down American claim to play a part in establishing 'peace without victory', through postwar order based on equality and the right of subject peoples to self-determination.

The US Enters the War

31 January 1917 Germany resumes all-out submarine war, offering sole concession of permitting one American passenger ship per week, without contraband, to travel unmolested from Falmouth, England. Wilson responds by severing diplomatic relations with Germany.

25 February 1917 British government dispatches to Washington intercepted note sent from German foreign secretary Arthur Zimmermann to the German minister in Mexico, instructing the latter to seek Mexican–German alliance and to urge reconquest of 'lost territory' in Texas, New Mexico and Arizona. Ironically, this message was relayed via Washington on 17 January on a line supplied by the US government, when German ambassador Count Johan von Bernstorff complained of difficulty in communicating confidentially with his government. Wilson releases the Zimmerman telegram to the press on 1 March, in the wake of which House of Representatives approves bill arming US merchant ships by an overwhelming 403–1 vote.

18 March German submarine sinks three unarmed US merchant vessels without warning.

6 April US enters the war.

The US Military Effort

Desperate for manpower on the western front, Allied commanders propose that US troops be decanted into British forces as they arrive. Commander of the American Expeditionary Force general

John J. Pershing, arriving in Paris on 14 June 1917, refuses, insisting that US forces retain their distinct identity and be allocated a portion of the front. Overall, some 4.8 million US citizens have enlisted by November 1918, of which 50,280 lose their lives; US presence on the western front gives Allied forces a decisive manpower majority in excess of 600,000.

21 March–17 July 1918 German Spring offensive, intended to drive through to the English Channel.

26 March 1918 Unified Allied command for the western front established under general Ferdinand Foch of France.

31 May 1918 American second division sent in to reinforce French forces at Chateau–Thierry, after German offensive reaches the Marne 50 miles from Paris, as had happened in August 1914. German troops are successfully pushed back beyond the Marne

15 July 1918 In counter-offensive to force German troops back through the Marne pocket between Rheims and Soissons, 85,000 US troops are involved.

August 1918–August 1920 Some 15,000 US troops take part in Allied occupation of Murmansk–Archangel in Russia in attempt to assist counter-revolutionary forces against Bolsheviks.

10 August 1918 Pershing commands 50,000 troops of the US 1st army allocated the St Mihiel section of the western front. By mid-September the German salient has been wiped out by first independent US action of the war.

26 September 1918 German line between Verdun and Sedan is attacked by 1.2 million US troops.

7 November 1918 Americans reach Sedan and isolate Sedan–Mezières railway.

US Naval Effort

10–11 April 1917 Agreement that US navy will patrol western hemisphere, leaving the British navy to safeguard submarine-infested waters around the British Isles. From February to April Allied shipping losses to German submarine attacks rise from 540,00 tons to over 880,000 tons per month.

Intervention of US navy renders the adoption of a convoy system more practical: by December shipping losses have been halved.

March 1918 North Sea barrage of anti-submarine mines laid at US suggestion.

'Peace without Victory'

27 May 1916 Wilson first declares himself explicitly in favour of US membership of a postwar collective security association of nations in a speech to the League to Enforce Peace at Washington. Favourable response encourages him to incorporate the theme into his 1916 presidential election campaign. His 'peace without victory speech' of 22 January 1917 (see above) expounds concept of a League of Nations.

8 January 1918 Wilson gives concrete form to that moral impetus he feels the war lacks, unveiling a fourteen-point package, devised by himself and colonel House, of peace proposals and conditions:

(1) No secret diplomacy: all covenants of peace to be openly arrived at and agreed.
(2) Freedom of navigation outside territorial waters, excepting cases of international collective action.
(3) Removal of economic barriers, as far as possible, and equality of trading conditions between nations partaking in the peace.
(4) Adequate guarantees that armament levels would be reduced to levels sufficient only for domestic security, not offensive action.
(5) Free, impartial adjustment of all colonial claims, according equal weight to the wishes of subject peoples.
(6) Evacuation of Russian territory to enable unhampered political development there.
(7) Complete evacuation of Belgium.
(8) Evacuation of French territory and restoration of Alsace–Lorraine.
(9) Readjustment of Italian borders along lines of nationality.
(10) Autonomy to the peoples of Austria–Hungary.
(11) Evacuation of Romania, Sebia and Montenegro, secure access to the sea for Serbia, an international guarantee of the political and economic independence and territorial integrity of the Balkan states.
(12) Sovereignty to the Turkish portions of the Ottoman empire, but self-determination for the other nationalities. Dardanelles to be opened freely to international commerce.
(13) Creation of an independent Polish state with secure access to the sea.
(14) Creation of an association of nations for the purpose of mutually guaranteeing political independence and territorial integrity.

Pre-armistice negotiations manage to blunt the edge of the Fourteen Points. David Lloyd-George (20 October) reserves British interpretation of article two regarding freedom of navigation, while Georges Clemenceau insists upon reparations for all civilian damages – this latter point conceded by the Supreme War Council on 4 November.

November 1918 Wilson attempts fatally to tie foreign policy to US party politics. Campaigning in mid-term Congressional elections, he alleges that anything but the return of a Democratic Congress will represent repudiation of Wilsonian war leadership and aims. Elections are lost more on basis of the tariff, wheat prices and general wartime disruptions, but Wilson's tactics irredeemably alienated new Republican majority in Congress.

The Paris Peace Conference, 1918–19

18 November 1918 US delegation is announced. It is headed by Wilson himself. Other members are: colonel Edward House, secretary of state Robert Lansing, General Tasker H. Bliss (a US member of the Supreme War Council) and Henry White (a very mildly Republican diplomat).

The notable exclusion of prominent Republicans serves only to insult them. Furthermore, the advice of Republican-controlled US Senate is at no point sought.

12 January 1919 Conference opens, attended by representatives of 27 nations. Wilson himself absent in US from 14 February until 12 March. Conference *structure* as follows:

- Council of Ten. An alter ego of the Supreme Allied War Council, composed of representatives of the Big Five (US, Britain, France, Italy and Japan), initially determines matters, consulting smaller powers as and when their interests come into play.
- The Big Four. Grossly overburdened, the Council is replaced on 24 March by the Big Four: Wilson, Lloyd George, Clemenceau and Orlando. The Four later becomes a triumvirate when Orlando quits over Italy's failure to acquire Fiume.

June 1919 The peace is signed at Versailles. It represents a considerable compromise of Wilson's original Fourteen Points:

- German Colonies. Ultimately the spoils go to the victors, under thin disguise of League of Nations mandates.
- French Buffer. In addition to Alsace–Lorraine, France granted 15-year Allied occupation of the left bank of the Rhine, a demilitarized zone extending 50 km into Germany and the Saar Valley, subject to a 1935 plebiscite. German navy and army to be severely restricted in size, and an Anglo-French–US treaty makes provision for mutual defence against Germany.
- Japan. Accorded title to German economic rights in the Shantung province of China.
- Poland. Polish state created and granted a territorial corridor to the Baltic, with Danzig established as a free city under League of Nations mandate.

- Italy. Receives the Brenner Pass, containing a population of 200,000 Germans, but not Fiume, on eastern Adriatic.
- Reparations. Greatest violation of the Fourteen Points. Germany acknowledges responsibility for all Allied losses during the war, and agrees to pay not only for all civilian damages, but also the cost of separation allowances and pensions for Allied veterans. To secure delivery, Allies to occupy the Rhineland until reparations are met in full.
- League of Nations. Created by covenant, each member to exercise one vote in the General Assembly. In addition an executive council to consist of the representatives of Britain, France, the US, Italy, Japan and four other powers. A permanent secretariat to sit at Geneva. Article X requires members to preserve each other's territorial integrity, while Article XVI provides for economic sanctions against aggressors.

Further Treaties

10 September 1919–20 August 1920 Five further treaties are imposed by the Allies:

(1) Balkanization of Austria-Hungary into states of Austria, Hungary, Czechoslovakia and Yugoslavia.
(2) Romania annexes land from Austria-Hungary and Russia.
(3) Italy recieves Trieste and the southern Tyrol from Austria-Hungary.
(4) Syria placed under French mandate and Palestine and Mesopotamia under British mandate; the Bosphorus and the Dardanelles are internationalized.
(5) Finland, Latvia, Lithuania, Estonia and Poland become independent states.

The US Rejects the League

10 July 1919 Wilson formally presents Versailles treaty to the Senate. 'There can be no question of our ceasing to be a world power. The only question is whether we can refuse the moral leadership that is offered, whether we shall accept or reject the confidence of the world.'

Main groups of senators:

- Extreme isolationists. About 12–15, including leading Progressives Hiram W. Johnson (California), William E. Borah (Idaho), James A. Reed (Missouri), Robert M. La Follette (Wisconsin) dominated Senate foreign relations committee.
- Democrat supporters. At least 43 of the 47-strong Democratic minority would back Wilson.
- Republicans. Most of these supported the League with reservations, but led by Henry Cabot Lodge, who had little desire to see Wilsonian peace approved.

6 November 1919 Having delayed matters by insisting upon reading entire treaty aloud, and packing the foreign relations committee with irreconcileables, Lodge presents *fourteen reservations* to the committee. The most important removed all US obligation to preserve the territorial integrity or political independence of any other country, or to interfere in controversies between nations, under Article X, or to use its armed forces to uphold any other article of the entire treaty without assent of Congress by joint resolution.

19 November 1919 Under Wilson's instructions, Democratic senators join irreconcileables to defeat ratification *with* the 12 reservations by 39–55. Republicans vote almost as a bloc with irreconcileables to defeat ratification *without* the 12 reservations by 53–38.

15 March 1920 Final vote on the treaty, after Wilson has declined compromise, declaring that non-ratification would render the presidential election of 1920 a referendum on the matter. Reluctantly obeying Wilson's instructions, 23 Democrats join the 12 irreconcileables to defeat treaty by 49–35 which, needing a two-thirds majority, received only 49 votes in favour with 35 against. A change of 7 Democratic votes would have put the US in the League.

2 July–18 October 1920 Congress by joint resolution ends state of war with Germany and Austria-Hungary. On 18 October Senate ratifies separate peace treaties with Germany, Austria and Hungary.

5. Republican Diplomacy

The Far East and the Pacific

August 1918 General William S. Graves leads 9,000 US troops sent to Vladivostock as part of contingent to rescue a Czech army from the Bolshevik forces. Some 75,000 Japanese troops dispatched to profit from chaos of Russian civil war, taking control of large tracts of eastern Siberia. Robert Lansing, Wilson's secretary of state, immediately demands Japanese withdrawal.

January–March 1919 At Paris peace negotiations, Wilson opposes both fortification of formerly German-owned Marshall, Mariana and Caroline Islands, seized by Japan in 1914, and Japanese occupation of Shantung Province.

2 July 1921 New US president Warren G. Harding signs joint resolution of Congress formally ending US state of war with Germany, and later Austria and Hungary. Though negotiations over reparations continue for some time, peace treaty is signed in August.

11 August 1921 Harding's secretary of state Charles Evans Hughes invites Britain, Japan, China, France, Belgium, the Netherlands, Portugal and Italy, all with interests in the Far East, to join US in conference in Washington.

12 November 1921 Washington disarmament conference convened to control naval power. Britain, France, Italy and Japan attend. Subsequent naval treaty fixes warships over 10,000 tons at ratio of US 5, Britain 5, Japan 3 France and Italy 1.67 each, with no large ships to be built for ten years. Conference also defines great power rights in the Far East and Pacific, which Japan ignores in 1931 by invading Manchuria.

10 April 1924 Ambassador Hanihara expresses Japan's distaste at House bill which seeks to end 'gentleman's agreement' over Japanese immigration to US by enforcing statutory exclusion of persons 'ineligible to citizenship'. Publication of Hanihara's letter to Hughes provokes anger at apparent threat against US.

16 April 1924 House bill approved 71 votes to 4, much to anger of Japan's moderate leaders.

18–19 September 1931 Fearing expansion of Russian power in Far East, and spread of Chinese nationalism into Manchuria, Japanese army attacks and occupies Mukden and Changchun in

Manchuria, using explosion on Manchurian railway as justification for 'Manchurian incident'.

21 September 1931 China appeals to League of Nations for protection after 'Manchurian incident'.

22 September 1931 Pursuing a cautious line, Hoover's secretary of state Henry L. Stimson summons Japanese ambassador and makes clear US interest in maintaining Chinese integrity. Nevertheless, US refuses to cooperate in any form of economic sanctions against Japan.

10 December 1931 League of Nations Council sends commission under Lord Lytton to report on Manchurian crisis. The report, published in September 1932, recommends restoration of Manchuria to China.

2 January 1932 Japanese army enters and occupies Chinchow, China's last stronghold in Manchuria.

7 January 1932 Stimson issues joint warning to Japan and China that US will recognize no territorial changes wrought by force which might impair territorial integrity of China or the 'Open Door', which had guaranteed European powers equal access to China since the 1890s. Japanese Foreign Office makes noncommittal reply on 16 January.

28 January 1932 Japan invades Shanghai in retaliation against Chinese boycott, killing thousands of citizens.

9 February 1932 Stimson appeals in vain to Britain for joint protest to Japanese.

22 February 1932 In public letter to senator William E. Borah, chairman of Senate foreign relations committee, Stimson declares that US will insist on its treaty rights in Manchuria.

11 March 1932 League of Nations unanimously adopts resolution of non-recognition of Japan's conquests in China and Manchuria.

15 September 1932 Japan establishes puppet state of Manchuko in Manchuria, ruled by last emperor of China.

24 February 1933 League assembly calls upon Japan to return Manchuria to China. Japan replies by withdrawing from the League on 27 March.

Latin America

Dominican Republic

12 July 1924 After inauguration of Santo Dominican president Horatio Vasquez, US occupation troops withdraw gradually, leaving US customs receivership in place.

Nicaragua

October 1924–August 1925 US marine guard withdrawn from Managua after liberal Carlos Solorzano is elected to presidency. Conservative leader Emiliano Chamorro reacts by expelling Solorzano from office and seizing presidency for himself. US immediately withdraws recognition.

October 1926 Nicaraguan Congress elects conservative pro-American Adolfo Diaz president. US reacts by according recognition.

April–May 1927 Exiled liberal vice-president Juan B. Sacasa returns to Nicaragua and leads revolt against Diaz government. Calvin Coolidge sends 5,000 US marines to support regime he had recognized and restore order. This intervention provokes powerful pro-liberal opposition in US when it becomes clear liberals are determined to fight.

Coolidge accordingly in April sent his personal representative Henry L. Stimson, who persuades liberals to lay down their arms, guaranteeing fair presidential election under US military supervision.

1927–1932 Liberals General Moncado and Juan B. Scasa elected to presidency as state department policy since 1909 of using military force to keep unpopular repressive but pro-US governments in power is reversed. US troops help Nicaraguan government suppress bandit leader Augusto Sandino, but are gradually withdrawn between 1931 and 1933.

Mexico

19 February 1918 President Venustio Carranza applies Article XXVII of the Mexican constitution, nationalizing all mineral and oil rights acquired by foreigners before 1917, and requiring all owners of such rights to seek new concessions from Mexican government. In response to protests from US and Britian, Carranza postpones the decree.

April 1920 Revolution deposes Carranza, replacing him by general Alvaro Obregon, who does not promise to respect and defend US holdings in Mexico. US withholds recognition until 1923, by which time US has secured compensation for land seized by revolutionary government prior to May 1917, validation of title to oil and mineral properties owned by US citizens before 1917, and establishment of joint commission to discuss American losses during Mexican revolution.

1 January 1927 More anti-American Plutarcho Calles government brings into force law limiting foreign concessions to 50-year leases. Coolidge's secretary of state Frank B. Kellogg prompts war scare by alleging that the Calles government is conspiring with Soviet Union to establish a 'Mexican-fostered Bolshevik hegemony intervening between the United States and the Panama Canal'.

September 1927 Coolidge dispatches Dwight W. Morrow as ambassador to Mexico, who obtains quick results.

November–December 1927 Mexican Supreme Court guarantees that US companies which had begun to work their properties prior to 1917 can retain ownership.

Intervention and Non-intervention

January 1928 At Pan-American conference in Havana, Cuba, Herbert Hoover refuses to make pledge of non-intervention.

17 December 1928 J. Reuben Clark of US state department drafts memorandum which, while falling short of renunciation of intervention, separates intervention from the Monroe doctrine. Published in March 1930.

19 November 1928–6 January 1929 President-elect Hoover makes goodwill tour of Latin America.

6 February 1931 Hoover's secretary of state Stimson renounces Wilsonian use of moral standards as test for recognition in Latin America.

Arms limitation

12 November 1921–6 February 1922 The Washington Conference:

- Four Power treaty (10 December 1921) sees Britain, US France and Japan pledge mutual respect for possessions in Pacific, and to confer jointly if peace is threatened.
- Nine Power treaty (4 February 1922) imposes unprecedented self-denial upon Japan and other signatories, recognizing Chinese sovereignty, independence and integrity while upholding traditional 'Open Door' policy giving powers equal access to China.
- Five Power naval treaty (6 February 1922) sets naval tonnage quotas for Britain, US, Japan, France and Italy. In addition, each agrees to abandonment of capital ship construction for ten years, and to limit auxiliary craft to 10,000 tons and aircraft carriers to 27,000 tons.

20 June–4 August 1927 The Geneva conference. Attended by Britain, US and Japan, after France and Italy decline to attend. Negotiations do not run smoothly. Britain is able to accept in principle heavy cruiser parity with US, but neither can agree upon light cruiser limitation.

26 July 1929 US ambassador Charles Dawes and British prime minister Ramsay MacDonald agree to equal combat strength in all categories of fighting ships.

7 October 1929 MacDonald expresses to US Senate British

willingness to purse naval limitations.

21 January–22 April 1930 The London conference. Representatives of US, Britain and Japan agree to:

- extension of holiday on constructing capital ships to five years
- scrap nine battleships
- ratios of 10 : 10 : 6 in heavy cruisers, 10 : 10 : 7 in light cruisers and destroyers, and parity in submarines. France and Italy reject all limitations without Anglo-American assurances of security. In response Britain inserts escalator clause allowing signatories to abrogate limitation agreements if their security should be threatened by naval construction of a non-signatory.

2 February 1932 World disarmament conference meets in Geneva. On 22 June, in effort to break deadlock, US delegation proposes abolition of all bombers, tanks, large mobile artillery and weapons of chemical warfare, and reduction of all land and naval forces by one-third. These proposals revive conference, and later US, Britain and France promise revision of the 1919 Versailles treaty and parity in land armaments to Germany. But on 30 January 1933, Adolf Hitler becomes chancellor of Germany and withdraws his delegates on 14 October.

6. The League of Nations and European Peace

1924 Though not a member of the League or the World Court, US begins to send delegates and observers to special League conferences on such topics as opium, trade restrictions and communications.

23 March 1925 House passes resolution urging US involvement in World Court established by League.

27 January 1926 Senate votes to join World Court, but adds reservations restricting Court's right to render advisory opinions which Court is unwilling to accept.

March 1927 James T. Shotwell of Carnegie Endowment for International Peace visits France, urging French foreign minister Aristide Briand to take lead in movement to outlaw war.

6 April 1927 On 10th anniversary of US intervention in first world war, Briand sends open letter to American people, proposing France and US join in pact to outlaw war between them.

21 May 1927 Charles Linbergh's solo trans-Atlantic flight, landing in Paris, provokes outpourings of Franco-American friendship.

28 December 1927 Coolidge and Kellogg propose that other nations join in treaty renouncing war as instrument of national policy, but permitting defensive war.

28 August 1928 Pact of Paris signed by fifteen nations, with notable exception of Soviet Union. The pact condemns 'recourse to war for the solution of international controversies'.

7. Economic Policy

Reparations

1918 At end of First World War, Allied governments seek to cancel all inter-governmental debt incurred as part of war effort. Allies owe US over $7 billion borrowed during war, and $4 billion in cash and supplies borrowed since Armistice. Britain is owed $4 billion by 17 nations, and France has lent to ten nations.

1 May 1921 Reparations commission presents German government with bill of $33 billion, plus entire Belgian war debt and costs of occupying armies.

9 February 1922 Establishment of world war foreign debt commission to negotiate with creditors on behalf of US, while insisting upon eventual repayment.

11 January 1923 France and Belgium occupy Ruhr valley in response to German failure to meet reparations payments, but gain nothing as galloping inflation makes the German mark valueless.

June 1923 Britain agrees to repay US $4.6 billion in principal and accrued interest over 62 years at 3 per cent during first ten years and 3.5 per cent thereafter. French and Italians refuse to accept such terms, but are forced to surrender in 1925–26 by US state department ban on all private loans.

November 1923 Reparations commission appoints Dawes committee headed by American banker Charles G. Dawes.

9 April 1924 Unveiling of Dawes Plan, aimed at restoring international financial stability. It arranges gold loan of $200 million by US to stabilize German currency on gold standard, and establishes new machinery to collect repayments and restructure schedule of repayments less onerous to Germany.

7 June 1929 Introduction of Young Plan, drawn up by committee headed by US banker Owen D. Young, reduces German reparations to $8 billion, with possibility of further reductions should US reduce war debts and an end to repayments set for 1988.

The Great Depression

March 1931 French bankers demand immediate repayment of short-term loans from Austria and Germany. Germany and Austria appeal to Britain and US for aid.

18 June 1931 German president Paul von Hindenburg appeals to Hoover for assistance.

21 June 1931 Hoover announces one-year moratorium on all inter-governmental and debt reparations payments. French bankers begin to make heavy withdrawals from British banks, prompting Britain to come off gold standard on 21 September. By March 1932 only US, France, Italy, Belgium, Holland and Switzerland remain on gold standard.

23 December 1931 Congress by joint resolution opposes any reduction or cancellation of war debts.

June 1932 Meeting of European powers in Lausanne agrees that German reparations obligations are to be cut to $714 million, on basis that the full sum will never, in reality, have to be paid. Hoover condemns the agreement and continues to press for repayment.

8. The Roosevelt Years

1933 Franklin D. Roosevelt, the new president, pursues conflicting policies abroad. Diplomatic cooperation, restraint and friendship with foreign nations are oddly combined with economic nationalism.

12 June 1933 London conference meets to discuss lower tariff barriers and stabilization of currencies. After a week of negotiations, Roosevelt sends economic adviser Raymond Moley with proposal to stabilize the dollar at between $4.05 and $4.25 to the pound. As Moley sets sail, the value of the dollar begins to fall. Convinced that dollar must be allowed to float free and depreciate, Roosevelt effectively scuttles conference on 3 July, declaring that the US will not agree to any kind of immediate currency stabilization.

Cordell Hull, FDR's secretary of state, believes US must act as good neighbour in both foreign and economic affairs and abandon economic and political autarchy of the kind Germany embarked on after January 1933.

12 June 1934 FDR signs Trade Agreements bill empowering president to raise or lower existing Hawley-Smoot tariff by as much as 50 per cent to obtain reciprocal concessions from other nations.

24 August 1934 First trade agreement with Cuba. By 1936 US has concluded trade agreements with Belgium, Canada, France, Finland, Holland, Sweden, Switzerland and six Latin American nations.

October 1936 British, French and US agree to stabilize their currencies, maintain their international exchange value and adopt a common gold standard for international trade.

1934–38 Federal government establishes Export–Import bank to stimulate foreign trade with Latin America and lends $66 million to help stabilize Latin American currencies and exchange rates.

Mexico

1934 Mexican government of Lazaro Cardenas expropriates all land held by US citizens. Without questioning their right to do this, Cordell Hull pressures Mexico City to obtain fair compensation. Friendly negotiations concluded in 1941 with payment of $40 million to settle outstanding US agrarian claims.

1936 Cardenas also launches campaign against British and US oil company interests, culminating in government-sponsored oil workers' union demands which would cripple companies.

Cardenas government orders them to comply, and Mexican Supreme Court upholds his decree. Companies make counter-proposal, which Cardenas accepts. But when companies demand he put his approval in writing, Cardenas nationalizes oil industry on 15 March 1938 and expropriates companies' property.

Enraged oil firms claim $450 million compensation, while some demand military intervention.

19 November 1941 General settlement of oil and land claims. As part of Mexican–US trade agreement, the *peso* is stabilized and all sides agree oil in ground belongs to Mexican people.

17 April 1942 Joint commission set up to value oil equipment and property awards American companies $24 million, which they grudgingly accept. Unlike some other Latin American nations, Mexico remains a loyal ally throughout the second world war.

The Road to War, 1933–40

FDR inherited a Far East situation where Japan had successfully defied the League of Nations in 1931 and established a puppet regime in Manchuria, and then quit the League. In Europe Germany's Nazi government was determined to overthrow the 1919 Versailles settlement, while the Italian fascist dictator Benito Mussolini was bent on building a new Roman empire in Africa.

14 October 1933 Germany withdraws from Geneva disarmament conference and announces it will resign from the League of Nations in two years.

17 October 1933 German physicist Albert Einstein, who evolved theory of relativity, flees anti-Semitism and anti-intellectualism of Nazi Germany to settle at Princeton, New Jersey, and play a crucial role in US decision to develop atomic bomb.

5 December 1934 Mussolini uses skirmish between Italian and Ethiopian troops to pick a quarrel with Ethiopia.

16 March 1935 Hitler denounces all provisions of the 1919 Versailles treaty, launches an expensive rearmament programme and reintroduces conscription. Britain, France and Italy, who have power to enforce treaty compliance, content themselves with verbal protests.

18 June 1935 Anglo-German naval treaty concedes parity to Germany in submarines and says she may build a surface fleet 35 per cent as great as Britain's.

21 August 1935 US Congress expresses mounting public mood of isolationism in face of foreign wars by passing Pittman resolution denying US presidents the right to discriminate in favour of victims of aggression when applying sanctions.

31 August 1935 Roosevelt signs Neutrality Act forbidding shipment of arms to belligerents once president has declared that a state of war exists and authorizing president to prohibit American citizens travelling on ships of belligerents.

3 October 1935 Mussolini orders Italian invasion of Ethiopia from Eritrea and Italian Somaliland.

5 October 1935 President Roosevelt applies arms embargo to Italy. On 7 October the League Council condemns Italy as aggressor and votes to impose sanctions.

18 November 1935 League sanctions go into effect, but exclude coal and oil (without which the Italian fleet would cease to function). Britain moves main fleet to Mediterranean, but fearing, like France, that coercion would drive Italy into alliance with Germany, does nothing. Collective security fails its first real test.

26 February 1936 *Nini roku jiken*, or 2.26 incident in Japan. Though this coup by junior army officers fails, it marks a decisive step towards a more aggressive foreign policy by Japan between 1937 and 1941.

7 March 1936 Hitler denounces 1925 Locarno treaty and occupies the demilitarized Rhineland.

18 July 1936 After five years of crisis following the overthrow of the Spanish monarchy, general Francisco Franco, supported by great landowners, Roman Catholic Church and big business leads overthrow of Popular Front government. Spanish Civil War begins.

9 September 1936 Representatives of 27 nations form Non-Intervention Committee in London to prevent men and supplies reaching either side in Spain. Naval blockade established in March. But Italy and Germany openly send forces to help Franco, while the Soviet Union aids part of brittle coalition of anarchists, communists, socialists and democrats ranged against him.

25 October 1936 Germany and Italy form Rome–Berlin axis, which soon becomes a political and military alliance between Hitler and Mussolini. French and British fears during Ethiopian crisis are thus fulfilled.

16 November Germany and Japan sign Anti-Comintern pact, setting stage for nations which seek to overthrow the existing balance of power.

6 January 1937 At Roosevelt's request, Congress hastily agrees by joint resolution (with only one dissenting vote) to extend existing Neutrality law to Spanish Civil War.

1 May 1937 Congress adopts new Neutrality Act (supplanting existing temporary measures) which, after careful work by secretary of state Cordell Hull, gives president more discretion in determining when a state of war exists and when a civil war endangers world peace. President signs this 'permanent' neutrality legislation.

7 July 1937 Japan launches full-scale invasion of China to conquer northern provinces.

16 July 1937 US condemns Japanese aggression and sends 1,200 marines to Shanghai to reinforce 2,000 American soldiers already on duty in China.

5 October 1937 In 'quarantine the aggressors' speech in Chicago, Roosevelt urges American people to face reality of mounting dangers of international situation and warns that peace-loving nations may have to join together to prevent anarchy. Public reaction is so adverse it rules out collective action.

6 October 1937 League of Nations condemns Japanese invasion of China and calls for conference of signatories of 1922 Nine Power treaty to enforce collective action. Roosevelt's refusal to defy overwhelming Congressional and popular mood, or risk war, wrecks first attempt at forceful resistance to aggression.

November 1937 British government, under new prime minister Neville Chamberlain, embarks on foreign policy aimed at appeasing Germany's legitimate grievances and securing European accord.

24 November 1937 Nine Power conference breaks up in Brussels.

12 December 1937 Japanese planes bomb and sink US gunboat *Panay* and three Standard Oil tankers on Yangtze River near Nanking. Chief reaction in United States is loud public demand for withdrawal of all American forces from China. Japan apologises and pays indemnity on 23 December.

11 January 1938 Roosevelt sends secret message to Chamberlain confirming US support for British attempt to come to understanding with Germany.

13 January 1938 Chamberlain replies that this will hamper his plan to appease Germany and recognize Italy's conquest of Ethiopia. US expresses disgust at Britain condoning Italian aggression in Africa.

20 February 1938 British foreign secretary Anthony Eden resigns in protest against Chamberlain's Italian policy.

12–13 March 1938 When Austrian chancellor Kurt von Schuschnigg is forced from office by pro-Nazi forces, Hitler sends German troops into Austria (his birthplace) to restore order and forcefully unite the two nations in the *Anschluss*.

August–September 1938 Mounting demands of German-speaking majority in Sudentenland, Czechoslovakia, for integration with Germany, orchestrated by Nazis, reaches climax.

15 September 1938 British prime minister Chamberlain flies to Germany to be told by Hitler that Germany will accept nothing less than cession of Sudetenland. When Hitler rejects Chamberlain's transfer arrangements it seems Britain and France will fight war.

27 September 1938 Roosevelt sends personal message to British, French, German and Czech governments urging peaceful settlement of crisis.

28 September 1938 Britain and France sign Munich agreement allowing Germany to occupy Sudetenland. On returning to London Chamberlain announces 'Peace in our time'. Polls show large majority of Americans approve the Munich agreement.

18 November 1938 US recalls its ambassador from Germany.

6 December 1938 In radio speech in America, Anthony Eden warns that expanding fascist regimes threaten all the world's democracies.

24 December 1938 In Peru, 21 nations of western hemisphere, meeting at Eighth International American conference, adopt Declaration of Lima. This reaffirms principle of mutual consultation, but not mutual defence against foreign threats.

4 January 1939 In annual State of the Union message, Roosevelt shifts emphasis from domestic to international affairs and warns democracies to be prepared.

5 January 1939 FDR submits budget to Congress, raising defence spending to $1.3 billion in a total of $9 billion.

14 March 1939 German army invades the rest of Czechoslovakia east of the Sudentenland, in clear violation of Munich agreement of September 1938. Appeasement policy is dead.

1 April 1939 With Spanish Civil War effectively over, US recognizes Franco's fascist government.

7 April 1939 Italian army invades Albania.

14 April 1939 Roosevelt writes open letter to Hitler and Mussolini demanding they promise not to invade any country in Europe or the Middle East in return for American pledge to cooperate over world trade and disarmament. Hitler replies with disdain and derision in a speech where a long list of countries he does not plan to invade omits Poland.

7–12 June 1939 King George VI and Queen Elizabeth visit US on goodwill trip designed to cement Anglo-American relations in face of growing fascist menace.

23 August 1939 German and Soviet foreign ministers J. von Ribbentrop and V. M. Molotov sign Nazi–Soviet pact.

1 September 1939 Germany invades Poland.

3 September 1939 Britain and France declare war on Germany in defence of Polish independence.

British liner *Athenia* sunk by German submarine off Hebrides with loss of 28 American lives. Roosevelt confirms 'this nation remains a neutral nation'.

17 September 1939 Soviet Union invades eastern Poland.

28 September 1939 Germany and Soviet Union sign new treaty dividing Poland between them.

2 October 1939 US government announces it does not recognize partition of Poland and maintains diplomatic relations with Polish government in exile in Paris.

3 October Inter-American conference issues Declaration of Panama, establishing safety zones in western hemisphere from which warships of belligerent powers are excluded.

4 November 1939 Roosevelt signs Neutrality Act of 1939. This repeals general embargo on arms contained in previous neutrality laws, replacing it with sale of arms to belligerents on cash-and-carry basis.

30 November 1939 Soviet Union invades Finland.

SECTION III

Constitution and Civil Liberties, 1910–1945

Since passage of the first ten amendments, or Bill of Rights, to the US constitution in 1791, and when *Marbury* v *Madison* established the Supreme Court's right to declare any law unconstitutional in 1803, civil rights and judicial review have been central to political and economic life.

This section covers the most important cases involving civil liberties and major Supreme Court decisions between 1910 and 1945.

25 February 1913 Adoption of 16th Amendment to the Constitution introduces federal income tax and provides basis for use of graduated, or progressive, taxes. This gives US government enhanced power to regulate and control the economy and redistribute wealth to the states and poorer people.

1 March 1913 Congress overrides president Taft's veto to uphold Webb-Kenyon interstate liquor Act, bringing Prohibition nearer.

8 April 1913 The 17th Amendment to the Constitution means that the Senate is thereafter elected directly by the voters of each state rather than indirectly by the state legislatures.

The First World War and the Red Scare

April 1917 Creation of Committee on Public Information under crusading journalist George Creel. Intended as an agency of publicity and voluntary censorship, as proposed by secretaries of war, navy and state, it distributes 75 million copies of more than 30 different pamphlets explaining America's relation to the war, sponsors war exhibitions attended by 10 million people, and issues 6,000 press releases.

15 June 1917 Espionage Act punishes by up to 30 years in jail and/or a fine of up to $10,000 obstruction of the draft, circulation of false rumours or incitement to rebellion among armed forces. Postmaster-general empowered to deny use of federal mails to any published material which could be shown to advocate treason or insurrection, under which *American Socialist, The Masses* and the *Milwaukee Leader* are all banned.

28 September 1917 Some 165 members of the IWW indicted on charges of subversion and conspiracy 'by force to prevent, hinder and delay the execution' of eleven different Acts of Congress and presidential proclamations covering the war programme. William D. (Big Bill) Haywood and 100 others IWWs are tried in federal court in Chicago and in August 1918 Haywood and fourteen other IWW leaders are sentenced to 20 years in jail and fined $30,000 each. By 1923 all had been released by presidential pardon, having spent six years in jail for their political beliefs.

6 October 1917 Trading with the Enemy Act empowers

president to censor all international communications and grants broad censorship powers to postmaster-general over all foreign language publications in US.

20 April 1918 Sabotage Act aims at the IWW (among others) who had fought a bitter labour campaign against Anaconda Copper Company. It renders sabotage of materials, utilities or transport a federal crime.

16 May 1918 Sedition Act, based upon Montana's Criminal Syndicalism Act, forbids any remarks detrimental to the US flag, government, uniform or war effort, regardless of whether injurious consequences can be shown to result. Postmaster-general empowered to deny use of the mails to anyone who, *in his opinion*, uses the mails to violate the Act.

Arrests under the Espionage and Sedition Acts are 1,532 for seditious utterances, 65 for threats against the president and 10 for sabotage.

Later California and a dozen other states pass 'criminal syndicalism laws' making it an offence to express or support syndicalist beliefs about role of organized labour in the US. Thousands are jailed for criminal syndicalism offences between 1918 and 1920, many for as long as ten years.

16 January 1919 Ratification of 18th Amendment making the manufacture, transport and sale (but not purchase) of alcohol unconstitutional. Congress passes the Volstead Act enacting this in October 1919 over Wilson's presidential veto. Prohibition begins.

10 March 1919 In *Schenk v United States*, US Supreme Court judges that Espionage Act does not violate First Amendment. Oliver Wendell Holmes joins the majority in finding that in time of war the 'clear and present danger' referred to in the Constitution does exist. The ten-year jail sentence given Socialist party leader Eugene Debs stands under this Supreme Court ruling. Debs receives presidential pardon in 1922 having served four years in jail for his political beliefs.

But in *Abrams v United States* Holmes files dissenting judgment that the Act does not bar the distribution of pamphlets protesting that US troops should not be in Siberia trying to overthrow the Bolshevik government.

7 November 1919 A. Mitchell Palmer, Wilson's attorney general, marks second anniversary of the Bolshevik Revolution by launching the 'Palmer raids' in 18 cities, most of them without legal warrants, on the homes of men and women suspected of holding left-wing views.

1 January 1920 Palmer arrests a further 10,000 people in 70 cities. Many are Russian, some are Communists and those who are not US citizens are ordered deported. Emma Goldman, the celebrated anarchist, is one of these expelled. However, 71 per cent of these orders are cancelled later in the year.

The Republican Ascendancy, 1920–32

1 March 1920 In *United States* v *US Steel* Supreme Court decides that one of the largest corporations in America is not an illegal monopoly under anti-trust legislation.

18 August 1920 Ratification of 19th Amendment makes denial or abridgement of right to vote on grounds of gender unconstitutional, enfranchising all women over 21.

23 April 1923 US Supreme Court decides in *Adkins* v *Children's Hospital* that minimum wage law adopted for women and children in Washington DC is unconstitutional.

The *Adkins* case is a significant indication of the direction of the Court's judicial thinking under chief justice Taft. Up to 1912, in deciding nearly a hundred cases involving social and economic legislation, the Supreme Court had interposed its veto only six times. Between 1913 and 1920, it decided adversely in nearly one-quarter of such cases. Between 1920 and 1930 it did so nearly one-third of the time.

2 June 1924 Congress sends an Amendment to the Constitution making child labour unconstitutional, but it is resisted by conservatives, not only in the south but in the American Federation of Labor, which also opposes federal unemployment insurance. Though the 1938 Fair Labor Standards Act outlaws child labour, the Constitutional Amendment is dropped in 1945 when only 25 States have ratified it.

5 May 1925 John T. Scopes, a schoolteacher in Dayton, Tennessee, is prosecuted for violating state law by teaching Darwin's theory of evolution. The fundamentalist Christian W. J. Bryan, three times Democratic candidate for president, leads for the prosecution with the great trial lawyer and socialist agnostic Clarence Darrow defending. The case is headline news all over the nation and the world. Bryan agrees to go into the witness stand, where Darrow destroys his literal interpretation of the Book of Genesis. Scopes is fined $100, but Tennessee Supreme Court reverses the decision.

July 1925 NAACP hires Darrow to defend Ossian Sweet, a black Detroit doctor, who had killed one of a white mob who invaded his home. Case is seen as a landmark in race relations, establishing principle of black right to self-defence.

1925–32 In early civil rights cases, such as *Gitlow* v *New York* 1925, the US Supreme Court extends the 14th Amendment to cover the First Amendment and other amendments in the Bill of Rights, thus reversing the *Slaughterhouse Cases* of 1873. However, *Plessey* v *Fergusson* 1896, establishing separate but equal facilities for black and white as being constitutional, remains until 1954.

27 May 1929 In the case of *United States* v *Schwimmer* the Supreme Court upholds lower court's denial of citizenship to a

Hungarian woman on grounds that she is an avowed pacifist. Dissenting, Oliver Wendell Holmes argues that freedom to think and express unpopular opinion is the most fundamental principle of the Constitution.

25 March 1931 Andrew Wright, aged 17, and eight other young African-Americans are arrested in Scottsboro, Alabama, and charged with raping two white girls on a freight train. After three trials based on unsatisfactory evidence before white juries, all nine are convicted and sentenced to death or life imprisonment. More even than the Sacco-Vanzetti case, 'the Scottsboro boys' become a *cause célèbre* in the United States and all over the world. The case rallies those seeking justice for black Americans. The United States Supreme Court overturns the convictions on 7 November 1932, but the boys are re-arrested and re-tried. On 1 April 1935, the US Supreme Court again overturns the convictions, but release from jail occurs slowly over many years, while Wright remains in prison until the 1950s.

The Supreme Court in Crisis, 1933–45

5 December 1933 The 21st Amendment, repealing the 18th Amendment, goes into effect when Utah becomes the 36th State to ratify. Prohibition, 'an experiment noble in purpose' as Herbert Hoover called it, comes to an end.

27 May 1935 After a series of decisions adverse to New Deal reforms, the Supreme Court in *Schechter* v *United States* rules 9–0 that the NIRA is unconstitutional because in seeking to regulate a Brooklyn poultry firm the executive branch of the federal government was interfering in intrastate commerce. This ends New Deal efforts to plan the industrial sector of the US economy.

6 January 1936 In *United States* v *Butler* the Supreme Court strikes down the AAA 6–3 on grounds that the tax it imposed on food processors to finance farm subsidies meant outright control of agriculture and thus exceeded government's proper role. The three dissenting judges hold that the majority are subverting the role of the legislature and deepening divide between Court and people.

6 February 1936 Supreme Court decides Ashwander case 7–2 in favour of public provision of hydro-electric power.

10 June 1936 In *Morehead* v *Tipaldo* the Supreme Court by 5-4 reaffirms its decision in the 1923 *Adkins* case that minimum wage laws are unconstitutional.

8 October 1936 In *West Coast Hotel* v *Parrish* the Court by 6–3 reverses the decision it took four months earlier in the *Tipaldo* case and approves of minimum wage legislation.

20 January 1937 Re-elected with the largest share of the popular vote in history, Franklin Roosevelt asks Congress to reform the Supreme Court by making it possible for the president to appoint a new justice (up to a total of six) for every serving justice who fails to retire on reaching 70. The 'court-packing' bill stimulates the most serious political crisis of his presidency. The bill fails, though the federal circuit courts are reformed, and by 1939 FDR has appointed new justices more favourable to social reform.

April–May 1937 In February 1936 the Supreme Court had upheld TVA 7–2. It now decided two other key areas of social reform. In *Jones and Laughlin* (April 1937) it found 6–3 in favour of free collective bargaining by labour unions, while in *Steward Machine Co* v *Davis* (May 1937) it upheld federally funded social security. It further reinforced its new position on minimum wage legislation, taken in *West Coast Hotel*, by upholding a minimum wage law in Washington DC.

26 May 1938 House of Representatives establishes committee to investigate un-American activities under the chairmanship of Martin Dies from Texas. Though designed to examine both Nazi and Communist influence, the committee pays attention only to the left of the political spectrum.

27 June 1940 Roosevelt revives 1917 Espionage Act by presidential proclamation.

29 June 1940 Alien Registration Act (Smith Act) requires all aliens to register and tightens deportation laws. The Smith Act also makes it illegal to advocate or teach the overthrow of any government of the United States by force or to organize a group for such purpose, and so makes the dissemination of ideas a crime.

April 1941 In *US* v *Darby* the Supreme Court upholds Fair Labor Standards Act (1938) 9–0, establishing minimum wage and outlawing child labour.

19 February 1942 President Roosevelt authorizes his secretary of war Henry L. Stimson to round up 110,000 Japanese or Japanese-Americans in California and the west coast and deport them to concentration camps in the interior. All lose their jobs, and most their property, while many are forced to work as manual farm labourers for the duration of the war.

In *Hirabayashi* v *United States* 1943 the US Supreme Court upholds military curfew on the west coast under which this deportation took place, and in *Korematsu* v *United States* 1944 the Supreme Court further upholds relocation programme, which ends on 2 January 1945. These Japanese-Americans are later compensated by the US government in a way which satisfies their claims.

SECTION IV

Economic and Social History, 1910–1945

Between 1910 and 1945 the United States transformed itself from a nation which was still predominantly agricultural into the industrial and financial powerhouse of the capitalist world. This section is designed to show how this happened, mostly through statistical tables. These have all been compiled from US Department of Commerce, Bureau of the Census, *Historical Statistics of the United States* (Washington DC, 1975).

1. Agriculture

1.1 Overview

American democracy, in Richard Hofstadter's phrase, had been born in the country but moved to the city. The value of the nation's total agricultural product had been overtaken by the value of its manufactured product in the 1890s. That same decade saw agrarian unrest express itself in the radical Populist movement. Ironically, as Populism reached its crest in 1896, farming was on the brink of a golden era which lasted roughly until 1920. Between 1920 and 1940, however, farming suffered severely from overproduction and adverse terms of trade, exacerbated by the Great Depression and ecological disasters of which the Dust Bowl of the 1930s was the best example.

During the New Deal and after, federal subsidies were used to control overproduction, while the decline of the sharecropping system, population shift and wartime demand between 1941 and 1945 helped stabilize agriculture and restore its prosperity.

Following the defeat of the Populist party at the polls in 1896, agrarian discontent, directed against falling prices and rising real debt, declined. The long-term figures for corn and wheat production show why the period between 1896 and 1915 was a golden era for American farming. In those years wholesale prices increased by two-thirds, production by one-half, and after 1900 debt burden was lightened by increased money supply.

The annual output of corn, wheat cotton and tobacco had increased as shown:

Corn	1860 800 million bushels
	1915 3 billion bushels
Wheat	1860 173 million bushels
	1915 1 billion bushels
Cotton	1915 record crop of 17 million bales.
Tobacco	1880 500 million bales
	1910 1 billion bales

1.2 The Farm Bloc

The depression which struck agriculture after the the wartime boom forced farmers to act together as a bloc in the 1920s. The farm bloc was headed by the conservative Republicans William S. Kenyon of Iowa in the Senate and Arthur Capper in the House, with the insurgent Progressive Robert La Follete running for president in 1924 and Floyd B. Olson as governor of Minnesota in the 1930s. The farm bloc had several important legislative achievements to its credit.

1921 War Finance Corporation revived to aid export of farm surpluses, with $433 million advanced for the purpose in the first year affecting commodities from 27 States.

Federal Land Banks enlarged.

Packers Stockyard Act gives secretary of agriculture power to prevent such abuses as manipulation of prices.

Grain-Futures Act gives secretary of agriculture supervision over traders in grain.

27 May 1921 Emergency Tariff Act places higher duties on wheat, corn, meat, wool and sugar for six months, which is later extended.

1922 Grain Futures Act replaced in order to conform with Supreme Court interpretation of farm legislation

Farm Cooperatives Act enables Farmers' Union and other cooperative stores to buy at current prices, with stockholders participating not only in profits from their own purchases but also from the business of outsiders. By 1926 a third of the nation's cheese is sold through 793 cooperatives in 21 States. By 1930 the California Fruit Growers' exchange controls 85 per cent of the citrus fruit of California, wheat cooperatives handle two-fifths of what goes into trade channels and the same is true in livestock and cotton. Cooperatives in the 1920s become big business.

4 March 1923 Intermediate Farm Credit Act allows US Treasury to provide capital for loans to farmers for between six months and three years, with a bank for such loans established in each Federal Reserve district. The Act essentially grants old Populist demand for a sub-treasury scheme.

1927 McFadden Banking Act authorizes the Federal Reserve Board to allow loans of up to ten months.

1.3 Farming and the Great Depression

The catastrophic impact of the Great Depression and the Dust Bowl during the 1930s forces the federal government to attempt to tackle farmers' problems through planning. The 1933 Agricultural Adjustment Act tries to solve the chronic problem of farming surplus by paying subsidies to farmers to grow fewer crops and rear less livestock.

Though the Supreme Court rules the AAA unconstitutional in the 1936 *Butler* decision, Congress later reintroduces subsidies through more carefully drafted legislation. In addition, the Federal Emergency Relief Administration pays millions of dollars in farm relief. The price is the collapse of sharecropping in the south, the decline of tenant farming and large scale rural depopulation. After 1940 the insatiable demands of the war economy restores prosperity to farming, but the consequence is a steady decline in the farm population. By 1945 subsidy is a permanent part of the agricultural economy.

1.4 Agricultural Statistics, 1910–45

1.4.1 Overview

	1910	1920	1945
Value of farm property (billions of 1929 dollars)	20.4	78.4	69.2
Wheat production (millions of bushels)	599	843	1,108
Corn production (millions of bushels)	2,622	3,071	2,869
Cotton production (millions of bales)	10.1	13.4	12.2
Number of farms (millions)	5.7	6.4	5.9
Gross private farm product (billions of 1929 dollars)	8.4	9.5	12.2

1.4.2 Value of Gross Farm Product, 1910–45 (in billions of current dollars)

1910	1920	1929	1934	1936	1937	1938	1939	1945
13.5	25.9	17.0	7.1	9.6	11.8	9.8	9.9	24.6

1.4.3 Acreage Value of Ten Leading Crops, 1910–44 (in dollars on 1910–14 base)

1910	1919	1924	1929	1930	1934	1939	1944
15.01	35.74	23.88	20.30	14.22	14.99	17.83	41.28

1.4.4 Index of Farms Costs and Prices, 1910–45 (Base: 1910–14 equals 100)

Year	Prices Received	Prices Paid	Ratio of two	Wages	Land taxes
1910	102	96	106	97	90
1915	99	107	93	103	118
1919	215	198	109	207	160
1921	124	165	75	155	244
1925	156	169	92	176	265
1929	149	167	89	180	279
1932	68	124	55	96	254
1937	122	133	92	126	181
1939	95	124	77	123	183
1940	100	125	80	126	186
1945	202	172	117	350	181

1.4.5 Farm Growth, 1910–45

Item	1910	1920	1930	1940	1945
Number of farms (in millions)	5.7	6.4	6.2	6.1	5.9
% of land in farms	46.2	50.2	51.8	55.7	59.9
Average acreage of farms	138.1	148.2	156.9	174.0	194.8
% of rural population to total US	54.2	48.6	43.8	43.5	37.5
% of farm to total US population	–	29.9	24.8	23.2	17.0
% of farm to rural population	–	61.5	56.6	53.4	45.2

1.4.6 Farm Income and Expenses, 1910–45 (in billions of current dollars, except as indicated)

Year	1910	1919	1929	1934	1936	1937	1938	1940	1945
Gross farm income	7.4	17.9	13.9	6.4	10.7	11.3	10.1	11.0	25.8
Personal income of farm pop.[1]	–	–	–	5.3	7.2	8.9	7.1	7.5	17.2
Net income of farmers from farming	4.1	9.0	6.1	2.0	4.3	6.0	4.3	4.4	12.3
Average per farm (dollars)	652	1,395	945	431	639	905	668	706	2,063
Per capita income of farm pop (dollars)[1]	–	–	–	167	228	287	232	249	705

[1] In each case, personal income from non-farm sources was often half the total.

1.4.7 Exports and Imports of Farm Products, 1910–45 (in millions of dollars, except %)

	1910	1920	1929	1933	1936	1937	1938	1945
Exports, domestic products	869	3,850	1,847	590	766	732	891	2,191
% of all exports	51	48	35	42	32	26	27	17
Imports for consumption	787	3,410	2,177	614	1,141	1,537	1,155	1,729
% of all imports	51	65	51	52	52	53	50	44

1.4.8 Direct Government Payments to Farmers, 1933–45 (in millions of dollars)

	1933	1935	1936	1938	1944	1945
Total[1]	131	573	278	446	776	742
Conservation[2]	–	–	24	309	378	259
Sugar Act	–	–	–	22	27	24
Cotton	–	15	41	114	–	–

[1] Includes programmes not shown separately.
[2] Includes Great Plains and other conservation programmes.

1.4.9 Index of Prices Received and Paid by Farmers, and Parity Ratio,[1] 1910–45 (1967=100)

	1910	1920	1929	1933	1937	1938	1939	1945
Prices received by farmers								
All farm products	41	83	58	28	48	38	37	81
Crops	46	93	65	31	54	43	42	92
Livestock and products	37	69	57	25	45	40	39	76
Prices paid by farmers								
Living	31	71	48	34	40	38	37	57
Production	34	68	51	34	46	43	42	61
Payable per acre								
Interest	17	45	45	34	24	23	22	16
Taxes	10	23	31	25	20	21	21	22
Wage rates	11	28	22	10	15	15	15	42
Prices paid, including tax, interest and wage rates	28	63	47	32	38	36	36	56
Parity ratio	107	99	92	64	93	78	77	109

[1] Ratio of prices received by farmers to prices paid, including interest, taxes and wage rates.

1.4.10 Farm - Mortgage Debt, Loans and Interest, 1910–45 (in millions of dollars, except as indicated)

	1910	1920	1929	1934	1940	1945
Total	3,207	8,448	9,756	7,685	6,586	4,940
Federal land banks & FFMC[1]	–	203	1,182	1,328	2,723	1,556
Life Insurance[1]	386	974	2,138	1,697	984	938
Commercial and savings banks[2]	406	1,204	1,046	710	534	449
Joint-stock land banks[2]	–	60	656.5	412.3	91.7	5.5
Farmers' home administration	–	–	–	–	32	195
Individuals and others	2,414	5,915	4,731	3,535	2,220	1,795
Loans foreclosed						
By Federal land banks & FFMC	–	66	63	1,283	100	120
By joint-stock land banks	–	19.3	18.2	.2	.1	**Z**
Interest payable						
Rates on loans[3]						
(i) recorded	6.4%	6.4%	6.3%	5.3%	**NA**	4.7%
(ii) outstanding	6.0%	6.1%	6.0%	5.8%	4.6%	4.5%
Total charges[4]	203	574	581	430	293	221
Taxes on farms						
Total						
Real estate	166	483	568	384	401	465
Amount per acre (dollars)	.19	.51	.58	.37	.39	.44
Personal property	–	–	84	40	50	92

[1] Beginning 1930, includes purchase-money mortgages and sales contracts in addition to regular mortgages.
[2] Includes soil and water conservation loans and farm-ownership loans insured by Farmers' Home Administration.
[3] Average contract rates, except for temporarily reduced rates on outstanding loans of Federal land banks 1933–44, and FFMC (Federal Farm Mortgage Corporation), 1938–45.
[4] Payable during calendar year on outstanding loans. Excludes amounts paid by secretary of the treasury to federal land banks 1933–34 and Federal Farm Mortgage Corporation 1937–45 on reimbursement for interest reductions granted borrowers.
Z Less than $50,000. **NA** Not available.

2. Conservation

The Progressive Era

1891 General Revision Act tightens up provisions for disposal of public lands, repealing a series of measures which had left glaring loopholes for fraud, for example the Desert Land Act (1877) and the Timber Cutting Act (1878). It also empowers the president to set aside forest reserves, with the result that between 1891 and 1900, 50 million acres of timberland are withdrawn from private entry.

1901 Creation of the Bureau of Forestry, which in 1905 becomes US Forest Service under Gifford Pinchot.

1902 Newlands Act enables receipts from land sales in arid states to be channelled into reservoir construction and irrigation schemes.

1908 National Conservation Commission, chaired by Gifford Pinchot, created as result of conference of state governors in May 1908.

1910 Withdrawal Act preserves all known coal, oil, gas and phosphate lands in the public domain.

1911 Weeks Act empowers federal government to purchase forest lands in the Appalachian and White Mountains for protection of watersheds and hence river navigability.

1916 Hydro-electric power: federal government compelled to evolve a policy towards this nascent private industry. Industrial lobbyists and southern and western congressmen urge conducive federal approach and dismantling of any obstructive legislation. Three alternative bills proposed, none of which is passed under president Wilson:

- The Ferris bill, approved by the House on 8 January 1916 would permit controlled construction of hydro-electric projects in the public domain and national forests on maximum 50-year leases, the government reserving right to purchase property at net cost on expiration of lease.
- The Adamson bill, approved by the House in August 1914, would empower secretary of war to license dam construction on navigable rivers, provided states in which they are located possess adequate machinery to regulate electric power rates.

- The Shields bill, approved by Senate on 8 March 1916, would give a virtually free hand to private power companies, offering perpetual leases for hydro-electric projects.

8 January 1916 Furore arises over Mineral Leasing bill, approved by the House. It offers relief to oil operators who have made improper but *bona fide* claims and are already producing oil in Californian naval reserves set aside in 1912 by President Taft.

Gifford Pinchot (who clashed with Ballinger over conservation in 1910 – see above) accuses department of interior of betraying the cause of conservation. No compromise reached until Mineral Leasing Act is approved on 25 February 1920.

1923 Teapot Dome scandal reveals twin problems of corruption and conservation.

1931 President Hoover vetoes Muscle Shoals bill, calling on federal government to take over hydro-electric power generation plant built during first world war. Within two years this very proposal becomes the basis for Franklin Roosevelt's Tennessee Valley Authority.

1933–1940 Creation of the Tennessee Valley Authority and many other New Deal initiatives bring conservation within the control of the federal government.

3. Commerce and the Tariff

Pre-1910

1890 McKinley tariff raises average level of protection to 50 per cent and greatly increases range of articles on the dutiable list.

1897 Dingley tariff raises average level to nearly 60 per cent – the highest tariff in American history.

Tariff Reform Movement 1900–13

1900–13 Tariff Reform Movement: spread of industrial combination fuels charges that high tariffs merely raise an umbrella under which trusts and monopolies flourish, a notion apparently lent additional proof by the fact that the cost of living increases by about one quarter between 1897 and 1907. In addition to Democrats, most midwestern Republicans, following Albert Cummins's 'Iowa Idea', favour downward revision.

1909 Payne-Aldrich tariff originally represents the Taft administration's will to reduce duties on iron and steel, agricultural implements, sugar and lumber, free listing certain raw materials, and imposes for the first time a small federal income tax to compensate for lost revenue. However, on 12 April 1909 Senate finance committee butchers the bill with 847 amendments, actually increasing *ad valorem* duties to 41.77 per cent. Taft accepts amendments in return for 2 per cent corporation tax and inclusion of income tax as a constitutional amendment.

8 April 1913 The new president Woodrow Wilson addresses both houses of Congress in favour of tariff reform.

8 May 1913 Approval of Underwood bill by the House. The bill by no means represents unadulterated free trade, but nevertheless is a genuine attempt to fulfil Democratic election pledges. It free lists most products manufactured under the aegis of trusts, for example iron and steel and agricultural machinery, and on most raw materials, shoes, food and so forth offers no more than incidental protection. Overall, average tariff rates are reduced from 40 to 29 per cent. In addition, the House ways and means committee adds a small graduated income tax as compensation, with rates ranging from 1 to 4 per cent for incomes over $100,000.

2 June 1913 In response to a resolution from Albert Cummins of Ohio, Senate select committee reports on lobbying activities of groups interested in acquiring favoured treatment under the tariff bill. For example, it is discovered that the beet sugar manufacturers' lobby spent $5 million over 20 years enlisting opinion makers for their campaign.

3 October 1913 Wilson signs tariff bill, after threatened rebellion of Progressive senators, including William E. Borah, Moses E. Clapp, George W. Norris and Robert M. La Follette, forces Senate finance committee to increase income tax to a maximum 7 per cent and reduce tariff by 4 per cent – the first material downward revision since the civil war.

1916 US Tariff Commission created, based upon shared notion that tariffs can be computed 'scientifically' to offset exactly the lower cost of production of a given article in a given country of origin.

1920s The Fordney-McCumber and Hawley-Smoot tariffs mark return to pre-1910 high tariff policies. European nations are unable to sell goods in US to repay war debt. During the Great Depression and New Deal, tariff policy is neglected while commerce, banking and finance are increasingly taken under control of Federal Reserve Board. Federal powers are enhanced through banking acts and control of the securities and exchange markets.

4. Banking and Finance

Pre-1910

1864 National Bank Act seeks to create uniform national currency and nationally chartered banks which, it is intended, will carry greater prestige and inspire customer confidence and hence stability. However, existing modes of operation under state charter – where required capital levels and reserves against deposits are generally lower, and rules governing lending and investment policy are slacker – remain attractive. Consequently, an uncoordinated dual system of national and state banks emerges, within which a huge number of small unit banks, as opposed to branch banking, is the rule.

The Progressive Era

1900 This tendency is further enhanced by a statute which reduces to $25,000 the capital requirement for a national bank in settlement of 3,000 persons or less, thus prompting creation of hundreds of small banks. Consquently, where in 1900 there are 5,007 state banks and 3,731 national banks, by 1914 there are 17,498 state banks and only 7,518 national banks.

1907 'Bankers' Panic': mass apprehension prompts depositors to rush to convert their deposits into cash. As banks compete to liquefy their assets, price of securities falls steeply, with result that banks are compelled to suspend payments or restrict withdrawals.

1908 Aldrich-Vreeland Act creates an unwieldy and ineffective emergency currency system and appoints National Monetary Commission headed by senator Nelson W. Aldrich (Rhode Island).

1912 Monetary commission's report, subsequently condemned by the Democrats in their election platform, advocates a central bank with 15 branches controlled entirely by bankers and banking interests as solution to alleged 'inelasticity' of money supply. While conservatives desire yet greater decentralization, Progressives contend that public control alone will suffice.

23 December 1913 Wilson signs Federal Reserve Act, the result of much compromise and revision. Twelve Federal Reserve Banks are created, each functioning as a central bank of its respective district, rediscounting commercial and agricultural paper and issuing federal reserve notes. National banks are accorded compulsory membership of the system, whereas state banks are permitted to join upon compliance with federal requirements. After 1917, all legal reserves of each member bank are to be held as deposits with the Federal Reserve Bank of their district.

Currency of the new system is federal reserve notes: each Reserve Bank is to back 40 per cent of its outstanding notes with gold reserves.

System is headed by Federal Reserve Board, consisting of seven members, including secretaries of the treasury and commerce, which can regulate credit supply by raising or lowering the rediscount rate, or by manipulating the sale of government securities.

In general, however, public interests receive no more than a supervisory role. For example, each Federal Reserve Bank is headed by a nine-man directorate, three of whom are Federal Reserve agents, the remaining six being elected by member banks. With this inbuilt majority, bankers are able to dictate selection of the operating head of the reserve bank, the governor.

Over time, governors acquire position of unrivalled supremacy within the Federal Reserve System, to the extent that a conference of governors is inaugurated in 1916, holding regular formal meetings to determine FRS policy.

Taxation and Financing the First World War

Emphasis upon indirect taxation leaves overall tax burden lying heavily on lower and middle classes, giving rise to such movements as the Association for an Equitable Federal Income Tax.

1916

6 September Senate adopts tax reform measure:

- Normal income tax doubles to 2 per cent.
- Surtax on incomes over $20,000 raised to a maximum of 13 per cent.
- Federal estate tax between 1 and 10 per cent on estates worth more than $50,000.
- Between 1 and 12.5 per cent tax on gross receipts of munitions manufacturers making net profits in excess of 10 per cent.
- Tax on corporation capital, surplus and undivided profits.

1917

23 April First War Loan Act: Treasury authorized to issue $2 billion in short-term notes and $5 billion in bonds to be sold by popular subscription; $3 billion to be lent to the Allies. By 1920 a total of $23 billion has been borrowed.

3 October War Revenue Bill:

- Normal income tax increased to 4 per cent, and exemptions reduced.
- Graduated excess profits tax levied up to 60 per cent.
- Maximum surtax up to 63 per cent.
- Estate taxes raised to maximum 25 per cent.
- New excise taxes on luxuries and services.

1919

24 February Revenue Act raises prevailing tax burden by almost 250 per cent, most deriving from large incomes, profits and estates:

- Normal income tax for incomes over $4,000 increased to 12 per cent, and surtax to an upper limit of 65 per cent, giving a maximum rate of taxation of 77 per cent.
- Excess profits tax raised to 65 per cent maximum.

1920s

In the 'bull market', nothing is done to deal with grave underlying monetary and tariff problems facing the United States, nor reform banking and commerce. Moreover, with both Germany and the Allies owing billions in war debt and reparations, there is no way they can pay their debts so long as America maintains her traditional high tariff policy.

1921

27 May Emergency Tariff Act. With postwar deflation and falling prices hurting farmers, special session of Congress rushes through emergency tariff fixing high duties on wheat, corn, meat, wool and sugar for six months – later extended.

1922

9 February Congress establishes world war foreign debt commission to settle vexed problem of Allied war and postwar loans. Britain owes $4 billion, France $3 billion, Italy more than $1.6 billion, while Germany has been saddled with entire cost of the war. Other countries are endebted to US, and some owe Britain a total of $10 billion. None can pay. Yet Wilson has blindly insisted on repayment in full. For second time, Britain offers to remit debts and reparations if US will do the same, but Harding and then Coolidge refuse.

The following year, French troops occupy the Ruhr in attempt to force Germany to pay, while German mark is destroyed by worst galloping inflation in history. Eventually, Congress agrees to reschedule repayment of $11.5 billion at 2 per cent over 62 years, but by the end of the decade Italy and France have had up to 80 per cent of debt cancelled.

24 March Fordney-McCumber Tariff, sponsored by Joseph W. Fordney of Michigan and Porter J. McCumber of North Dakota, carries old 1909 Republican idea of equalization to absurd extremes, raising tariffs to their highest rate in history. Unabashed, senator Robert N. Stanfield boasts he would favour duties of 5,000 per cent if necessary.

1924

Congress sets up special commission to advise on tariff question. In presidential election campaign Democrats denounce Fordney-McCumber Act as 'the most unjust, unscientific and dishonest tariff tax measure ever enacted in our history'.

1924–29

Tariff commission, with added powers, promises to take tariff out of politics, but recommends increased duties.

1928

July–November Republican candidate Herbert Hoover campaigns for presidency on promise to increase only those tariffs which will help ailing agriculture.

1929

7 May Willis C. Hawley of Oregon, chairman of House Ways and Means committee, presents bill which far exceeds president Hoover's recommendations by raising almost every tariff to new heights. Passes House at end of month.

1930

24 March After amendment by Senate finance committee, headed by Reed Smoot of Utah, bill sent to conference committee, which votes 1,253 amendments mostly by accepting highest rate recommended by either house of Congress.

14 June Hawley-Smoot Tariff, the highest in US history, passes Senate 44–42 and is signed by Hoover on 17 June.

11 December Bank of the US, a major private bank with some 60 branches and 400,000 depositors, fails. Approximately 1,300 banks have failed since October 1929. By March 1933 some 6,000 have failed, and there is hardly a sound bank in America.

1931

20 June Hoover proposes one-year moratorium on all inter-governmental debts and reparations, following collapse of *Kreditanstalt*, major bank of Austria. This only briefly halts collapse of world economy. By 1932 this is spiralling down more viciously than ever.

8 December Hoover asks Congress to establish an emergency reconstruction finance corporation to lend money to banks, insurance companies and other bodies which would then be invested in industry.

1932

22 January Reconstruction Finance Corporation created with more than $500 million in funds and authorization to borrow up to $2 billion by tax exempt bonds.

21 July Hoover signs Relief and Reconstruction Act, an emergency bill designed to enlarge RFC programmes by increasing amount it can loan to $3 billion and extending loans to state and local agencies in order to finance public works.

22 July Congress adopts Federal Home Loan Bank Act authorizing a dozen regional banks to provide cheaper home loans for house purchase.

26 August Controller of the Currency declares moratorium on foreclosures of first mortgages thus helping millions of unemployed Americans who are unable to maintain their home repayments.

1933

5 March President Franklin D. Roosevelt declares national four-day bank holiday while Emergency Banking Act, which saves the nation's banking system, is drafted. Congress passes Act in seven hours.

20 March Roosevelt signs Economy Act, reducing salaries of all federal employees and payments to army veterans.

19 April By presidential proclamation, Roosevelt takes US off gold standard. Net effect is to increase money supply and start economic recovery through reflation.

12 May Federal Emergency Relief Act (FERA) authorizes immediate grants to states for relief programmes – unlike Hoover who gave only loans. Through its administrative agency FERA plays a major part in reducing unemployment and stimulating economic recovery over the next seven years.

12 June–27 July London economic conference fails when Roosevelt decides he must put national economic recovery before international financial recovery and refuses to stabilize the dollar.

13 June Home Owners Loan Refinancing Act provides money for more than one million desperate home owners in danger of repossession.

1934

4 January President asks Congress for $10.5 billion to advance recovery programmes during the next 18 months.

30 January Congress passes the Gold Reserve Act, empowering president to fix value of US dollar in terms of gold. Gold fixed at $35 an ounce, where it remains until 1971.

31 January President signs Farm Mortgage Refinancing Act, establishing Federal Farm Mortgage Corporation to help farmers reschedule debt incurred buying their land.

2 February By executive order president creates Export–Import Bank to encourage commerce between US and other nations.

6 June Securities Exchange Act creates Securities and Exchange Commission (SEC) to regulate Wall Street stock market. Wealthy Democrat and Roosevelt-backer Joseph P. Kennedy becomes first chairman of SEC, classic case of poacher turned gamekeeper.

28 June National Housing Act establishes Federal Housing Administration to ensure finance for massive programme of home construction.

1935

8 April Congress appropriates $5 billion for huge programme of public works organized by the Works Progress Administration (WPA).

30 August Congress passes the Revenue Act, increasing taxes on higher incomes, gifts and inheritance. Asking for this legislation, FDR observes 'Our revenue laws have operated ... to the unfair advantage of the few, and they have done little to prevent an unjust concentration of wealth and economic power.' Taxation becomes increasingly progressive during the next ten years.

In summary, following collapse of Wall Street stock market in 1929–31, the 1933 Emergency Banking Act, the 1933 Glass-Steagall Act and the creation of the Federal Deposit Insurance Commission and Securities and Exchange Commission, passage of the 1935 Revenue Act or wealth tax, together with the enhanced role of the Federal Reserve Board, all combine to bring banking and finance under greater federal regulation. This is increased by war powers after 1941.

Finance Between the Wars

The Republican ascendancy of the 1920s sees determined policy of raising tariffs and reducing taxation and public spending as a means of eliminating public debt incurred during first world war. Budget deficit is reduced from $25 billion in 1919 to $16 billion in 1930.

But when the Great Depression strikes, despite Franklin Roosevelt's pledge to cut the cost of federal government by 25 per cent, New Deal reforms inevitably raise public spending and debt from $16 billion in 1930 to $43 billion in 1940. When public spending is cut by just $1.5 billion in 1937–38, the result is a sharp downturn in the economy and a rapid rise in unemployment.

Financing the Second World War

However, the real cause of increased federal budget deficits is not welfare but warfare. Total public debt rises from $1.4 billion in 1910 to $25 billion in 1919, almost entirely because of war expenditure. But this is to be dwarfed by spending after 1940, when the second world war transforms the American economy and its financial basis. Federal spending during the war exceeds $320 billion, nearly twice the previous total of all government spending since 1789. The national debt, which rose by $27 billion during the emergency years of the Great Depression and New Deal between 1930 and 1940, went up by $215 billion between 1941 and 1945.

5. Industry

Pre-1910

Start of shift from an agricultural to an industrial economy.

1860–1918 Precision in metalworking increased from 0.01 inch to 0.001 inch toleration limit.

1882 Construction of Thomas Edison's central power plant in New York, although by 1914 less than half electric motors in use are driven by power from a central plant.

1895 Northrup Automatic Loom introduced.

1908 Henry Ford's plans for a low-priced car to furnish cheap transport with minimum frills produces first example of progressive line production, initially by means of sub-assembly at several stationary points.

Industrial Concentration

1910 By now, economic concentration has slowed considerably: the formation of such monopolistic giants as Standard Oil (1869), American Tobacco (1890) and US Steel (1901) belong to previous decades.

Between 1888 and 1905, 328 major combinations had been formed, and by 1905 around two-fifths of US manufacturing capital is controlled by some 300 companies. But between 1905 and 1920, only 30–40 new combinations are formed.

Nevertheless, the Progressive impulse towards anti-monopolistic legislation is not blunted. Indeed, it is given additional impetus by the findings of the Pujo Committee in February 1913 which, for example, reports that J.P. Morgan & Co, the First National Bank and the National City Bank together hold 341 directorships in 112 banks, railroads, industries and other corporations worth over $22 billion.

1911 The Taylor philosophy of 'scientific management' popularized by Louis D. Brandeis. He argues before Interstate Commerce Commission in favour of logically ordered industrial operations, planned according to scientific principles.

1913 Henry Ford's adoption of moving assembly: sub-assemblies are performed as the car is pulled by a windlass. By

1914, a chassis which previously took 12 hours to assemble was put together along a 250-foot line in one-and-a-half hours.

1914

26 September Wilson signs Federal Trade Commission Act, written largely by Louis D. Brandeis. The Act does not attempt to define unfair trade practices, but establishes an independent, bipartisan Federal Trade Commission of five members, empowered to move against corporations accused of suppressing competition via cease and desist orders or by going to trial.

15 October Presidential approval of the Clayton Act. Original bill sought to list and define illegal trade practices, which included price cutting to destroy competitors, tying contracts, refusal to sell to responsible firms and interlocking directorates, and rendered owners and directors criminally responsible for civil violations. After much pressure from the American Federation of Labor, an amendment is approved exempting labour, farm fraternal and cooperative organizations from definition as illegal combinations in restraint of trade, and forbidding courts to issue injunctions in labour disputes unless to prevent irreparable injury to property. Workers are given right to trial in cases of criminal contempt.

However, once cut adrift in the Senate, the bill loses many of its teeth by inclusion of a long catalogue of qualifying phrases, elimination of criminal penalties for civil violations and exemption of banks with resources under $5 million from ban on interlocking directorates.

Industry and Mobilization

1915

15 October Wilson approves naval equality plan, prepared by general board of the navy and the army War College in response to a presidential request of July 1915. It aims at achieving naval parity with Britain by 1925, constructing $500 million worth of vessels.

1916

7 September Shipping bill effectively gives birth to US merchant navy, appointing a shipping board empowered to spend up to $50 million on construction and purchase of merchant ships, operate shipping lanes and regulate rates and services of all vessels engaged in interstate, coastal and foreign trade of the US.

1917

31 March Establishment of Munitions Standards Board in wake of an inventory of US industrial capacity undertaken by Council of National Defense. Shortly after it becomes the General Munitions

Board, entrusted with control of purchase and supply of armed forces' ammunition.

16 April Federal government charters Emergency Fleet Corporation as subsidiary of US Shipping Board, in order to construct ships quickly enough to beat submarine blockade.

July After jurisdictional squabbles between Emergency Fleet Corporation and the Shipping Board, Edward N. Hurley, chairman of Federal Trade Commission, is appointed as single head. Progress, however, remains slow: Atlantic seaboard's largest new shipyard, at Hog Island, does not produce a serviceable vessel until December 1918.

28 July Unsatisfactory General Munitions Board abolished, and is supplanted by War Industries Board, a bureaucratic clearing house for purchases, allocation of raw materials, and supervision of labour relations, but without authority over the war and navy departments.

December Investigation of mobilization by Senate military affairs committee, under chairman George E. Chamberlain, reveals breakdowns in rail transport and soldiers left unhoused and unfed, prompting Republican demands for a coalition war cabinet.

In response, Wilson writes Overman bill (adopted April 1918) granting himself unprecedented and virtually unlimited power to marshal national resources and manpower.

28 December All railroad transport brought under control of US Railroad Administration, headed by William G. McAdoo, who spends more than $500 million on long overdue improvements.

1918

4 March Wilson appoints Bernard M. Baruch (a Wall Street broker) head of War Industries Board, vesting in him wide authority over prices, purchasing for the Allies and setting production priorities. The rest of the story of industrial growth is best told through statistics.

6. Industrial Production, 1910–45

6.1 Major Fuels

	1910	1920	1930	1940	1945
Coal (m. of tons)	373	568	518	417	577
Petroleum (b. of barrels)	172	443	896	1,242	1,714
Natural Gas (t. cubic feet)	437	762	1,638	2,402	3,919
Natural Gasoline (m. of gallons)	30	268	1,852	2,105	3,291

6.2 Electric Power Production for Public Use

	1920	1930	1940	1945
Million Kw. Current Produced				
Total	39.4	91.1	142	228
Water Power	15.7	31.1	47.3	80
Consumption of Fuels Producing Current				
Coal (m. of tons)	32	40.2	51.5	75
Fuel Oil (m. of barrels)	13	9	16.3	36.3
Gas (t. of cubic feet)	22.1	120	180	326.2
Coal (equivalent of all fuels m. of tons)	36	46	63	99.2
Capacity of Generators (m. of Kw,)	13	32.3	40	50.1

6.3 Steel Production (millions of tons)

	1910	1920	1930	1940	1945
Total	26.1	42.1	40.6	60	71.1
Bessemer	9.4	8.9	5	3.3	3.8
Open Hearth	16.6	32.7	35	55	64
Crucible	00.12	00.07	00.22	00.02	–
Electric	00.05	00.50	00.61	1.52	3.08

6.4 Index of Manufacturing Production (1947=100)

1910	1920	1929	1931	1936	1937	1938	1940	1945
24	32	65	40	52	58	54	56	103

6.5 Index of Manufacturing Production by Industry Group (1947=100)

	1909	1919	1929	1933	1937	1939
All manufacturing industries	24	34	56	35	58	57
Durable manufactures						
Primary metals	28	40	65	27	58	52
Fabricated metal products	–	–	–	–	51	50
Machinery except electrical	–	–	–	–	38	38
Electrical machinery	–	–	–	–	35	35
Transportation equipment	7	40	66	22	60	49

Table 6.5 (Cont.)

	1909	1919	1929	1933	1937	1939
Stone, clay and glass products	–	70	89	42	88	87
Lumber and furniture	75	71	91	42	69	72
Nondurable manufactures						
Textiles and apparel	41	45	67	57	72	80
Rubber products	–	30	57	39	51	55
Leather	65	142	79	68	86	87
Paper	19	27	52	44	63	68
Printing and publishing	25	39	72	52	73	69
Chemicals	11	18	35	29	43	46
Petroleum and coal products	9	21	54	42	61	65
Food	28	32	46	37	61	65
Tobacco	24	38	55	48	65	66

6.6 Wholesale Commodity Price Index (1926=100)

1910	1920	1925	1933	1936	1937	1938	1940	1945
70.4	154.4	103.5	65.9	80.8	86.3	77.1	78.6	105.8

6.7 Index of National Productivity, 1910–45 (per worker hour; 1929=100)

	1910	1920	1931	1933	1936	1937	1938	1940	1945
Total economy	65	78	98	91	109	109	112	120	145
Farm	90*	86**	103	105	99	108	116	115	128
Non-farm	–	80	97	93	111	110	113	122	141

* 1915 = 101
** 1927 = 101

6.8 Growth Rate Gross National Product (GNP), 1910–45 (annual %)

1910	1921	1922	1929	1932	1936	1937	1938	1939	1940	1943
+2.6	–8.6	+16	+6.7	–15	+14	+5.3	-5.0	+8.6	+8.5	+16

6.9 Gross National Product (GNP), Total and Per Capita, 1910–45

	1910	1920	1929	1933	1936	1937	1938	1940	1945
Current prices									
Total (billion $)	35	91	103	55	82	90	84	98	213
Per capita ($)	382	860	847	442	643	701	651	754	1515
1958 prices									
Total (billion $)	120	140	203	141	193	203	192	227	355
Per capita ($)	1,299	1,315	1,671	1,126	1,506	1,576	1,484	1,720	2,538
Implicit price index (1958=100)	29.4	65.4	50.6	39.3	42.7	44.5	43.2	43.9	59.7

6.10 Exports and Imports, 1910–45 (billions of current dollars)

	1910	1920	1925	1930	1935	1940	1945
Total exports	1.7	8.2	4.9	3.8	2.2	4.0	9.8
Exports of US merchandise	1.7	8.0	4.8	3.7	2.2	3.9	9.5
General imports	1.5	5.2	4.2	3.0	2.0	2.6	4.1

6.11 United States Expenditures and Receipts, 1910–45 (billions of current dollars)

	Budget receipts	Budget expenditures	Surplus or deficit	Total public debt
1910	0.67	0.69	–0.18	1.14
1919	5.13	18.49	–13.36	25.48
1920	6.54	6.35	+0.29	24.29
1925	3.64	2.92	+0.17	20.51
1927	4.01	2.85	+2.73	19.48
1930	4.05	3.32	+0.73	16.18
1932	1.92	4.65	–2.73	19.48
1934	3.01	6.64	–3.62	27.05
1936	3.99	8.42	–4.42	33.77
1937	4.95	7.73	–2.77	38.42
1938	5.58	6.76	–1.17	37.16
1939	4.97	8.84	–3.86	40.43
1940	5.15	9.05	–3.90	42.93
1945	44.45	98.15	–53.70	258.63

1. 6.12 Unemployment, 1910–45[1]

	1910	1929	1933	1937	1938	1940	1945
Total (millions)	2.1	1.5	12.8	7.7	10.4	8.1	1.0
% of working population	5.9	3.2	24.9	14.3	19	14.6	1.9
% of non-farm working population	11.6	5.3	37.6	21.3	27.4	25.2	2.7

[1] The link between cuts in public expenditure and unemployment between 1936 and 1940 is clear from the two tables above. But see Table 8.6 below, for the extent to which wages rose and fell with public spending. Indeed the whole economy both agricultural (Tables 1.4.2 to 1.4.9 above) and industrial (Tables 6.6 to 6.9, 6.13 and *passim*) reacted to relatively small changes in the federal deficit. Moreover, the really large increases in public debt were incurred not by spending on public works, relief or social welfare, but on armaments during the first and second world wars.

6.13 Money Supply, 1910–45 (currency + both demand and time deposits in billions of dollars)

1910	1920	1929	1933	1937	1938	1940	1945
13	35	47	32	31	30	40	127

7. Demography

7.1 Population of the United States, 1910–45 (in millions)

	1910	1920	1930	1940	1945
Total	92.4	106.4	123.1	132.1	139.9
Afro-American	9.8	10.4	11.8	12.8	13.1
Immigration	1.0	0.43	0.24	0.07	n.a.

7.2 Net Migration of Afro-Americans out of the South, 1900–50 (in millions)

1900–10	1910–20	1920–30	1930–40	1940–50	Total
1.86	4.95	7.83	4.04	13.22	31.90

7.3 Population of the United States, 1910–45 (% of total)

	1910	1920	1930	1940	1945
Urban	46	51	56	57	n.a
White native-born	74	77	78	81	n.a
White foreign-born	15	13	11	9	n.a.
Non-white	11	10	10	10	n.a.

7.4 Population by Gender and Race, 1910–50 (in millions)

	1910	1920	1930	1940	1950
Male					
All races	47.3	53.9	62.1	66	74.8
White	42.1	48.4	55.9	59.4	67.1
Black	4.9	5.2	5.8	6.2	7.3
Native American	0.13	0.12	0.17	0.17	0.18
Japanese	0.06	0.07	0.08	0.07	0.08
Chinese	0.06	0.05	0.06	0.06	0.08
Female					
All races	44.6	51.8	60.6	65.6	75.8
White	39.5	46.3	54.3	58.7	67.8
Black	4.9	5.2	6.0	6.6	7.7
Native American	0.13	0.11	0.16	0.16	0.16
Oriental	–	0.03	0.06	0.07	1.00

7.5 Total Number of Immigrants Arriving Annually, 1910–45 (in millions)

1910	1915	1920	1925	1930	1940	1945
1.0	0.32	0.43	0.3	0.2	0.07	0.03

7.6 Total Number of Immigrants Arriving by Decade, 1901–50 (in millions)

1901–10	1911–20	1921–30	1931–40	1941–50
7.9	5.7	4.1	0.5	1.0

7.7 Number of Immigrants by Country and Decade, 1910–50 (in millions)

	1901–10	1911–20	1921–30	1931–40	1941–50
Britain	0.53	0.34	0.33	0.03	0.13
Ireland	0.39	0.15	0.22	0.01	0.03
Scandinavia	0.51	0.20	0.12	0.01	0.26
Germany[1]	0.34	0.14	0.41	0.11	0.23
Poland	n.a.	n.a.	0.23	0.02	0.007
Russia and Baltics	1.6	0.92	0.09	0.007	0.004
Italy	2.5	1.1	0.46	0.07	0.06
China	0.02	0.02	0.03	0.004	0.16
Japan	0.13	0.08	0.03	0.002	0.02
Canada and Newfoundland	0.18	0.74	0.92	0.11	0.17
Mexico	0.05	0.22	0.46	0.22	0.60
Australia and New Zealand	0.12	0.08	0.02	0.13	0.11
Asia	0.16	0.08	0.15	0.08	0.13
Africa	0.07	0.08	0.06	0.02	0.08
West Indies	0.11	0.12	0.07	0.02	0.05

[1] Although Germany sent few immigrants between 1910 and 1945, between 1820 and 1950 some 6.25 million immigrants came from there, easily the largest single source. Together with immigrants from Austria-Hungary, 10 million of an estimated 40 million immigrants came from German-speaking parts of the world during this longer period. This meant that of the native white population of foreign or mixed parentage, 4 million were of German descent and 3 million of Italian in 1940 (the year before Germany and Italy declared war on the United States).

8. Industrial Workers and Labour Unions

8.1 Labour Force and its Components 1910–45

	1910	1929	1933	1937	1939	1945
Total civilian labour force (millions)	36.7	47.7	50.8	53.7	55.2	53.8[1]
Farm labour force (millions)	11.2	10.5	10.0	10.0	9.7	8.5
Non-farm labour force (millions)	23.2	35.6	27.9	36.0	36.0	44.2
Farm labour as % of total	30.5	22	19.6	18.6	17.5	15.7
Non-farm labour as % of total	63.2	74.6	54.9	65.2	66.9	82.1

[1] Fell by 750,000 from 54.6 million in 1944, presumably in part because 11.4 million had been mobilized for war. The only other fall this century, by 350,000, occurred between 1916 and 1918 when 2 million had been similarly mobilized.

8.2 Labour Union Membership, 1910–45 (in millions)[1]

1910	1915	1920	1930	1933	1937	1939	1945
2.1	2.5	5.0	3.6	2.8	7.2	8.9	14.7

[1] As with all labour union figures, these include Canadian members of US unions.

8.3 Labour Union Membership, 1910–45 (as % of non-farm employment)

1910	1915	1920	1930	1933	1937	1939	1945
9.0	9.9	17.4	10.6	11.7	22.6	28.6	33.25

8.4 Labour Union Membership by Affiliation, 1910–45

	1910	1920	1933	1937	1940	1945
Total (millions)	2.1	5.0	2.8	7.2	8.9	14.7
Number of AFL unions	120	110	108	102	105	102
AFL members after 1937 schism (millions)	–	–	–	4.5	4.5	6.9
CIO members after 1937 schism (millions)	–	–	–	1.9	3.6	6.1
Number of CIO unions	–	–	–	42	45	40
Membership of independent unions, like rail brotherhoods (millions)	0.5	0.9	0.7	0.8	0.8	1.7

8.5 Prices and Incomes, 1910–45

	1910	1920	1929	1934	1937	1940	1945
Average annual real earnings (1914 dollars)	607	672	834	800	880	943	1,318
Consumer price index (1914=100)	94.7	199.7	170.9	133	143	139.5	179

8.6 Annual Income by Industry, 1910–45 (current dollars)

	1910	1920	1929	1934	1937	1938	1940	1945
Farming and (after 1929) fisheries	223	528	401	253	360	369	407	1,125
Manufacturing	651	1,532	1,543	1,153	1,376	1,296	1,432	2,517
All mining	668	1,684	1,526	990	1,366	1,282	1,388	2,621
Anthracite	604	1,777	1,728	1,452	1,388	1,315	1,297	2,685
Bituminous	657	1,633	1,293	748	1,170	1,050	1,235	2,629
Metal	865[1]	1,639	1,613	1,040	1,630	1,453	1,610	2,551
Construction	827	1,710	1,674	869	1,278	1,193	1,330	2,600
All transport	607	1,645	1,643	1,334	1,644	1,676	1,756	2,734
Rail	662	1,807	1,749	1,439	1,774	1,849	1,906	2,711
Water	430	1,499	1,275	1,038	1,536	1,299	1,648	3,538
Local	575	1,435	1,598	1,219	1,505	1,529	1,559	2,596
Communication and utilities	516	1,238	1,478	1,351	1,600	1,673	1,717	2,446
Gas & electric	616	1,489	1,589	1,453	1,705	1,749	1,795	2,596
Telephone, telegraph	461	1,115	1,386	1,245	1,481	1,508	1,610	2,246

[1] 1908 figure is given here as the one for 1910 is not available.

8.7 Average Earnings and Hours by Gender and Skill, 1914–45[1] (weekly rate in 25 manufacturing industries)

	1914	1920	1929	1934	1937	1940	1945
All production workers							
hours	51.5	48.2	48.3	34.7	38.7	38.6	44.2
pay($)	12.68	29.39	28.55	17.05	26.80	28.54	48.46
Male							
hours	52.2	49.2	49.1	34.4	39.3	39.2	45.2
pay($)	13.65	31.69	30.64	18.69	28.72	30.64	53.47
Female							
hours	50.1	43.0	44.2	34.0	36.1	35.5	40.8
pay($)	7.75	17.71	17.61	11.73	17.02	17.43	32.18
Unskilled male							
hours	52.9	49.2	50.2	34.4	39.6	39.3	44.8
pay($)	10.71	26.06	24.40	14.48	22.41	23.91	41.08
Skilled and semi-skilled male							
hours	51.7	49.4	48.8	35.1	39.3	39.2	45.2
pay($)	14.99	34.10	32.60	19.48	37.1	39.2	45.2

[1] No figures available before 1914.

8.8 Work-Injury Rates in Manufacture, Mine and Rail, 1926–45[1] (per million man-hours)

	1926	1931	1936	1940	1945
Manufacturing	24.2	18.9	16.6	15.3	18.6
Mining					
Coal	n.a.	89.9	74.4	70.4	60.7
Metals	n.a.	58.0	76.3	66.8	44.9
Non-metals		n.a.	47.5	48.6	44.247.2
Stone quarries	58.0	41.0	39.5	35.7	32.8
Railways	23.9[2]	7.5[2]	13.7	11.5	20.5

[1] No figures available before 1922, full figures only after 1931.
[2] Excluding 1–3 day injuries.

8.9 Industrial Disputes, 1914–45[1]

	1914	1919	1930	1937	1940	1945
Total number of strikes (in thousands)	1.2	3.6	0.6	4.7	2.4	4.6
Total number of strikers (in millions)	n.a.	n.a.	0.18	1.8	0.57	4.75
Strikes per million non-farm workers	120	150	25	95	63	130
Strikers as % of total employed	n.a.	n.a.	0.8%	7.2%	1.7%	8.2%
Strikers per thousand non-farm workers	47	75	10	48	35	73
Man-days lost (in millions)	n.a.	n.a.	3.3	28.4	6.7	38.0
Man-days lost per worker involved	n.a.	n.a.	18.1	15.3	11.6	11.0
Man-days lost as % of total working time of non-farm economy	n.a.	n.a.	0.05	0.43	0.10	0.47
Average duration (in days)	n.a.	n.a.	22.3	20.3	20.9	9.9

[1] Full strike figures are not available for the years before 1914, and in many cases before 1927.

SECTION V

Principal Officeholders, 1910–1945

This section lists all cabinet officers, US Supreme Court justices and leaders of Congress between 1910 and 1945. It has been compiled from material in Erik W. Austin, *Political Facts of the United States since 1789* (New York, 1986).

Presidential Cabinet Officers

President WILLIAM HOWARD TAFT (Republican, 1909–13)

Vice President	James S. Sherman*
Sec. of State	Philander Chase Knox 1909–13
Sec. of Treasury	Franklyn MacVeagh
Sec. of War	Jacob McGavock Dickinson 1909–11
	Henry L. Stimson 1911–13
Sec. of Navy	George von Lengerke Meyer
Attorney General	George W. Wickersham
Sec. of Interior	Richard Achilles Ballinger 1909–11
	Walter L. Fisher 1911–13
Sec. of Agriculture	James Wilson
Sec. of Commerce and Labor	Charles Nagel
Postmaster-General	Frank Harris Hitchcock

* Died 30 October 1912.

President THOMAS WOODROW WILSON (Democrat, 1913–21)
First Administration, 1913–17

Vice President	Thomas Riley Marshall
Sec. of State	Philander C. Knox 1913
	William Jennings Bryan 1913–15
	Robert Lansing 1915–17
Sec. of Treasury	William Gibbs McAdoo
Sec. of War	Lindley M. Garrison 1913–16
	Newton D. Baker, 1916–17
Sec. of Navy	Josephus Daniels
Attorney General	James C. McReynolds 1913–14
	Thomas W. Gregory 1914–17
Sec. of Interior	Franklin Knight Lane
Sec. of Agriculture	David Franklin Houston
Sec. of Commerce	William C. Redfield
Sec. of Labor*	William Bauchop Wilson
Postmaster-General	Albert Sidney Burleson

* New cabinet post.

Second Administration 1917–21

Vice President	Thomas Riley Marshall
Sec. of State	Robert Lansing 1917–20 Bainbridge Colby 1920–21
Sec. of Treasury	William Gibbs McAdoo 1917–18 Carter Glass 1918–20 David F. Houston 1920–21
Sec. of War	Newton D. Baker
Sec. of Navy	Josephus Daniels
Attorney General	Thomas W. Gregory 1917–19 A. Mitchell Palmer 1919–21
Sec. of Interior	Franklin Knight Lane 1917–20 John B. Payne 1920–21
Sec. of Agriculture	David Franklin Houston 1917–20 Edward T. Meredith, 1920–21
Sec. of Commerce	William C. Redfield 1917–19 Josh W. Alexander 1919–21
Sec. of Labor	William Bauchop Wilson
Postmaster-General	Albert Sidney Burleson

President WARREN GAMALIEL HARDING (Republican, 1921–23)

Vice President	Calvin Coolidge
Sec. of State	Charles E. Hughes
Sec. of Treasury	Andrew W. Mellon
Sec. of War	John W. Weeks
Sec. of Navy	Edwin Denby
Attorney General	Harry M. Daugherty
Sec. of Interior	Albert B. Fall 1921–23 Hubert Work 1923
Sec. of Agriculture	Henry C. Wallace
Sec. of Commerce	Herbert C. Hoover
Sec. of Labor	James J. Davis
Postmaster-General	Will H. Hays 1921–22 Hubert Work 1922–23 Harry S. New 1923

President JOHN CALVIN COOLIDGE (Republican, 1923–29)

Vice President	Charles G. Dawes*
Sec. of State	Charles E. Hughes 1923–25 Frank B. Kellogg 1925–29
Sec. of Treasury	Andrew W. Mellon
Sec. of War	John W. Weeks 1923–25 Dwight F. Davis 1925–29
Sec. of Navy	Edwin Denby

Attorney General	Harry M. Daugherty 1923–24
	Harlan F. Stone 1924–25
	John G. Sargent 1925–29
Sec. of Interior	Hubert Work 1923–29
	Roy O. West 1929
Sec. of Agriculture	Henry C. Wallace 1923–24
	Howard M. Gore 1924–25
	W.M. Jardine 1925–29
Sec. of Commerce	Herbert C. Hoover 1923–28
	William F. Whiting 1928–29
Sec. of Labor	James J. Davis
Postmaster-General	Harry S. New

* Coolidge succeeded to the presidency on Harding's death and accordingly was without a vice president from 3 August 1923 until 4 March 1925, when Dawes was inaugurated.

President HERBERT CLARK HOOVER (Republican, 1929–33)

Vice President	Charles Curtis
Sec. of State	Frank B. Kellogg 1929
	Henry L. Stimson 1929–33
Sec. of Treasury	Andrew W, Mellon 1929–32
	Ogden L. Mills 1932–33
Sec. of War	James W. Good 1929
	Patrick J. Hurley 1929–33
Sec. of Navy	Charles Francis Adams
Attorney General	William D. Mitchell
Sec. of Interior	Ray Lyman Wilbur
Sec. of Agriculture	Arthur M. Hyle
Sec. of Commerce	Robert P. Lamont 1929–32
	Roy D. Chapin 1932–33
Sec. of Labor	James J. Davis 1929–30
	William N. Doak 1930–33
Postmaster-General	Walter F. Brown

President FRANKLIN DELANO ROOSEVELT (Democrat, 1933–45)

President Roosevelt was elected four times. The following lists cabinet offices and their holders with dates between 1933 and 1945. Only Harold L. Ickes (secretary of the interior) and Frances Perkins (secretary of labor) held office unchanged.

Vice President	John Nance Garner 1933–41
	Henry A. Wallace 1941–45

	Harry S. Truman 1945
Sec. of State	Cordell Hull 1933–45
	Edward R. Stettinius, Jr. 1945
Sec. of Treasury	William H. Woodin 1933–34
	Henry Morgenthau, Jr. 1934–45
Sec. of War	George H. Dern 1933–37
	Harry H. Woodring 1937–40
	Henry L. Stimson 1940–45
Sec. of Navy	Claude A. Swanson 1933–40
	Charles Edison 1940
	Frank Knox 1940–44
	James V. Forrestal 1944–45
Attorney General	Homer S. Cummings 1933–39 (Thomas A. Walsh was nominated but died before FDR's inuaguration on 4 March 1933)
	Frank Murphy 1939–40
	Robert H. Jackson 1940–41
	Francis Biddle 1941–45
Sec. of Interior	Harold L. Ickes
Sec. of Agriculture	Henry A. Wallace 1933–40
	Claude R. Wickard 1940–45
Sec. of Commerce	Daniel C. Roper 1933–39
	Harry L. Hopkins 1939–40
	Jesse Jones 1940–45
	Henry A. Wallace 1945
Sec. of Labor	Frances Perkins*
Postmaster-General	James A. Farley 1933–40
	Frank C. Walker 1940–45

*First woman to hold cabinet office.

President HARRY S. TRUMAN (Democrat, 1945–1953)*

Vice President	Alben W. Barkley**
Sec. of State	Edward R. Stettinius 1945
	James F. Byrnes 1945–47
	George C. Marshall 1947–49
	Dean G. Acheson 1949–53
Sec. of Treasury	Fred M. Vinson 1945
	John W. Snyder 1946–53
Sec. of War	Robert P. Patterson 1945–47
	Kenneth C. Royall 1947 (War Department then became part of Defense Department)
Sec. of Navy	James V. Forrestal 1945–47 (Navy Department then became part of Defense Department)
Sec. of Defense	James V. Forrestal 1947–49
	Louis A. Johnson 1949–50
	George C. Marshall 1950–51
	Robert A. Lovett 1951–53
Attorney General	Tom C. Clark 1945–49
	J. Howard McGrath 1949–52

	J.P. McGranery 1952–53
Sec. of Interior	Harold L. Ickes 1945
	Julius A. Krug 1946–50
	Oscar L. Chapman 1950–53
Sec. of Agriculture	Clinton P. Anderson 1945
	Charles F. Brannan 1948–53
Sec. of Labor	L.B. Schwellenback 1945–49
	Maurice J. Tobin 1949–53
Sec. of Commerce	Henry A. Wallace 1945–47
	W. Averell Harriman 1947–48
	Charles Sawyer 1948–53
Postmaster-General	Robert E. Hannegan 1945–47
	Jesse M. Donaldson 1947–53

* The S stood for nothing: it was a compromise between two names.
** Truman succeeded to the presidency on Roosevelt's death, and had no vice-president between 14 April 1945 and 20 January 1949, when Barkley was inaugurated.

Justices of the Supreme Court

The following table lists all justices who served on the Supreme Court between 1910 and 1945. When the position of chief justice fell vacant, presidents usually nominated someone not currently serving on the court, rather than elevating an associate justice. Exceptions to this rule are noted below. Where an individual's name is followed by an asterisk, it shows that he served as Chief Justice.

John M. Harlan (Kentucky) served from 29 November 1877 until his death on 14 October 1911.

*Melville W. Fuller** (Illinois) served as chief justice from 20 July 1888 until his death on 4 July 1910.

*Edward D. White** (Louisiana) served from 19 February 1894 until his death on 19 May 1921, as associate justice 1894–1910 and as chief justice 1910–21.

Joseph McKenna (California) served from 21 January 1898 until he resigned on 1 May 1925.

Oliver Wendell Holmes (Massachusetts) served from 4 December 1902 until he resigned on 12 January 1932.

William R. Day (Ohio) served from 23 February 1903 until he resigned on 13 November 1922.

William H. Moody (Massachusetts) served from 12 December 1906 until he resigned on 20 November 1910.

Horace H. Lurton (Tennessee) served from 20 December 1909 until his death on 12 July 1914.

Charles E. Hughes (New York) served as associate justice from 2 May 1910 until 10 June 1916, when he resigned to run unsuccessfully for president against Woodrow Wilson.

Joseph R. Lamar (Georgia) served from 15 December 1910 until his death on 2 January 1916.

Willis Van Devanter (Wyoming) served from 15 December 1910 until he resigned on 2 June 1937.

Mahlon Pitney (New Jersey) served from 19 February 1912 until he resigned on 31 December 1922.

James C. McReynolds (Tennessee) served from 29 August 1914 until he resigned on 31 January 1941.

Louis D. Brandeis (Massachusetts) served from 1 June 1916 until he resigned on 13 February 1939.

John H. Clark (Ohio) served from 24 July 1916 until he resigned on 18 September 1922.

*William H. Taft** (Connecticut) served as chief justice from 30 June 1921 until he resigned on 3 February 1930.

George Sutherland (Utah) served from 5 September 1922 until he resigned on 17 January 1938.

Pierce Butler (Minnesota) served from 21 December 1922 until he died on 16 November 1939.

Edward T. Sanford (Tennessee) served from 29 January 1923 until he died on 8 March 1930.

*Harlan F. Stone** (New York) served from 5 February 1925 until he died on 22 April 1946, as associate justice 1925–41 and as chief justice 1941–46.

*Charles E. Hughes** (New York) served as chief justice from 13 February 1930 until he resigned on 1 July 1941.

Owen J. Roberts (Pennsylvania) served from 20 May 1930 until he resigned on 31 July 1945.

Benjamin N. Cardozo (New York) served from 24 February 1932 until he died on 9 July 1938.

Hugo L. Black (Alabama) served from 17 August 1937 until he resigned on 17 September 1971.

Stanley F. Reed (Kentucky) served from 25 January 1938 until he resigned on 25 February 1957.

Felix Frankfurter (Massachusetts) served from 17 January 1938 until he resigned on 28 August 1962.

William O. Douglas (Connecticut) served from 4 April 1939 until he resigned on 12 November 1975.

Frank Murphy (Michigan) served from 15 January 1940 until he resigned on 19 July 1949.

James F. Byrnes (South Carolina) served from 12 June 1941 until he resigned on 3 October 1942.

Robert H. Jackson (New York) served from 7 July 1941 until he died on 9 October 1954.

Wiley B. Rutledge (Iowa) served from 8 February 1943 until he died on 10 September 1949.

Harold H. Burton (Ohio) served from 19 September 1945 until he resigned on 13 October 1958.

National Leadership: The Legislative Branch

Presidents Pro Tempore of the US Senate, 1910–45

The presiding officer of the Senate is the vice president of the United States, who may vote only to break a tie. But the Senate elects one of its members president pro tempore, who becomes presiding officer in the absence of the vice president. Figures in brackets denote the number of the Congress when they presided.

William B. Frye (Rep., Maine, 54th–62nd) 1896–1911. After Frye's resignation on 27 April, and death on 8 August 1911, the Senate failed to elect a successor for the remainder of the 62nd Congress. Temporary designations were made from time to time, and Augustus O. Bacon (Democrat) and Jacob H. Gallinger (Republican) alternated in office for most of 1912 and 1913.

Charles Curtis (Rep., Kansas, 62nd) 1911.

Henry Cabot Lodge (Rep., Mass., 62nd) 1912.

Frank B. Brandegee (Rep., Connecticut, 62nd) 1912.

Augustus O. Bacon (Dem., Georgia, 62nd) 1912–13.

Jacob H. Gallinger (Rep., New Hampshire, 62nd) 1912–13.

James P. Clark (Dem., Arkansas, 62nd–64th) 1913–15.

Willard Saulsbury (Dem., Delaware, 64th–65th) 1916–19.

Albert B. Cummins (Rep., Iowa, 66th–68th) 1919–25.

George H. Moses (Rep., New Hampshire, 69th–72nd) 1925–33.

Key Pittman (Dem., Nevada, 73rd–76th) 1933–40.

William H. King (Dem., Utah, 76th) 1940–41.

Pat Harrison (Dem., Mississippi, 77th) 1941.

Carter Glass (Dem., Virginia, 77th–78th) 1941–45.

Kenneth McKellar (Dem., Tennessee, 79th) 1945–47.

Speakers of the House of Representatives, 1910–45

At the beginning of each Congress, members of the House of Representatives elect the Speaker of the House, who serves as their presiding officer. Speakers, who in practice are members of the majority party in the House, have a right to vote, and are frequently re-elected if their party retains its majority.

Joseph G. Cannon (Rep., Illinois, 58th–61st) 1903–11.

Champ Clark (Dem., Missouri, 62nd–65th) 1911–19.

Frederick H. Gillett (Rep., Mass., 66th–68th) 1919–25.

Nicholas H. Longworth (Rep., Ohio, 69th–71st) 1925–31.

John N. Garner (Dem., Texas, 72nd) 1931–33.

Henry T. Rainey (Dem., Illinois, 73rd) 1933–35.

Joseph. W. Byrns (Dem., Tennessee, 74th) 1935–36.

William B. Bankhead (Dem., Alabama, 74th–76th) 1936–40.

Sam Rayburn (Dem., Texas, 76th–79th) 1940–47.

Majority Leaders of the US Senate, 1910–45

Since 1911, respective political parties in both Senate and House have elected floor leaders, known as Majority and Minority Leaders and Whips, who mobilize members and organize voting. Seniority and the ability to influence individual members are important attributes in leaders of the two chambers.

Shelby M. Cullom (Rep., Illinois, 62nd) 1911–13.

John W. Kern (Dem., Indiana, 63rd–64th) 1913–17.

Thomas S. Martin (Dem., Virginia, 65th) 1917–19.

Henry Cabot Lodge (Rep., Mass., 66th–68th) 1919–24.

Charles Curtis (Rep., Kansas, 68th–71st) 1924–29.

James E. Watson (Rep., Indiana, 71st–72nd) 1929–33.

Joseph T. Robinson (Dem., Arkansas, 73rd–74th) 1933–37.

Alben W. Barkley (Dem., Kentucky, 75th–79th) 1937–47.

Majority Whips of the US Senate, 1913–45

J. Hamilton Lewis (Dem., Illinois, 63rd–65th) 1913–19.

Charles Curtis (Rep., Kansas, 66th–68th) 1919–24.

Wesley L. Jones (Rep., Washington, 68th–70th) 1924–29.

Simon D. Fess (Rep., Ohio, 71st–72nd) 1929–33.

J. Hamilton Lewis (Dem., Illinois, 73rd–75th) 1933–39.

Sherman Minton (Dem., Indiana, 76th) 1939–41.

Lister Hill (Dem., Alabama, 77th–79th) 1941–47.

Minority Leaders of the US Senate, 1911–45

Thomas S. Martin (Dem., Virginia, 62nd) 1911–13.

Jacob H. Gallinger (Rep., New Hamp., 63rd–64th) 1913–17.

Henry Cabot Lodge (Rep., Mass., 65th) 1917–19.

Thomas S. Martin (Dem., Virginia, 66th) 1919.

Oscar W. Underwood (Dem., Alabama, 66th–67th) 1919–23.

Joseph T. Robinson (Dem., Arkansas, 68th–72nd) 1923–33.

Charles McNary (Rep., Oregon, 73rd–78th) 1933–45.

Wallace H. White, Jr. (Rep., Maine, 79th) 1945–47.

Minority Whips in the US Senate, 1915–45

James W. Wadsworth, Jr. (Rep., New York, 64th) 1915.

Charles Curtis (Rep., Kansas, 64th–65th) 1915–19.

Peter G. Gerry (Dem., Rhode Island, 66th–70th) 1919–29.

Morris Sheppard (Dem., Texas, 71st–72nd) 1929–33.

Felix E. Hébert (Rep., Rhode Island, 73rd–77th) 1933–43.

Kenneth Wherry (Rep., Nebraska, 78th–79th) 1943–47.

Chairmen of Major Congressional Committees, 1910–45

Much of the business of each of the two chambers of Congress is carried out by committees, which hold hearings frequently involving searching investigative activity, collect information, draft legislation and strongly influence whether, in what order and on which timetable legislation is considered by the full House or Senate. The chairmen of these committees, chosen by the majority party in each chamber, are powerful figures who between 1910 and 1945 usually had the greatest seniority on the committee.

Chairmen of Major Committees in the US Senate, 1910–45

Judiciary Committee

Clarence D. Clark (Rep., Wyoming, 59th–62nd) 1905–13.

Charles A. Culberson (Dem., Texas, 63rd–65th) 1913–19.

Knute Nelson (Rep., Minnesota, 66th–67th) 1919–23.

Frank B. Brandegee (Rep., Connecticut, 68th) 1923–25.

Albert B. Cummins (Rep., Iowa, 69th) 1925–27.

George W. Norris (Rep., Nebraska, 70th–72nd) 1927–33.

Henry F. Ashurst (Dem., Arizona, 73rd–76th) 1933–41.

Frederick Van Nuys (Dem., Indiana, 77th–78th) 1941–45.

Pat McCarran (Dem., Nevada, 79th) 1945–47.

Foreign Relations Committee

Shelby M. Cullom (Rep., Illinois, 57th–62nd) 1901–13.

Augustus O. Bacon (Dem., Georgia, 63rd) 1913–15.

William J. Stone (Dem., Missouri, 64th–65th) 1915–19.

Henry Cabot Lodge (Rep., Mass., 66th–68th) 1919–25.

William E. Borah (Rep., Idaho, 69th–72nd) 1925–33.

Key Pittman (Dem., Nevada,73rd–77th) 1933–41.

Walter F. George (Dem., Georgia, 78th) 1941–43.

Tom Connally (Dem., Texas, 79th) 1943–47.

Appropriations Committee

Eugene Hale (Rep., Maine, 61st) 1909–11.

Francis E. Warren (Rep., Wyoming, 62nd) 1911–13.

Thomas S. Martin (Dem., Virginia, 63rd–65th) 1913–19.

Francis E. Warren (Rep., Wyoming, 66th–71st) 1919–31.

Frederick Hale (Rep., Maine, 72nd) 1931–33.

Carter Glass (Dem., Virginia, 73rd–79th) 1933–47.

Armed Services Committee

Francis E. Warren (Rep., Wyoming, 59th–61st) 1905–11.

Henry A. Du Pont (Rep., Delaware, 62nd) 1911–13.

Joseph F. Johnston (Dem., Alabama, 63rd) 1913–15.

George E. Chamberlain (Dem., Oregon, 64th–65th) 1915–19.

James W. Wadsworth (Rep., New York, 66th–69th) 1919–27.

David A. Reed (Rep., Pennsylvania, 70th–72nd) 1927–33.

Morris Sheppard (Dem., Texas, 73rd–76th) 1933–41.

Robert R. Reynolds (Dem., N. Carolina, 77th–78th) 1941–45.

Elbert D. Thomas (Dem., Utah, 79th) 1945–47.

Majority Leaders of the US House of Representatives, 1910–45

Sereno E. Payne (Rep., New York, 56th–61st) 1899–1911. Payne was the first House member to be officially designated Majority Leader. Until 1911 the Speaker selected the Majority Leader, usually the chairman of the Ways and Means Committee, but occasionally somebody else. After a revolt against Speaker Joseph G. Cannon in 1909–10, House members selected a leader through party caucuses or conferences.

Oscar W. Underwood (Dem., Alabama, 62nd–63rd) 1911–15.

Claude Kitchen (Dem., N. Carolina, 64th–65th) 1915–19.

Franklin W. Mondell (Rep., Wyoming, 66th–67th) 1919–23.

Nicholas Longworth (Rep., Ohio, 68th) 1923–25.

John Q. Tilson (Rep., Connecticut, 69th–71st) 1925–31.

Henry T. Rainey (Dem., Illinois, 72nd) 1931–33.

Joseph W. Byrns (Dem., Tennessee, 73rd) 1933–35.

William B. Bankhead (Dem., Alabama, 74th) 1935–37.

Sam Rayburn (Dem., Texas, 75th–76th) 1937–41.

John W. McCormack (Dem., Mass., 76th–79th) 1941–47.

Majority Whips of the US House of Representatives, 1910–45

John W. Dwight (Rep., New York, 61st) 1909–11; (62nd) 1911–13.

Thomas M. Bell (Dem., Georgia, 63rd) 1913–15; (64th–65th) 1915–19.

Harold Knutson (Rep., Minnesota, 66th–67th) 1919–23.

Albert H. Vestal (Rep., Indiana, 68th–71st) 1923–31.

John McDuffie (Dem., Alabama, 72nd) 1931–33.

Arthur H. Greenwood (Dem., Indiana, 73rd) 1933–35.

Patrick J. Boland (Dem., Pennsylvania, 74th–77th) 1935–42.

Robert Ramspeck (Dem., Georgia, 77th–78th) 1942–45.

John J. Sparkman (Dem., Alabama, 79th) 1945–47.

Minority Leaders of the US House of Representatives, 1910–45

Champ Clark (Dem., Missouri, 61st) 1909–11. Although first identifiable as early as 1883, the position of Minority Leader was not officially recognized until 1899. After 1911, following the revolt against Speaker Joseph G. Cannon, which led to House members selecting their leader, party conferences or caucuses decided, usually choosing the candidate the minority party had nominated for Speaker.

James R. Mann (Rep., Illinois, 62nd–65th) 1911–19.

Champ Clark (Dem., Missouri, 66th) 1919–21.

Claude Kitchen (Dem., North Carolina, 67th) 1921–23.

Finis J. Garrett (Dem., Tennessee, 68th–70th) 1923–29.

John N. Garner (Dem., Texas, 71st) 1929–31.

Bertrand H. Snell (Rep., New York, 72nd–75th) 1931–39.

Joseph W. Martin, Jr. (Rep., Mass., 76th–79th) 1939–47.

Minority Whips of the US House of Representatives, 1910–45

John W. Dwight (Rep., New York, 62nd) 1911–13.

Charles H. Burke (Rep., South Dakota, 63rd) 1913–15.

Charles M. Hamilton (Rep., New York, 64th–65th) 1915–19; (66th) 1919–21.

William A. Oldfield (Dem., Arkansas, 67th–70th) 1921–28.

John McDuffie (Dem., Alabama, 70th–71st) 1928–31.

Carl G. Bachman (Rep., West Virginia, 72nd) 1931–33.

Harry Englebright (Rep., California, 73rd–77th) 1933–43.

Leslie C. Arends (Rep., Illinois, 78th–79th) 1943–47.

Chairmen of Major Committees in the US House of Representatives, 1910–45

Ways and Means Committee

Sereno E. Payne (Rep., New York, 56th–61st) 1899–1911.

Oscar W. Underwood (Dem., Alabama, 62nd–63rd) 1911–15.

Claude Kitchen (Dem., North Carolina, 64th–65th) 1915–19.

Joseph W. Fordney (Rep., Michigan, 66th–67th) 1919–23.

William R. Green (Rep., Iowa, 68th–69th) 1923–27.

Willis C. Hawley (Rep., Oregon, 70th–71st) 1927–31.

James W. Collier (Dem., Mississippi, 72nd) 1931–33.

Robert Doughton (Dem., North Carolina, 73rd–79th) 1933–47.

Rules Committee

Joseph G. Cannon (Rep., Illinois, 58th–61st) 1903–11.

Robert L. Henry (Dem., Texas, 62nd–64th) 1911–17.

Edward W. Pou (Dem., South Carolina, 65th) 1917–19.

Philip Campbell (Rep., Kansas, 66th–67th) 1919–23.

Bertrand H. Snell (Rep., New York, 68th–71st) 1923–31.

Edward R. Pou (Dem., South Carolina, 72nd–73rd) 1931–35.

John J. O'Connor (Dem., New York, 74th–75th) 1935–39.

Adolph J. Sabath (Dem., Illinois, 76th–79th) 1939–47.

Appropriations Committee

James A. Tawney (Rep., Minnesota, 59th–61st) 1905–11.

John J. Fitzgerald (Dem., New York, 62nd–65th) 1911–19.

James W. Good (Rep., Iowa, 66th–67th) 1919–23.

Martin R. Madden (Rep., Illinois, 68th–69th) 1923–27.

Daniel R. Anthony (Rep., Kansas, 70th) 1927–29.

William R. Wood (Rep., Indiana, 71st) 1929–31.

Joseph W. Byrns (Dem., Tennessee, 72nd) 1931–33.

James P. Buchanan (Dem., Texas, 73rd–75th) 1933–39.

Edward T. Taylor. (Dem., Colorado, 76th–77th) 1939–43.

Clarence Cannon (Dem., Missouri, 78th–79th) 1943–47.

Armed Services Committee (Military Affairs)

John A.T. Hull (Rep., Iowa, 54th–61st) 1895–1911.

James Hay (Dem., Virginia, 62nd–64th) 1911–17.

S. Herbert Dent (Dem., Alabama, 65th) 1917–19.

Julius Kahn (Rep., California, 66th–68th) 1919–25.

John M. Morin (Rep., Pennsylvania, 69th–70th) 1925–29.

W. Frank James (Rep., Michigan, 71st) 1929–31.

John McSwain (Dem., South Carolina, 72nd–74th) 1931–37.

Lister Hill (Dem., Alabama, 75th) 1937–39.

Andrew J. May (Dem., Kentucky, 77th–79th) 1939–47.

SECTION VI

Biographies

This section provides brief biographical sketches of people who played a significant part in the US political economy between 1910 and 1945, plus most of the American writers, active during that period, who won the Nobel prize for literature.

Addams, Jane (1860–1935): Gifted, hardworking and pragmatic, Jane Addams was the most influential female reformer of her time. Graduating in 1881 from one of the first women's colleges in the US, she studied economics and sociology abroad. Helped by campaigning from the British journalist W.T. Stead, and by Ellen Gates Starr, she founded Hull House in Chicago in 1889 and made it the nation's most celebrated settlement house. It became the model for similar places established in major American cities during the Progressive era. Designed to give the urban poor practical advice and survival skills to help them out of poverty, social settlements acted as 'spearheads for reform', challenging political bosses for the votes of the urban poor and so forcing them to become more socially responsive, but making reformers more realistic too. She wrote many books, chaired the 1928 international congress of women at the Hague and won the 1931 Nobel peace prize.

Baruch, Bernard M. (1870–1965): Born in Camden, South Carolina, Bernard Mannes Baruch graduated from City College, New York, in 1889 and entered business, becoming one of America's leading financiers and most successful Wall Steet speculators. From 1916 onwards Baruch, like Herbert Hoover, came to personify the new breed of managerial technocrat taking command of business, economic and financial affairs during the Progressive period. He headed the war industries board between 1917 and 1919; was adviser to presidents Wilson and Harding; and a member of the supreme economic council which, under Hoover's direction, helped feed and reorganize starving, demoralized Europe after the first world war. A leading figure in the New Era of prosperity in the 1920s, he fell out of favour during the economic depression which followed and rejected Franklin Roosevelt's invitation to head AAA in 1933. Lifelong friend of Winston Churchill, Baruch became adviser to the war mobilization director after 1943 and devised the Baruch plan for controlling atomic weapons via the UN which was discussed but not adopted.

Berle, Adolph A. (1895–1971): Trained as a lawyer, Berle was, like Raymond Moley and Rexford Tugwell, a Columbia professor who joined FDR's Brains Trust on the campaign trail in 1932. With Gardiner Means he had in 1931 published *The Modern Corporation and Private Property*, charting the ground between public and private economic spheres. On the question of planning during the first New Deal, Berle struck a middle course between Moley's belief that private enterprise should hold the upper hand in any partnership with government, and Tugwell's belief in planning where government took the initiative. Critics said unkindly that Berle had been an infant prodigy who stopped being a prodigy, but unlike Moley and Tugwell he remained in government service as assistant secretary of state during the crucial years of war and peace between 1938 and 1944 and was US ambassador to Brazil from 1945 until 1946.

Black, Hugo L. (1886–1971): Born in the south and trained as a lawyer, Hugo Black was a liberal southern Democrat elected senator from Alabama in 1927. Prominent backer of the New Deal in the Senate, he joined with William P. Connery Jr to sponsor the 30-hour week bill in Congress to try to share work, which was subsumed by the National Industrial Recovery Act. In 1937, in the midst of the struggle over Supreme Court reform, Black was an obvious choice to take Van Devanter's place and increase the number of liberals on the bench. However, it emerged during confirmation hearings that as a young lawyer he had belonged to the Ku Klux Klan. The Senate nevertheless confirmed Black, who went on to become the most liberal member of the Court, especially on First Amendment freedoms, until his death in 1971.

Borah, William E. (1865–1940): The grand old man of western Progressivism, Borah was Republican senator from Idaho from 1903 until his death. Noted for scalding attacks on left-wing radicals like the IWW, he was equally hostile to big business, trusts and corporations, especially those with interests in the west or his own state. Opposed to US involvement in the first world war, and even more to the 1919 Versailles treaty and US membership of the League of Nations, Borah combined patriotic isolationism, hostility both to big business and organized labour and demand for reform found in a significant group of western and midwestern opinion makers acting within the Populist/Progressive tradition between 1910 and 1940.

Brandeis, Louis D. (1856–1941): The outstanding jurist of his generation, Brandeis believed in Woodrow Wilson's political philosophy of the New Freedom, which aimed at breaking up corporations and monopolies and re-establishing fair competition. Appointed to the Supreme Court in 1916, Brandeis became the most illustrious liberal on a Court dominated between 1916 and 1937 by pro-business conservatives like McReynolds, Sutherland and Van Devanter. Close friend of the legendary Oliver Wendell Holmes, Brandeis often joined him in dissenting judgments and accepted the Court's limitations. 'Sonny, when I first came to this Court,' he told James M. Landis in the 1920s, 'I thought I would be associated with men who really cared whether they were right or wrong. But sometimes, Sonny, it just ain't so.' When Holmes retired and Hughes succeeded Taft as chief justice, Brandeis was the bench's senior and most liberal judge during FDR's long, bruising battle to reform the Court. However, when he resigned in 1939, a changed intellectual climate and new judges had created a Court more in tune with the times.

Bryan, W.J. (1860–1925): Born in Illinois and moving to Nebraska, William Jennings Bryan was a life-long Democrat who spoke for debt-ridden midwestern farmers. Though he studied law, his real talent was for Baptist preaching and Chautauqua tent oratory. Campaigning for free and unlimited coinage of silver at the ratio of 16 to 1 against gold, Bryan came into his own. His 'cross of gold' speech to the 1896 Democratic convention is one of the great speeches of US history. Yet Bryan frightened voters and, after two decades of close elections, was so badly beaten in 1896, 1900 and 1908 that Democrats remained largely a sectional minority party until 1932. He had many enemies. 'Six inches deep and six miles wide at the mouth,' one commented, while the journalist Oswald Garrison Villard regarded him as 'the most ignorant' politician of his era. Woodrow Wilson made Bryan secretary of state in 1913, but he resigned in protest at Wilson's pro-British neutrality in 1915 and never held office again. By then he was involved in real-estate speculation, the campaign for Prohibition and the crusade against the Darwinian theory of evolution. Not a member of the Ku Klux Klan, he fought attempts to denounce it and was named 'the greatest Klansman of our time'. The following year he prosecuted John Scopes, who had violated Tennessee law by teaching the Darwinian theory of evolution, and died a few days after securing his conviction.

Bullitt, William C. (1891–1967): A charming, energetic, enthusiastic political maverick, Bullitt travelled widely in his youth. He was in Moscow when war broke out in 1914, on Woodrow Wilson's staff at the 1918 Paris peace conference, and was sent to Soviet Russia to try to coax Lenin and the Bolsheviks back into Europe. As an internationalist when Republicans resumed America's historic isolationism in the 1920s he was out of favour but, when Democrats recaptured the White House, Roosevelt made him special assistant to secretary of state Cordell Hull and delegate to the 1933 London world economic conference, which FDR torpedoed by refusing to stabilize the dollar. Bullitt was ambassador to the Soviet Union from 1933 until 1936, and then in Paris from 1936 until 1941, seeing Germany conquer France.

Byrnes, James F. (1879–1972): James F. ('Jimmy') Byrnes personified that small but influential minority of liberal Democrats who emerged from southern politics during the Progressive period. Trained as a lawyer, he represented South Carolina in the House from 1911 until 1925, and in the Senate from 1931 until 1941. A keen New Dealer, he was unlike many southern Democrats in supporting Roosevelt's bid to reform the Supreme Court. It was Byrnes, indeed, who memorably explained that with Black replacing Van Devanter, and Roberts changing sides, the Court now had a 6–3 liberal majority. 'Why run for a train after you've caught it?' he asked. Byrnes himself served briefly on the Court between 1941 and 1942, and then became director of economic stabilization and later war mobilization from 1942 until 1945. He attended the February 1945 Yalta conference and, when FDR died, Truman made him secretary of state in succession to Edward Stettinius in July 1945. Byrnes served during the crucial early period of the Cold War, and though criticized for being soft on the Soviet Union, he promised US troops would not leave Germany until peace was signed. He resigned in January 1947 having lost Truman's support and was replaced by Dean Acheson.

Cermak, Anton J. (1873–1933): Born in the US of Bohemian parents, Cermak entered Chicago politics and was elected mayor when the formidable Republican political machine of William Hale ('Big Bill') Thompson was finally broken in 1931. His election was significant because voters of recent ethnic origin – the last great wave of unrestricted immigrants between 1900 and 1914, and their sons and daughters – supported him as a Democrat. He might have become a reforming political boss in the style of Detroit's Hazen Pingree a generation earlier, but on 15 February 1933, accompanying president-elect Roosevelt to Miami, he was assassinated by Giusseppe Zangara, a gunman who had apparently been aiming at FDR. His last words were, 'Thank God they got me and not you.' After his death Edward J. Kelly was mayor until 1945 and, with Thomas Nash and Jacob Arvey, laid the foundations for Democrats to control Chicago politics for two more generations.

Cohen, Benjamin V. (1894–1983): Good lawyers were vital if first New Deal reforms were to be effective, and Ben Cohen was one of the best. He was associate general counsel to PWA and the public works programme, crucial to stopping rising unemployment between 1933 and 1934. When political controversy flared over TVA, Cohen was general counsel to the national power policy committee between 1934 and 1941, helping establish the principle of public power exemplified by TVA and similar projects. He drafted securities control legislation in 1933 and 1934, the Public Utility Holding Company Act of 1935 and the landmark 1938 Fair

Labor Standards Act, which established the minimum wage and effectively outlawed child labour for the first time. Between 1941 and 1945 Cohen attended every important foreign diplomatic conference, and was a delegate to the United Nations in 1945.

Coolidge, Calvin (1872–1933): Born in tiny Plymouth Notch, Vermont, Calvin Coolidge read law at Amherst, joined the Massachusetts bar in 1891 and embarked on a political career. He was mayor of Northampton from 1909 until 1914, lieutenant governor and then governor of Massachusetts, where he made his name crushing the 1919 Boston police strike, coining the aphorism, 'There is no right to strike against public safety anywhere, any time.' Elected Republican vice-president in 1920, he succeeded Harding when he died in 1923. An immaculate, laconic Yankee, he was, in public at least, a man of few words: his 1924 inaugural was the shortest in history. He said little because he had little to say, but he limited the damage the Teapot Dome scandal caused, and desired above all to diminish presidential power and advance business. The journalist, William Allen White, said that Coolidge was as convinced of the divine character of wealth as Lincoln had been of the divine character of man – 'crazy about it, sincerely, genuinely, terribly crazy'. He chose not to run for president in 1928 and died during the Great Depression.

Corcoran, Thomas C. (1900–81): Unusually for the kind of lawyer who joined the New Deal in its early stages, Tom Corcoran's first government job was as special counsel to Herbert Hoover's RFC in 1932. When Roosevelt took office in March 1933 he made Corcoran assistant secretary to the treasury during the banking crisis, when his boss Will Woodin, in Moley's view, 'saved capitalism in seven days'. Woodin, compromised by personal financial dealings before 1929, resigned and then died later in 1934, and his successor at the treasury, Henry Morgenthau, found Corcoran's reflationary views far less congenial. Budget-balancer Morgenthau remained in post until April 1945, but when Lewis W. Douglas resigned as budget director in 1934, Roosevelt thought of replacing him with Corcoran. Instead, he returned him to the RFC where he remained until 1941, during which time Corcoran was associated with Ben Cohen in drafting more reform legislation.

Cummings, Homer (1870–1956): Appointed attorney general by Roosevelt in March 1933 when Tom Walsh died, Cummings's position was crucial. He had to ensure that New Deal legislation was properly drafted to avoid costly legal battles, and that New Deal agencies were staffed with good lawyers for the same reason. Despite this, the Supreme Court declared both the AAA and NIRA unconstitutional, along with other reforms, so Roosevelt asked

Cummings to help him in utmost secrecy draft a bill to reform the Supreme Court. When sent to Congress in January 1937 this bill led to the most serious constitutional crisis between 1910 and 1945. What made Roosevelt especially gleeful about Cummings's bill was that it was based on one James McReynolds, the most conservative member of the Court in 1937, had drafted as Woodrow Wilson's attorney general in 1913. The reform bill failed to pass Congress, however, and Cummings left office to return to private practice in 1939.

Curley, James M. (1874–1958): Mayor of Boston in 1914–19, 1922–26, 1930–34 and 1946–50, Jim Curley was the archetypal big city political boss, whose Democratic political machine ran Boston for a generation. Of Irish descent, Curley spoke for an ethnic group which exercised great political influence between 1910 and 1945. Resisted by Republican interests dominant in Massachusetts as a whole, Curley delivered the state's vote to Roosevelt in every election between 1932 and 1944, and was elected governor between 1935 and 1937, and to the House of Representatives between 1943 and 1946. Edwin O'Connor's influential novel *The Last Hurrah* was based on Curley's colourful career.

Currie, Lauchlin (1902–1993): Born in Nova Scotia, Canada, on 8 October 1902, and educated by Jesuits and at the London School of Economics, Lauchlin Currie was intellectual leader of a small band of Keynesian economists who helped transform public policy during the New Deal. Teaching international economics at Harvard, he so impressed senior colleagues that they arranged secondment to the treasury department. There he met Harry Dexter White and Marriner Eccles, of the Federal Reserve Board. All three agreed that the Fed bore major blame for the Great Depression because, as central bank, it had restricted money supply, and, after a short break during which he completed his Harvard Ph.D, Currie transferred to the Fed, which Eccles now governed. Because Currie never advocated a position before putting analysis and data together, he now did the work for which he is best remembered by documenting the contradictory actions of the Federal Reserve since 1929. He helped draft the 1935 Banking Act, which enhanced the power of the Board's governors over both policy-making and reserve requirements, which he said should be doubled. From now on his advice on spending and lending was crucial in demonstrating its link with economic prosperity and unemployment, and by 1940 treasury secretary Henry Morgenthau, who believed in balanced budgets, had been isolated. That year Currie became the first professional economist in the White House where, as government spending rose exponentially in wartime, his impeccable statistical work helped control wages, prices and inflation. However, what really made his reputation in those years was undertaking several wartime missions to the Far East and Europe, and helping set up Claire Chennault's Flying Tigers, which caused such havoc to Japan's airforce. He remained in the White House until FDR died in 1945, but by 1948 his friendship with Harry Dexter White, and advice that general Stillwell be recalled from China, so enraged Communist-hunting congressmen that he emigrated to Colombia, where he advised the government until his death. He loved rearing plants, especially irises, because he said they never tried to resist his policy prescriptions.

Cutting, Bronson M. (1888–1935): Bronson Murray Cutting came from a wealthy New York family and went to school at Groton and Harvard University. Like many prominent New Deal politicians, his roots were in the Progressive period. Indeed, he led the New Mexico Progressive party in 1912 when Theodore Roosevelt bolted Republican ranks, having failed to win nomination for president, and joined TR's insurgent Bull Moose campaign. Ill-health sent him to the southwest, where he became Republican senator for New Mexico in 1927. He survived the Democratic landslide of 1932 and as a reform Republican was, like Robert La Follette, largely sympathetic to the New Deal. He did not live to see its legacy, dying aged only 47 in 1935.

Darrow, Clarence (1857–1938): Born in Kinsman, Ohio, son of an ex-minister who ran a funeral parlour, Clarence Darrow was the most celebrated trial lawyer of his day. Agnostic and socialist, he made his name defending socialists and labour union leaders, like Debs, Haywood, Moyer, Pettibone and the McNamara brothers. However, the guilty plea he entered in this last case, in which the McNamaras had been accused of dynamiting the *Los Angeles Times* building in 1911, ruined his credit with organized labour. He won later notoriety defending child-murderers Leopold and Loeb in 1924; and John Scopes, who taught Darwinian theory in Tennessee in 1925, when his opponent was W.J. Bryan. When a black Detroit doctor, Ossian Sweet, killed one of a white mob who invaded his home, Darrow won his acquittal. He debated capital punishment, child labour, Prohibition, socialism and other issues of the day before large audiences across the US throughout the 1920s. In his last case, aged 77, he conducted a legal investigation of proposed NRA codes in 1933, concluding that they were unworkable. This conclusion Roosevelt himself reluctantly endorsed two years later.

Davis, Chester (1887–1975): An experienced agricultural expert, Chester Davis had stood with George Peek in defence of the McNary-Haugen tariff in 1927–28. After the depression he was more open-minded about new farm policies. So when Peek rejected Tugwell's idea of paying farmers subsidies to stop overproduction, Davis was the obvious man to replace him as head of AAA in October 1933. Helped by Tugwell and the agency's legal counsel Jerome Frank, Davis stayed until 1936, when the Supreme Court declared AAA unconstitutional in the *Butler* case. Congress reassembled most of its policies in more carefully drafted law, while Davis moved on to become one of the most influential figures in the New Deal. He was a member of the industrial emergency policy committee of the Temporary National Economic Committee (TNEC) from 1934 until 1936 when it vainly sought an effective anti-trust policy. Davis was also a governor of the Federal Reserve Board from 1936 until 1941, when the central bank adopted a Keynesian approach to economic management.

Debs, Eugene V. (1855–1926): Born in Terre Haute, Indiana, Debs became a railway locomotive driver. He founded the American Railway Union in 1894 as an industrial union to challenge the railway brotherhoods and company unions he believed weakened worker bargaining power. Jailed that year for his part in the Pullman strike, he was converted to socialism and in 1901 helped found the Socialist Party of America. Always an industrial unionist, Debs joined the anarcho-syndicalist IWW in 1905, but soon left because it rejected political action. Five times candidate for president, he polled 6 per cent of the national popular vote in 1912 and a million votes in 1918 campaigning from jail, where he had been sent for opposing US involvement in the first world war. He remained leader of the SPA until he died, when he was succeeded by Norman Thomas.

Douglas, Lewis W. (1894–1974): Born into an Arizona copper-mining family, Lewis Douglas graduated from Amherst, served with distinction in France and Flanders in the first world war and in the state legislature after 1918. Elected to the House of Representatives in 1927 he became Roosevelt's director of the budget in March 1933 and impressed FDR, who spoke of him as a future president. His job was to help redeem FDR's firm campaign pledge to cut the cost of government by 25 per cent. By summer 1933 the administration had abandoned this goal in favour of reflation. When the US took the dollar off gold, Douglas remarked, 'Well, this is the end of Western civilization.' In fact it marked the start of a generation in which controlled inflation became an acceptable answer to mass unemployment. Resigning in 1934, he was deputy war shipping administrator between 1942 and 1944 and ambassador to Britain from 1947 until 1952.

Du Bois, W.E.B. (1868–1963): This intellectually distinguished African-American political leader was born in Barrington,

Massachusetts, went to Fisk University and was the first black to complete a Harvard Ph.D. From 1897 until 1910 he taught history and economics at Atlanta University, publishing a pathfinding social history of Philadelphia blacks in 1899. In his 1903 classic *The Souls of Black Folk*, Du Bois predicted that 'the problem of the 20th century [will be] the problem of the color line' and dedicated himself to solving it. Impatient with the compromising gradualism of Booker T. Washington, he founded the Niagara Movement to train an elite black leadership, and joined the biracial NAACP. As editor of the NAACP's journal *Crisis*, Du Bois became the most respected spokesman for justice for black Americans and a prolific writer of articles, books, pamphlets and poems. His beliefs changed in the 1930s, when he left the NAACP to espouse Pan-Africanism, and though he rejoined the NAACP after 1945 his sympathy for Soviet communism marginalized him in the US.

Eccles, Marriner S. (1890–1977): Born to a Mormon banking family in Utah, Marriner Stoddart Eccles was unknown to the Washington DC establishment when he jolted the 1933 Senate finance committee hearings by testifying that the federal government should forget about trying to balance its budget during the depression and spend heavily on relief, public works, the domestic allotment plan, refinancing farm mortgages and cancelling what debt remained from the first world war. When Henry Morgenthau became secretary of the treasury on Woodin's death in 1934, FDR made Eccles his assistant, but on Morgenthau's recommendation he was appointed head of the Federal Reserve Board, or central bank, later that year. In the next six years he played a leading part in transforming US monetary policy by combining a belief in deficit spending with a sustained programme of public works. With Lauchlin Currie and Leon Henderson he persuaded Roosevelt to resume government spending after the 1937–38 cuts had been accompanied by sharp recession and rapidly rising unemployment. He remained in charge of the Fed throughout the second world war, and was on the board until 1951 when he returned to banking in Utah.

Eisenhower, Dwight D. (1890–1969): Born in Texas, Dwight David Eisenhower (Ike) grew up in the frontier town of Abilene, Kansas, where his father was a mechanic, and graduated from West Point military academy in 1915, sixty-first out of 165. He was not on active service in the first world war, and thereafter much of his military career was spent on training stations. Genial, modest, pious, reliant on hard work, he was quite unlike general MacArthur, but became special assistant on MacArthur's Far East staff in 1935, with the rank of lieutenant-colonel. Here he became what MacArthur repeatedly described as 'The best staff officer in the Army. When war comes he should go straight to the top.' The day after the attack on Pearl Harbor general George Marshall ordered him to Washington to plan the war and Ike rose to five star general in three years. He was a major-general on the staff planning Torch, the US invasion of North Africa in 1942, and by 1943–44 was in London co-ordinating the Allied invasion of France. As supreme commander Allied powers in Europe he controlled multi-national forces and the vast engine of war which invaded France in June 1944, and deftly repulsed the German army's last counter-offensive in the Ardennes that winter (see Map 3). When Germany surrendered unconditionally in May 1945 his reputation as the man who won the war was much higher than MacArthur's, and he was to enjoy the political power MacArthur craved as Republican president between 1953 and 1961.

Eliot, T.S. (1888–1965): Born in St Louis, Missouri, and educated in New England, Eliot settled in Britain after 1915, working as a bank clerk and writing *The Waste Land* which, when published in 1922, became the twentieth century's most influential poem written in English. The part played in its composition by another American poet, Ezra Pound, was crucial; but as editor of the literary magazines *The Egoist* and *The Criterion,* and as a member of the publishing house Faber & Faber, Eliot exerted much greater influence than Pound on poetry, prose and criticism on both sides of the Atlantic between 1922 and 1945. His political views, like those of Pound, were right-wing, but not as pro-fascist as Pound's became, nor so anti-Semitic. Other Eliot poems include *Four Quartets, The Love Song of J. Alfred Prufrock* and plays such as *Murder in the Cathedral* and *The Cocktail Party.* He was awarded the Order of Merit and the Nobel prize for literature in 1948.

Fall, Albert B. (1861–1944): Republican senator from New Mexico from 1912 until 1921, Albert Fall became Harding's secretary of the interior between 1921 and 1923 and was at the centre of Teapot Dome – the biggest financial/political scandal in US history. Close observers were not surprised. The journalist William Allen White said he looked like a snake-oil salesman, 'a cheap and obvious faker. I could hardly believe my eyes.' But Fall had something more valuable than snake-oil to trade. When millionaire Edward Doheny handed him a satchel containing $100,000, Fall gave him government oil leases in Elk Hills, California. Later indicted and convicted of bribery and conspiracy, along with other Harding appointees, Fall was fined $100,000 and sentenced to a year in prison, the first US cabinet member to go to jail.

Farley, James A. (1888–1976): As chairman of the Democratic national committee in 1932, Jim Farley was Roosevelt's campaign manager in his landslide victory and became a legendary political operator. He deserved much of the credit for organizing the party's astonishing national and local victories during the New Deal, and as national chairman and postmaster-general had ample power of patronage to reward supporters. He claimed to know 60,000 key people nationwide who could test local opinion and help him get out the vote. In the days before modern opinion polls, Farley's judgement on voting intention was unrivalled, and he sealed his reputation by predicting the 1936 election precisely. He fell out with FDR over the third term and became chairman of Coca Cola Export Corporation in 1940.

Flynn, Edward J. (1891–1953): As chairman of the Bronx Democratic county committee in New York city from 1922 until his death in 1953, Ed Flynn held a key post in the most populous city and state in the US. As New York's governor, Roosevelt relied on him during the 1928–29 scandal involving mayor Jimmy Walker, and then as president during the New Deal often asked his advice. Flynn was secretary of state of New York from 1929 until 1939, national committeeman from New York from 1930 until 1953 and succeeded James Farley as Democratic national committee chairman from 1940 until 1942. His book *You're the Boss,* published in 1947, gives his shrewd views on politics, Roosevelt and the New Deal.

Ford, Henry (1863–1947): Born in Greenfield Township, Michigan, of Irish farming stock, Henry Ford personified the American myth: a man of ordinary birth who becomes rich and powerful. He did this by making something everyone wanted: a cheap, reliable motor car. Mechanically adept as a child, he qualified as an engineer in 1891 with a Detroit company owned by Thomas Edison, who became a close friend. Early experiments led to Ford's first four-horsepower automobile in 1896 and an improved version in 1899, when he founded the firm which became the Ford Motor Company in 1903. His Model T put cheap motoring within the grasp of almost everyone. It remained in production until 1927 and is the second best-selling car in history. Ford's early success depended on standardization and assembly line production based on the Taylor system of work measurement. By doubling wages to $5 a day he could hire the best craftsmen, and compensate them for the monotony of the production line. He gave blacks greater opportunities than most employers, but was ruthlessly anti-union. His newspaper, the *Dearborn Independent,* expressed his reactionary anti-Semitism, while his autocratic style meant that Ford fell behind the competition in the 1930s.

Frankfurter, Felix (1882–1965): Professor at Harvard Law School between 1914 and 1939, Frankfurter taught generations of students who became influential in the US political economy. Prominence came in the 1920s campaigning for the convicted anarchists Sacco and Vanzetti. But his real impact on public affairs sprang from his long friendship with Franklin Roosevelt. A liberal Democrat, he placed scores of young lawyers in government service, and during sabbatical leave in Britain in 1933–34 sent advice from British economists about the importance of public works in ending unemployment which had a decisive impact on policy. His own economic views were essentially Keynesian, but he gave only qualified support to FDR's bid to reform the Supreme Court in 1937. FDR appointed him to the Court in 1939. *Roosevelt and Frankfurter: Their Correspondence, 1928–1945*, edited by Max Freedman, is a revealing source for New Deal historians.

Garner, John N. (1868–1967): A Texan Democrat in the House of Representatives from 1903 until 1933, Garner was FDR's vice president during his first two terms. At the Chicago Democratic convention in June 1932 Garner had been a candidate, but switched his votes to enable FDR to win on the fourth ballot. In return, he was given the vice presidential spot. As a southern conservative he balanced the ticket and was retained in 1936, but fell out with Roosevelt over Supreme Court reform in 1937, and even more seriously over FDR's decision to run for a third term in 1940, when he was replaced by Henry A. Wallace. Keen on poker, Garner said the vice presidency was 'not worth a pitcher of warm spit' and on leaving office remarked that when he first came to Washington the total cost of government was $486 million. 'Any appropriation item that small now is merely interim'.

Garvey, Marcus M. (1887-1940): Marcus Moziah Garvey was born in St Ann's Bay, Jamaica and moved to Kingston when he was 16 as an apprentice printer. He led an unsuccessful printers' strike aged 19 and lived in Britain from 1912 until 1914, returning to Jamaica to organize the Universal Negro Improvement Association and African Communities League (UNIA). Emigrating again, this time to the US, he established a New York branch of UNIA and published the *Negro World* as a focus for African-American political action at a time when New York was an important centre of immigration from the Caribbean. There he helped found the Black Star Line, a steamship company which traded with black communities in the Caribbean, Africa and other parts of the world. When Black Star went bankrupt, Garvey was jailed for mail fraud. On release from jail in 1927 he launched the Negro Factories Corporation, which also failed, and began advocating that black Americans could only win political and economic equality by leaving the US. For his work with this Back to Africa movement he was deported to Jamaica, whence he returned to

Britain, publishing his autobiography before his death. Buried in Kensal Green, London, he had been fogotten by 1945, though his reputation revived in the 1960s.

Glass, Carter (1858–1946): Carter Glass was an old school conservative from Virginia who became one of the founders of the Federal Reserve when the central bank system was founded in 1913. Democratic representative from Virginia from 1902 until 1918, he was president Wilson's secretary of the treasury from 1918 until 1920 and senator from Virginia from 1920 until his death in 1946. He co-sponsored the April 1934 Glass-Steagall Act which, by creating the Federal Deposit Insurance Corporation, guaranteed bank deposits under $7,000. The FDIC was a landmark in banking history. Where bank failures averaged 600 a year before 1933, fewer than 600 occured between 1934 and 1945.

Gompers, Samuel (1850–1924): The most influential figure in shaping organized labour in the first quarter of the twentieth century, Samuel Gompers was born in Britain, the son of Dutch-Jewish parents who had settled in London's east end. They took him to the US aged 13, when he began work as a cigar wrapper and started trade union activities in early manhood. He was one of the craft union leaders who between 1881 and 1886 established the American Federation of Labor to focus the activities of all American unions. He was elected first AFL president, a position he held until his death except in 1894, when he was unseated at an election by the mineworkers' leader John McBride. Brought up on socialism, Gompers became firmly anti-socialist; brought up on politics, he saw that in the US partisan political action could be divisive. 'Reward friends and punish enemies' was his political slogan, and while he believed in strikes over pay, hours and conditions, he saw that the AFL's real problem was to secure legal security and bargaining rights from employers. Despite the 1914 Clayton Act, this was not achieved in his lifetime. Though he was a member of war production boards after 1917, and represented the AFL at the Paris peace conference, he lacked executive power. He saw AFL membership rise to some 10 per cent of the non-agricultural workforce by 1919, but then decline after the employers' offensive which began in 1919–20. His craft unionism and cautious conservatism, which characterized the AFL, were sustained after his death but abandoned in the turbulent radicalism of the 1930s.

Green, William (1870–1952): As Gompers's successor, William Green presided over the American Federation of Labor during the years of decline, upheaval and rapid growth which American unions experienced between 1924 and 1945. Born in Coshocton, Ohio, he quit school at 16 to work as a coalminer, joined the

United Mineworkers and quickly won local elective office. He became AFL statistician in 1911, national secretary–treasurer from 1912 until 1924, AFL vice-president from 1913 and president from 1924 until his death. Unlike Gompers, a gregarious, beer-drinking Jewish immigrant, or John L. Lewis, the most powerful labour leader of his generation, Green was a devoted Baptist, capable, decent, a good administrator and bitterly anti-communist. What he lacked was imagination, vision or the will to resist the craft unionists who dominated AFL membership and refused to help organize the unorganized. Nevertheless, he helped create an Ohio workman's compensation scheme, and did back the June 1935 Wagner and Social Security Acts. In the long run the AFL benefited from Lewis and Hillman launching the Congress of Industrial Organizations; in the short run, Green expelled the CIO in 1937. When war came in 1941 Green, like Hillman and Murray, served on the War Labor Board and most of the other federal government boards which planned the war economy. Lacking Hillman's executive ability, he tried, with limited success, to make the No-Strike pledge effective.

Hague, Frank (1876–1956): The most brutal political boss in the US, Frank 'I am the law' Hague ran the politics of New Jersey for a generation. Mayor of Jersey City for 30 years between 1917 and 1947, and member of the Democratic national committee from 1922 until his death, Hague's connections with the New York/New Jersey waterfront criminal underworld were notorious and his methods violent. He helped break independent waterfront labour unions ruthlessly, while the socialist Norman Thomas was attacked by Hague's goons when he exposed his machine's methods. Hague was also an open admirer of Mussolini and Hitler in the 1930s. Yet, as with other bosses such as Tom Pendergast in Kansas City and Edward Crump in Tennessee, FDR worked happily with Hague and never challenged him, though New Deal social reform had greatly weakened this style of leadership in politicians like Hague by 1945.

Harding, Warren G. (1865–1923): Every ten years American historians place past presidents in rank order. Warren Harding always fills last place. A handsome, genial, gregarious incompetent from Ohio, Harding became a partner in the Marion *Star* and married a banker's daughter. Thanks to the contacts this brought, and the backing of Harry Daugherty, the Ohio Republican boss, Harding became state senator, lieutenant governor and US senator between 1899 and 1914, rising without trace. Calvin Coolidge believed he could not be blamed for what he did not say; Harding felt the same about action. But he did sponsor an absurd bill to enable Theodore Roosevelt to raise a volunteer army in the first world war. The bill failed, but a grateful TR promised Harding second spot on his 1920 presidential ticket, should he be nominated. Then TR's death in 1919 helped make Harding 'the available man'. Promising a return to 'normalcy', Harding won the greatest popular victory in history in 1920. With business interests dominant, his Ohio cronies lined their pockets and his administration became a byword for corruption when the Teapot Dome scandal broke after his death.

Hayden, Carl (1877–1967): Arizona sent the Democrat Carl Hayden to Washington to serve in the House of Representatives from 1912 until 1927, and then in the Senate until 1966. His seniority gave him influence in Congress, while his Progressive origins and domicile in a desert state combined to make him a specialist in legislation dealing with the irrigation of dry lands. This became a national priority during the Dust Bowl emergency in the 1930s, when the federal government had to spend millions on reclamation and conservation in the Plains States of the Dakotas, Nebraska, Kansas, Oklahoma and Texas.

Haywood, William D. (1869–1928): Born in the Colorado, 'Big Bill' Haywood lost his ranch to the government as a young man and took work in the metal mines. A radical trades unionist, he joined the Western Federation of Miners in 1896 and became secretary–treasurer in 1900. In 1905 he helped launch the Industrial Workers of the World, a syndicalist industrial union, merging the WFM with it, and by 1908 was an executive member of the Socialist Party of America. But Haywood's aim to organize the unorganized and overthrow capitalism proved too radical. The WFM left the IWW in 1908, while the SPA expelled him in 1913. By then Haywood, hero of the 1908 Boise murder trial and Lawrence and Paterson textile strikes of 1912–13, was one of the working class's most prominent international figures. When the US joined the war in 1917, Haywood and 100 other IWW leaders suffered arrest and eventually long jail sentences and huge fines. Jumping bail in 1921 Haywood fled to the Soviet Union, but this destroyed his credit with American workers and, despite organizing in the Kuznetsk and writing the ghosted autobiography *Bill Haywood's Book*, he neither returned to the US nor found a proper role in Russia.

Hearst, William Randolph (1863–1951): This newspaper editor and publisher founded the Hearst newspaper chain and became one of the richest and most powerful publishers in the US. Like most media tycoons, however, his political influence was far less than he wished. Demagogic and self-seeking, he ran unsuccessfully for mayor of New York in 1905 and for governor in 1906, but never held elective office. He backed FDR for president in 1932, helping him win both nomination and presidency, and hoped for preferment. Ignored, he quarrelled violently over the increasingly left-wing direction of the New Deal, and then supported Alf Landon's disastrous 1936 campaign. It was typical of his impatience and bad political judgement. Immensely rich, Hearst entertained world celebrities at his vast estate at San Simeon in California. In 1941 he tried, with partial success, to suppress Orson Welles's film *Citizen Kane*, largely based on Hearst's life.

Hemingway, Ernest (1899–1961): Born in what is now suburban Chicago, Hemingway had a country boyhood around Lake Michigan and joined the Kansas City *Star* on leaving high school. His simple, precise prose, so different from that of Henry James, helped change the style of twentieth-century US fiction. When America went to war in Europe in 1917 an injured eye kept him from fighting, but he served as an ambulance driver on the Italian front and was badly wounded in the Italian collapse at Caporetto. After the war he joined American expatriates like Ezra Pound and Gertrude Stein in Paris, and his picture of this 'lost generation' in *The Sun Also Rises* had made him world famous by 1926. *A Farewell to Arms* in 1929 vividly evokes the first world war, while the Spanish Civil War, which he reported from the Republican side, was the setting of *For Whom the Bell Tolls* in 1940. Second world war reporting, more novels and short stories followed; but after 1945, the macho-man legend, based on travel, hunting, fishing, obsessive love of bull fighting, childish behaviour and excessive drinking began to take its toll, choking his creative talent. *The Old Man and the Sea* (1952) sold millions of copies, and he won the Nobel prize for literature in 1954, but after that he virtually stopped writing and became prone to depression and despair, killing himself (as his father had done) in 1961.

Hillman, Sidney (1887–1946): Born in the Baltic states of Tsarist Russia, Sidney Hillman attended a Lithuanian rabbinical school but was jailed for his minor part in the 1905 Revolution and fled to the US where he worked as a cutter in the Chicago garment industry. A labour activist, he joined the United Garment Workers and, during a strike of women workers, brokered the 1910 Hart, Schaffner and Marx contract which became a garment industry bargaining benchmark. First president of the Amalgamated Clothing Workers in 1914, he led successful strikes in New York, Philadelphia and Chicago and, as war orders gave ACW members better bargaining power, pay packets and benefits, built a powerful union. The ACW suffered serious reverses in the 1920s, but Hillman, a working-class intellectual, regained authority when he joined John L. Lewis, David Dubinsky and others to found the CIO in 1935. After launching TWOC in an abortive bid to organize southern textile workers between 1937 and 1940, Hillman was picked by FDR to head the labour division of the National Defense Administration between 1940 and 1943, when, despite ill health, he exerted more influence than AFL president William Green. He helped shape the US war economy, and played a role which anticipated the corporate political structure American unions adopted after his death in 1946.

Hiss, Alger (1904–): Born in Baltimore, Maryland, Alger Hiss graduated from the local high school, Johns Hopkins and Harvard Law School to become clerk to the distinguished Supreme Court justice Oliver Wendell Holmes in 1932. He was counsel for Senator Nye's committee which investigated the role the arms industry played in bringing the US into the first world war, and in 1934 Lee Pressman hired him to work for the Agricultural Adjustment Administration. By 1936 he had transferred to the state department as war clouds darkened and had a brilliant career, travelling with President Roosevelt to the conference of the Big Three at Yalta and serving as secretary to the San Francisco conference which set up the United Nations in 1945. Then he became president of the Carnegie Endowment for International Peace, but in 1948 was accused by journalist Whittaker Chambers of having been a fellow Communist spy who helped him send state department secrets to the Soviet Union in the 1930s. His case acted as midwife to McCarthyism. Jailed for perjury for having denied Chambers's charge to a congressional committee, Hiss strenuously maintains his innocence, first published in his book *In the Court of Public Opinion*, though historian Allen Weinstein's book *Perjury*, and files found in Hungarian Communist archives since the Cold War ended, seem to prove his guilt.

Holmes, Oliver Wendell (1841–1935): Holmes, the most distinguished jurist of his generation, fought for the Union in the civil war yet, like many of old Yankee stock, was deeply critical of postwar values, famously observing that 'the 14th amendment does not legislate Herbert Spencer's *Social Statics*'. Holmes had to wait until Theodore Roosevelt became president to be elevated to the Supreme Court, when he was 61. There he sided with Brandeis in years of dissenting liberal judgments, but set limits to free speech. The First Amendment, he wrote, does not give the right 'falsely to cry fire in a crowded theater'. Holmes's reputation was legendary when he retired aged 89, and he lived long enough to see Franklin Roosevelt ('a second-class intellect but a first-class temperament') try to tackle aspects of capitalism Holmes deplored, but not his abortive attempt to reform the Supreme Court. When Holmes died he left the bulk of his estate to the federal government.

Hoover, Herbert C. (1874–1964): Herbert Clark Hoover's life and reputation hinged on the Great Depression. His outstanding career before 1929 personified American virtues, just as its decline afterwards appeared a crisis of that same individualism. Hoover was born in Iowa to an old Quaker family of modest circumstances, was orphaned in childhood and, after graduating from Stanford in 1895, travelled the world for the next fifteen years to win an international reputation as a mining engineer. Heading the vast US programme of relief during and after the first world war so enhanced his reputation that both Democrats and Republicans were eager to have him run for president in 1920. Had he done so he would doubtless have left office in 1929 more highly regarded than ever. Instead, after serving as secretary of commerce to Harding and Coolidge, his defeat of the liberal, anti-Prohibitionist Al Smith in the 1928 presidential election meant he was in charge when the economic crash came after 1929. By 1932, millions of homeless job seekers squatting in tar-paper shanty towns all over the nation called them 'Hoovervilles' as Franklin Roosevelt swept to power promising 'a New Deal'. Hoover was as much victim as cause of the depression, and did more to tackle it than he was given credit for. His Reconstruction Finance Corporation helped fund the early New Deal and lasted until the 1950s. But he refused to sanction relief payments to the chronic jobless for fear of destroying their self-respect, and never questioned his simplistic belief in market forces which caused the crash. Bitter and disappointed after 1933, he remained active and lived long enough to see his presidency partially vindicated in the 1960s.

Hoover, J. Edgar (1895–1972): Born, bred and educated in Washington DC, J. Edgar Hoover devoted his life to making the Federal Bureau of Investigation the most feared and powerful branch of the federal bureacracy. Yet he is a classic case of how dedication to the high ideal of national security can degenerate into fear and intolerance of all but the most reactionary beliefs. From a minor post, Hoover helped attorney general Mitchell Palmer launch his 'Red Scare' raids in 1919. By 1924, aged only 29, he was FBI director, holding the job until his death. Giving top priority to forensic science and rigorous selection and training, he made the FBI an efficient law enforcement agency during Prohibition, but in the 1930s was criticized for harrying Communists and the Popular Front, not the Ku Klux Klan or organized crime. After 1941 Hoover switched FBI attention from Communists to Nazi spies, and by 1945 his legendary reputation was at its peak. Communism remained his great hate, however, and the crisis of the Cold War fed this obsession until, in old age, his suspicion all but destroyed him and the bureau he had built.

Hopkins, Harry L. (1890–1946): The son of a saddle maker, Harry Hopkins trained as a welfare worker and so was exactly the kind of man Franklin Roosevelt welcomed to his closest political circle. His first-hand experience of the seamier side of life filled a gap in FDR's patrician view. As head of the Federal Emergency Relief Administration from 1933 until 1935, Hopkins spent $5 million in his first afternoon and was a powerful force in favour of reflating economic recovery. Yet he always drew a clear distinction between work and welfare, and as director of the Works Progress Administration from 1935 until 1938 greatly advanced the vast programme of public works on which Harold Ickes had cautiously embarked until the Supreme Court ruled the National Industrial Recovery Act unconstitutional in 1935. With the death of Louis Howe in 1936, Hopkins became FDR's closest confidant. As secretary of commerce, and head of Lend-Lease in 1941, he was the president's constant companion throughout the tragedies and triumphs of war.

House, Colonel Edward M. (1858–1938): Trained as a diplomat, Edward House became so close a personal friend, adviser and representative that Woodrow Wilson could not function properly without him. When Wilson was elected president in 1912, he was the first to set up a modern-style staff, which House effectively headed. He came into his own handling foreign affairs, especially during the period of increasingly un-neutral neutrality Wilson tried to sustain between 1914 and 1917, and even more so with the Armistice and Paris Peace Conference in 1918–19. In Paris, House tried to take staff work off his chief's shoulders, but Wilson obsessively felt responsible for everything, refused to delegate and insisted on doing it all. Yet when Wilson went home to Washington DC to win votes in Congress, House was left in Paris to deal with diplomacy. After Wilson's stroke in 1919–20, his second wife Edith Galt and House hid the president's incapacity and effectively ran the White House for months. He long outlived Wilson and became an elder statesman in Democratic party affairs.

Howe, Louis M. (1871–1936): From the day the journalist Louis Howe met Franklin Roosevelt at Albany he believed FDR should be president and spent his life helping him fufil his destiny. His aide at the navy department from 1913 until 1920, and on the doomed 1920 presidential campaign, he helped Roosevelt's wife and mother nurse him back to private and then public life when polio crippled him in 1921. Personal secretary and closest confidant, he sustained FDR through two terms as New York governor between 1928 and 1932. Howe's experience of life, like that of Harry Hopkins later, put the aristocratic FDR in touch with realities he could not know at first hand. His political judgement was excellent, and he was FDR's senior speech writer. But after 1932 his influence waned. Raymond Moley vividly recalled Howe toiling without sleep at the Chicago convention to help win the nomination on the fourth ballot. Yet the acceptance speech, pledging 'a New Deal', was written by Moley who, as chief-of-staff, displaced Howe. Moley, however, had himself gone by 1935 and when Howe died the following year Hopkins replaced him. Deprived of Howe's advice, FDR badly mishandled his bid to reform the Supreme Court in 1937.

Hughes, Charles E. (1862–1948): Born in upstate New York, Charles Evans Hughes graduated from Brown and Columbia Law School to practice commercial law. Rooting out corruption in New York insurance and public utilities, he was elected Republican governor in 1906 and pursued Progressive policies. Taft put him on the Supreme Court in 1910, but his liberal influence there ended when he resigned to run unsuccessfully against Wilson for president in 1916. With Herbert Hoover and Henry C. Wallace he lent substance to the Harding-Coolidge cabinets as secretary of state, concluding an arms reduction naval treaty and withdrawal of some US troops from Latin America. Returning to private practice in 1925, he was named chief justice in 1930 and had the thankless task of trying to organize consistent judicial response by a deeply divided Supreme Court to a flood of emergency New Deal legislation. Meticulous yet flexible, he resisted FDR's bid to reform the Court and, helped by the retirement of conservative justices like Van Devanter and their replacement by liberals like Black, he coaxed the Court into accepting left-wing reforms such as the Social Security and Wagner Acts. Thus, before retiring in 1941, he was able to secure his belief that the Court must interpret the Constitution not as a static document but as a living one.

Hull, Cordell (1871–1955): A conservative Democrat, Cordell Hull represented Tennessee in the House of Representatives from 1907 until 1921, and from 1923 until 1931, when he moved to the Senate. As Franklin Roosevelt's secretary of state from 1933 until 1944, he handled American diplomatic responses to all the crises which led to war in Asia, Europe and the Pacific by 1941; and was involved in the complex diplomacy of the wartime alliances with Britain, China, France and the Soviet Union which culminated with the total capitulation of the Axis powers in 1945. The award of the Nobel prize for peace that year crowned his lifetime's work in the field of foreign affairs.

Ickes, Harold L. (1874–1952): Trained as a lawyer, Harold Ickes was a Progressive Republican and partner in the same Chicago law firm as Donald Richberg and David Lilienthal. The

Ballinger/Pinchot scandal persuaded him to back Theodore Roosevelt in 1912 and, lacking sympathy with 1920s Republicanism, he gladly became secretary of the interior to 'the other Roosevelt' in 1933 when Hiram Johnson refused. During the depression this was a key post and 'the old curmudgeon', as he called himself, filled it to perfection. Given control of NRA's $3.3 billion public works programme, Ickes was criticized for putting the Public Works Administration into effect so slowly. Yet his overriding fear was that local political bosses might steal or waste the money, discredit the New Deal and so prevent the programme gaining the solid basis on which Harry Hopkins was able to build with the Works Progress Administration from 1935 until 1938. As head of the department of the interior, Ickes played a crucial role in dealing with the ecological catastrophe of the Dust Bowl and finally implementing the kind of conservationist programme which had brought him into politics as a Bull Mooser in 1912. With Frances Perkins, he was the only cabinet member to serve throughout FDR's dozen years as president. He kept a long, detailed journal (published in 1953 after his death as *The Secret Diary of Harold Ickes*) which is full of mordant comments on people and events and is a major source for New Deal historians.

Johnson, Hiram W. (1866–1945): Governor of California from 1911 until 1917, Hiram Johnson was one of the insurgent Republican founders of the Progressive party and its candidate for vice president in 1912. Clearly the ablest and most prominent western Progressive, his disloyalty in 1912 denied him the regular Republican nomination in 1916 and 1920. Yet as senator from California from 1917 until his death in 1945, Johnson belonged to an elite group of national legislators. When he refused Franklin Roosevelt's offer of secretary of the interior in 1933, the president gave the job to Harold Ickes who filled it with distinction for twelve years.

Jones, Jesse H. (1874–1956): A banker and federal government official, Jesse Jones held the key post of director of the Reconstruction Finance Corporation from its birth in 1932 until 1939, when the depression was widely believed to have ended. In addition to heading RFC, membership of the Temporary National Emergency Committee (TNEC) from 1933 until 1939 gave him general oversight of the whole New Deal. As secretary of commerce between 1940 and 1945 he worked with the Economic Stablization Board, trying to control wages, prices and profits and thus inflation in the booming war economy.

Jones, Mary Harris (1830–1930): 'Mother' Jones as she was universally known was by 1910 one of the greatest legends of the American labour movement, and although she was then aged 80 still had another 20 active and influential years. Born in Cork, Ireland, on May Day 1830, she emigrated to the US as a teenager worked as a dressmaker and teacher and married an iron moulder in 1861. From then onwards she was tirelessly active trying to improve working conditions in coal, metal mining and other industries with the National Labour Union, the Knights of Labor and the American Railway Union. The death of her husband and children of yellow fever in 1867, and loss of all her worldly goods in the 1871 Chicago fire, merely redoubled her dedication. A founder member of the Industrial Workers of the World in 1905 she was interviewed by presidents Taft and Wilson as they sought the causes of mounting labour unrest. Her conviction for conspiracy to murder during the 1912–13 West Virginia coal strike was set aside and replaced by congressional investigations which led to reforms. A little grey-haired old woman with black bonnet and handsome face, she spoke eloquently and movingly in a falsetto voice which combined defiance with wit. During presidential commission hearings into the 1914 Ludlow massacre, John D. Rockefeller Jr greeted her warmly and asked her to come to his office as there 'are so many things on which you can enlighten me'. She offered to show him Colorado's mining communities. 'What you see will make you do things which will make you one of the country's greatest men.' When he smiled and said she was inclined to throw compliments she replied, 'I'm more inclined to throw bricks.' She remained active in the coalfields of both Colorado and Virginia, and on her hundredth birthday received thousands of messages, including one from Rockefeller, and made a vigorous speech for talking-picture cameras.

Keller, Helen (1880–1968): Born to a prominent Georgia family, Helen Keller was struck by illness at the age of two which left her blind and deaf. State-of-the-art medical therapy could do nothing, but her desperate parents hired the Boston blind school teacher Anne Sullivan, whose direct method taught Helen to read and write. At ten she began speech classes and graduated from Radcliffe in 1904. Tirelessly organizing, lecturing and writing, she was prime mover in launching the first state commission for the blind in Massachusetts and seeing it spread throughout the US. She also became a left-wing socialist and supported the IWW when it was one of the most feared and hated labour unions in the land. Chronically short of funds, she toured in vaudeville theatre, made films and started the Helen Keller Endowment Fund for the American Foundation for the Blind in 1932. Though Anne Sullivan died in 1936, Helen Keller's work spread round the world and she became an international figure showing what the blind and deaf could do.

Kelly, Edward J. (1876–1950): Anton Cermak's assassination in 1933 made Democrat Edward Kelly mayor of Chicago, enabling this former engineer to build the formidable 'Kelly machine'. This kept him in office until 1947 and ran city hall for two more generations. It also made Kelly a powerful politician and member of the Democratic national committee from 1940 to 1944. The machine's reliability was due partly to the fact that Chicago, like Detroit, had a strong-mayor constitution, but also to the city's importance in Illinois politics, and the state's importance in the politics of the nation.

Kennedy, Joseph P. (1888–1969): Son of an Irish immigrant saloon-keeper, Joseph Patrick Kennedy graduated from Harvard University in 1910 and made a vast fortune from banking, distilling, real estate and Hollywood moving pictures. One of Wall Street's most ruthless raiders, he was also one of the few to emerge from the 1929 stock market crash with his huge fortune intact. Though much hated, even in his own party, he had been for Roosevelt before Chicago and as a rich, lifelong Democrat he was a natural choice for the Securities and Exchange Commission established during the New Deal, becoming its chairman in 1935. As ambassador to Britain from 1937 until 1941 he was less assured. From the Munich crisis in September 1938 until the fall of France in June 1940 his diplomatic advice was like that of a broker:, buy German stock and sell British. Convinced Hitler would win the war, he lost favour with Roosevelt and was replaced as ambassador on the eve of US involvement in 1941.

Keynes, John M. (1883–1946):The most influential economist of the twentieth century, John Maynard Keynes was part of that remarkable Cambridge generation which included Bertrand Russell and Alfred Whitehead, though he also moved among the Bloomsbury set of Clive Bell and Virginia Woolf. He made his name with *The Economic Consequences of the Peace*, published in 1920, a sardonic analysis of men and events at the 1919 Paris peace conference, where he had been Lloyd George's economic adviser. But his serious influence on the political economy came after 1929, in a world desperately seeking a way out of economic depression. His use after 1931 of 'the multiplier', the mathematical link between levels of government spending and economic activity, provided the theoretical basis for a reflationary solution to mass unemployment. Though his first meeting with Franklin Roosevelt in 1934 appeared unproductive, New Deal economic policy became increasingly Keynesian, especially after his vastly influential *General Theory*, published in 1936, which orchestrated the theory of 'managed capitalism' on which the wealth of nations rested. His last political contribution to the capitalist system came at the 1944 Bretton Woods conference, where he helped put together the banking, financial and trade arrangements by which the postwar world would be run.

La Guardia, Fiorello (1882–1947): Born in Arizona of Italo-American parents, Fiorello La Guardia became as celebrated and effective a reformer as Al Smith had been in New York. After two terms in the House as a Republican between 1917 and 1921, and again from 1923 until 1933, he ran for mayor of New York city against a Democratic party hopelessly split by fallout from the Jimmy Walker scandal and Seabury investigation which followed in 1930. Putting together a crazy-quilt coalition, united only by resentment against generations of Tammany Hall rule, his fusion ticket managed to keep the coalition together and win him re-election in 1937 and 1941. Blessed with a genius for publicity, 'the Little Flower' became almost as famous as FDR in the 1930s and a musical comedy about his life ran successfully on Broadway after his death.

La Follette, Robert M. (1855–1925): Even more so than Theodore Roosevelt or Hiram Johnson, 'Fighting Bob' La Follette was the true voice of Progessive reform between 1900 and 1925. Born and educated in Wisconsin, he practised law and represented the state for three terms in the House as an unremarkable conservative. Losing his seat in 1891 he completely reshaped his ideas, coming to see monopoly and special interests as his enemy. After years of political struggle he was elected governor of Wisconsin in 1900, just as Progressivism was about to bloom. La Follette's 'Wisconsin idea' turned the state and its institutions into a laboratory for reform of tax, electoral law, railroads and other services and utilities. As senator after 1905 he saw the Wisconsin idea become that of the nation, but doubted Theodore Roosevelt's commitment and challenged him unsuccessfully for presidential nomination in 1912. He supported the reforms which came during Wilson's presidency, culminating with federal income tax and creation of the Federal Reserve which gave national government much greater power to control the US economy. However, he opposed Wilson's war policy and he was appalled by restored business dominance in the 1920s. Running for president in 1924 he won 16 per cent of the popular vote, carrying only Wisconsin, in a campaign which was a last hurrah for Progressivism and himself.

La Follette, Robert M. Jr. (1905–53): The younger of two sons, he was part of the formidable La Follette dynasty in Wisconsin. His brother Philip served three terms as governor from 1931 until 1939, while as Republican senator from 1925 until 1947 Robert Jr. chaired the celebrated Senate civil liberties investigation which was a model of how a Senate investigation should be conducted. It revealed that major employers, like Ford and Republic Steel, spied on their workers, fired them for their political beliefs and hired thugs to stop them joining unions. Later he reorganized the Senate committee system and in the 1940s was voted best senator by political analysts. In 1946 he lost his party's nomination in Wisconsin to senator Joe McCarthy, who was voted the worst senator in 1948.

Landon, Alfred M. (1887–1989): Republican governor of Kansas from 1933 until 1935, Alf Landon was an honest, if limited, spokesman for the middle American values Republicanism aspired to articulate before the Great Depression devastated the system in which they grew. Nominated by his party to run for president in 1936 on a programme of outright opposition to the New Deal, he was swept away, winning only in Maine and Vermont. Thereafter the party endorsed much New Deal reform, especially social security. Thereafter, too, Landon lived as a private citizen and died aged 101.

Laski, Harold (1893–1950): Born in Manchester and educated at Manchester Grammar School and New College, Oxford, Harold Laski taught at Amherst, Harvard, McGill and Yale universities, frequently visited the US, wrote prolifically for American publishers and serious magazines, and came to exercise great influence during the economic depression of the 1930s. He was professor of politics at London University from 1926 until his death and had long associations with the London School of Economics and Sidney and Beatrice Webb. A Fabian socialist and for a time the most influential intellectual in the British Labour party, his network of contacts spanned the world and he was intent on bringing welfare socialism to Western democracies after 1945.

LeHand, Marguerite (1898–1944): Appointed personal secretary to Franklin Roosevelt when polio struck him in 1921. 'Missy' Le Hand lived at the family home at Hyde Park and became a close personal friend of both Franklin and Eleanor. She remained with FDR in the same post throughout his presidency, came to exercise the political influence of a close courtier and died less than a year before the president in July 1944.

Lewis, John L. (1880–1969): The son of a Welsh coalmining father in an Iowan coal community, John Llewellyn Lewis was the most autocratic and influential labour leader of his generation. He began work underground but quickly joined the staff of the United Mineworkers of America. The UMW was an industrial union frequently at odds with the craft concerns of the AFL, but as the only national union covering the nation's largest extractive industry it was the most important union in the AFL. By 1920 Lewis – large, beetle-browed, eloquent and self-dramatizing – was UMW president and on the AFL executive. He led a series of disastrous coal strikes in the 1920s, and by 1933 he was the discredited leader of a bankrupt union. Moreover, as a lifelong Republican, he had voted for Hoover (another Iowan) and so had no friends at FDR's court. Nevertheless, he served as a labour adviser to the NRA. But what made his name in the 1930s was leading that astonishing eruption of rank-and-file activism which, aided by the 1935 Wagner Act, created the Congress of Industrial Organizations and tripled labour union membership by 1940. However, the CIO's industrial unions threatened AFL craft jurisdictions, and in 1937 the two labour federations split. An isolationist in foreign affairs, Lewis was the first US union leader to be spoken of as a possible presidential candidate. However, when he opposed FDR's decision to run for a third term in 1940 he put his own CIO presidency on the line by endorsing the Republican Wendell Willkie; and had to resign in favour of Philip Murray when Willkie lost. Despite leading successful coal strikes in 1943–44, he never recovered the national influence he had exercised in the 1930s, and by 1945 had become a hated figure, blamed for creating wartime labour unrest in the coal industry.

Lewis, Sinclair (1885–1951): Born in a small town in Minnesota, Harry Sinclair Lewis was the son of a country doctor who grew up in the midwest and in 1907 graduated from Yale University, where he had edited the student literary magazine. He worked as a freelance writer and editor on the east coast, and in California, before leaving paid employment in 1914 to work full time as a novelist after a few short stories and his first novel *Our Mr Wrenn* had been published. *Main Street*, published in 1920, made his name. It gently satirized midwestern middle-class values in the very year Warren Harding, who personified those values, took power in Washington DC. The novel made Lewis rich and *Babbitt*, published two years later, was a sharper satire. Lewis refused to accept a Pulitzer prize for *Arrowsmith* (1926), but became the first American writer to win the Nobel prize for literature in 1930. The books he wrote afterwards failed to win the commercial and critical success he had enjoyed in the 1920s, but he travelled widely, lived in Europe and died in Rome in 1951.

Lilienthal, David E. (1899–1981): A corporation lawyer, David Lilienthal was a country boy from Indiana who after university and law school joined the Chicago firm where Harold Ickes and Don Richberg were partners. On the recommendation of Felix Frankfurter and Jerome Frank, he was invited to become one of three directors of the Tennessee Valley Authority, a post he held until 1946. TVA was set up to fulfil the long-held conservationist ambitions of men like George Norris and FDR himself to make hydro-electric power available universally and change the ecology of a whole river basin (see Map 2). Simply building the huge dam stimulated work on a large scale, and at least six other dams were built. Yet public power struck at private enterprise, and in many ways TVA was the most radical and long-lasting of New Deal projects. Lilienthal was the archetypal New Deal technocrat, and fought decisive political battles about TVA's purpose with co-directors A.E. Morgan and Harcourt Morgan and other policy makers, such as Rex Tugwell. The importance of TVA is shown in another way: Wendell Willkie, who made his name resisting TVA on behalf of private utilities, ran against Roosevelt as a Republican in 1940. *The Journals of David E. Lilienthal* are a reflective diary of these events.

Lindbergh, Charles A. (1902–75): The first man to fly the Atlantic solo, in 1927, Lindbergh was the most acclaimed popular American hero of the 1920s. Born in Detroit, Michigan, he had done some army flying and worked as an air mail pilot before trying for the $25,000 prize on offer to the first non-stop pilot from New York to Paris. For that purpose he helped design *The Spirit of St Louis* and tested it between California and New York before starting his 33-hour flight on 20 May 1927. He lived much of the rest of his life in the harsh glare of publicity. His son was kidnapped and murdered in 1932, and he was unsuccessful in his attempts to persuade the federal government to let him fly private enterprise air mail services. Later Lindbergh's isolationism, visits to Nazi Germany, from where he brought back favourable reports and a medal from Goering, kept him in the headlines. Despite the importance of air power, no significant role was found for him during the second world war.

Long, Huey P. (1893–1935): Described by FDR in the 1930s as 'the most dangerous man in America', Huey Pierce Long was a southern politician in the Populist tradition, but with a national following and bizarre personality unmatched by any other in his lifetime. Born on a prosperous farm, he worked as a travelling salesman, but studied law at night and in 1915 passed the Louisiana bar examinations. He based his political career on the machine he built in 1920s Louisiana, running unsuccessfully for governor in 1924 but serving as governor from 1928 until 1931, and as senator from 1931 until his death. He spent taxpayers' money to give Louisiana a welfare state without equal in the south, arguing that the tax system should be used to redistribute wealth under the slogans 'Every man a king' and 'Share our wealth'. By

1934 'the kingfish', as he was known, and dangerous Southern demagogues like Gerald L.K. Smith were attacking the New Deal as a failure. Private polls commissioned by Roosevelt's campaign manager James Farley revealed that if Long ran as a third-party candidate in 1936 he would win 10 million votes – enough to deny FDR re-election. The president's backing for the reforms of the second New Deal, which began in 1935, stemmed partly from that fear, but in September 1935 Long was assassinated in Baton Rouge by a deranged doctor. At his funeral the wreaths covered three acres of land.

Luce, Henry (1898–1967): Born in China, educated at Yale and Oxford, Henry Robinson Luce founded *Time* magazine in 1923 and made it the most widely read and successful weekly news magazine in the US by 1945. In 1930 he founded *Fortune*, an authoritative popular journal reflecting the interests of big business, and *Life*, the best photo-journalism magazine in the world. The huge circulation enjoyed by *Time* and *Life*, the prestige won by *Fortune*, and his serious political interests made Luce the most formidable publisher of his generation. He aimed at bringing evangelical Christian values to public life, and became the leading journalistic spokesman of the China lobby, which argued that US influence over the affairs of the world's largest nation state should have first priority in foreign affairs, both in peace and war. In 1940, three years after Japan invaded China, he organized a large China relief programme and lobbied tirelessly on behalf of Chiang Kai-shek and the Kuomingtang government against the internal threat of the Communist army in China from 1941 until 1949. After Pearl Harbor he and general MacArthur argued strongly but unsuccessfully that Hitler was Europe's problem and that defeat of militarism in Japan and the Pacific should be given priority over defeat of Germany in Europe.

MacArthur, Douglas (1880–1964): Born in Little Rock, Arkansas, Douglas MacArthur graduated from West Point with the best record in the history of the military academy since the civil war. Twice wounded in the first world war, he won many decorations for gallantry and after 1918 became head of West Point, which he transformed and modernized. Bombastic, egotistical, flamboyant, he was an intellectual with a remarkable memory and tireless attention to detail. After duty in the Philippines from 1922 until 1930, MacArthur was made army chief of staff, and he became notorious for using mounted cavalry and tear gas to rout the 'Bonus Army' – unemployed war veterans demonstrating for earlier payment of their first world war bonus in 1932. Three years later FDR put him in command of US forces in the Far East, with headquarters in the Philippines, where Dwight Eisenhower was his chief of staff with the rank of lieutenant-colonel. After Pearl Harbor, Japanese invaders forced him to evacuate the Philippines in March 1942, when he vowed 'I shall return'. He argued unsuccessfully that defeat of Japan in the Pacific be given priority over defeat of Hitler in Europe, but played a major part in devising the strategy which defeated the Japanese in the Pacific, organized his own publicity and took their surrender on 2 September 1945 (see Maps 4 and 5). As postwar leader of Japanese reconstruction, he held a proconsular position unique in US history which gave him the kind of power and influence he relished. But his lifelong ambition for a career in US politics came to nothing.

McAdoo, William G. (1863–1941): Born in Georgia, William Gibbs McAdoo lived in New York, trained as a lawyer and became a promoter who helped finance the first tunnel under the Hudson river. A leading member of the business community, he was also a Jeffersonian Democrat who married Woodrow Wilson's daughter and became his secretary of the treasury from 1916 until 1918. A strong contender for Democratic presidential nomination in 1924 and 1928, he helped swing California's convention vote to Franklin Roosevelt on the third ballot in 1932 to get John Nance Garner on the ticket. McAdoo was Democratic senator from California between 1933 and 1939.

Marshall, George C. (1880–1959): The only US career soldier to win the Nobel peace prize, George Catlett Marshall was best known for organizing the programme of economic recovery and relief which restored war-ravaged Europe after 1945. Born in Pennsylvania, he graduated from Virginia Military Institute and served in the Philippines and then as Pershings's chief of operations during the first world war. Experience as an army instructor in the US and China was followed in the 1930s by work with the Civilian Conservation Corps, which gave a generation of jobless young Americans work experience. From 1941 he was in charge of organizing victory in a truly global war for which the US was totally unprepared, ranking seventeenth among the military powers with armed forces smaller than those of Romania in 1940. He was an outstanding chief of staff during the second world war, especially noted for his judgement in using Eisenhower's unique gifts, and by 1945 was probably the most admired living American, at least among the nation's political elite.

Mencken, H.L. (1880–1956): The most sardonic writer of his generation, H.L. Mencken was born into a comfortable German-American family in Baltimore, Maryland, and became a newspaper reporter on graduating from high school in 1896. Within ten years he was editor-in-chief, and then joined the *Baltimore Sun*, where he remained until 1948. His greatest days were the 1920s, when he campaigned tirelessly against ignorance, philistinism, Prohibition, politicians as a class, the 'blue' laws and what he called 'the booboisie'. His real target was the tyranny of the majority inherent in any democracy. 'No one has ever gone broke,' he observed, 'underestimating the intelligence of the American public.' He founded a magazine called *The Smart Set* and edited the influential *American Mercury*. The new agenda facing the US after 1929 made Mencken's favourite, easy targets suddenly dated, and his humour empty, so his influence waned and he was never at ease with Roosevelt and the New Deal. His lasting legacy was his dictionary *The American Language*, which explored distinctions between American and British usage.

Moley, Raymond (1886–1975): Appointed professor of public law and government at Columbia University in 1923, Raymond Moley caught the attention of New York's governor Franklin Roosevelt, who made him chief-of-staff of his 'Brains Trust' when he ran for president in 1932. His pragmatic conservatism matched FDR's patrician opportunism and common touch, and for a time Moley replaced Louis Howe as FDR's closest confidant. Regarded by everyone, including himself, as the president's most conservative adviser, Moley was sent to the London economic conference as assistant secretary of state in June 1933. There he had the ground cut from under his feet by the president's sudden decision not to stabilize the dollar, and thereafter grew more and more disillusioned with the New Deal and with Roosevelt's increasingly demagogic style, writing a perceptive critical account in 1939 called *After Seven Years*. Returning to academic life, he was also editor of *Today* and contributing editor of *Newsweek*.

Morgan, J. Pierpont (1837–1913): Though J.P. Morgan died in 1913 he was the founder of the kind of finance capitalism which was crucial in shaping US history between 1910 and 1945. A banker and son of a banker, Morgan expanded the family business until it reached into every branch of commercial enterprise. The trusts, vast conglomerates of manufacturing, transport, marketing and services which spread horizontally and vertically across the economy and society after 1910, were largely of his creation; especially in the years between 1899 and 1901, when Morgan, Harriman and Carnegie put together the first 'billion dollar' trust combining coal, steel and railways. Henceforth, Progressive and New Deal reformers struggled with the problem of trusts and how to diminish, or at least control, their power – with little success. In 1931 the House of Morgan alone controlled about one-quarter of US corporate assets, and efforts by the federal government during the New Deal to break the power of trusts were notably unsuccessful.

Morgenthau, Henry (1891–1967): Son of a New York lawyer who made a fortune in real estate, Henry Morgenthau studied architecture and then agriculture at Cornell University but did not take a degree. He met Franklin Roosevelt in 1913, visited him frequently when he was learning to cope with being crippled by polio, and held New York state office when FDR was governor between 1929 and 1933. When Will Woodin resigned as secretary of the treasury Morgenthau replaced him in 1934. A budget balancer, Morgenthau loyally accepted the need for deficit financing in 1933 and had helped stabilize the dollar against foreign currencies by 1938. Between then and 1940, however, he lost the key argument about the need to cut public spending and by 1945 this had risen to $98 billion a year. Aided by J.M. Keynes and other Allied economists, he helped shape postwar world banking and financial policy at Bretton Woods in 1944, when the International Monetary Fund and World Bank were set up, but the Morgenthau plan to dismantle German industry after the war was disowned by Roosevelt, and when Harry Truman became president he went to the Potsdam conference without Morgenthau and forced his resignation in July 1945.

Moses, Robert (1888–1981): Born at Yale, Robert Moses studied political science there and at Columbia but became a public works planner who transformed the New York landscape. Governor Al Smith made him head of state reconstruction in 1919, head of New York and Long Island state park commissions in 1924 and secretary of state in 1927, which gave him unprecedented planning power. However, he clashed bitterly with Smith's successor Roosevelt, who sacked him, but he retained his park jobs and was able to work better with FDR as president. Chairman of New York Emergency Public Works Commission in 1933, Moses was so widely popular that he was offered the chance to run against La Guardia for mayor of New York, and did run as a Republican for governor in 1934, when Herbert Lehman beat him by 800,000 votes. La Guardia made him head of City Parks and the Triborough Bridge and Tunnel Authority, which he used to transform New York into one of the most stunning cities in the world, as the 1939 World's Fair revealed. The influence this had on other cities in the US and around the world was immense, and Moses supervised work on two hydro-electric dams, a network of highways, 12 bridges, millions of acres of parkland and was instrumental after 1945 in bringing the United Nations complex to Manhattan.

Moskowitz, Belle Lindner Israels (1877–1933): Born the daughter of Isidor Lindner, a Jewish watchmaker, on the east side of New York City, Belle Moskowitz, with Polish, German and Russian ancestry, became an outstanding welfare worker and political leader, and one of the most remarkable women of her generation. Ambitious and clever, she completed high school and Teachers College before working for social welfare agencies helping the mass of recent immigrants to integrate into American life. There she met, and in 1903 married, Charles Henry Israels, an architect of Dutch descent, and began to specialize in providing playgrounds for slum children. She was instrumental in getting much regulatory law covering workplace, tenement housing and places of recreation through the New York legislature. The Triangle Shirtwaist Factory fire, which killed some 147 young women in 1911, told a shocked nation the importance of her work and redoubled her commitment, despite the fact that the early death of her husband that same year left her alone to support three children. She became an expert on factory legislation and in 1914 married another former associate in settlement work, Dr Henry Moskowitz. Hitherto she had been essentially non-partisan. But when Al Smith ran for governor of New York in 1918 she chaired the women's section of his campaign committee and began a relationship which was vastly influential to both of them and lasted the rest of her life. Not only did she attract many votes from outside the Democratic party; more important, she reorganized the whole structure of New York government in the next ten years and became governor Smith's most trusted adviser on social and economic problems, though never in the public eye. 'I read a book once,' Smith explained. 'It was called Belle Moskovitch.' The relationship between them personified the fact that as urban reformers became more realistic, so machine politicians became more responsible. Though she died prematurely following an accident in 1933, and did not live to see her local agenda become national during the New Deal, her legacy ranks with that of Jane Addams and Frances Perkins.

Murphy, Charles F. (1872–1924): Born in New York of poor Irish immigrants, Charles Francis Murphy left school before graduating to do a series of manual jobs in and around the city's dockyards. He organized a successful boys' baseball team and opened a saloon which became headquarters for the team and his street gang. His political career was based on the contacts this brought him, and the work he did on behalf of dockers, gas workers, clerks and other politicians who lived on the lower east side. He became a ward leader of the Democratic party machine, Tammany Hall, at 24 and mayor Van Wyck appointed him dock commissioner when he was under 30. Like his predecessors, Murphy used this office to grant lucrative contracts to Tammany supporters. But though this was the only salaried political office he ever held, Murphy used it to take control of Tammany when political scandal forced Richard

Croker to retire in 1901. Under his leadership Tammany was transformed for a time into a more responsive, and responsible, political organization than it had been under Croker or Tweed. The 'new Tammany', as it was called, controlled the politics of the city, and often of the state, and in 1918 helped Al Smith become an outstanding reforming governor; a post he held until after Murphy's death.

Norris, George (1861–1944): George Norris was one of the leaders of the midwestern Progressive movement, who represented Nebraska as a Republican in the House from 1903 until 1913 and in the Senate from 1913 until 1943. He embraced central Progressive beliefs about the need to regulate public services in the public interest and was public spokesman for his generation of the need to generate power through hydro-electric dam projects. He was legislative father of the Tennessee Valley Authority, and the first dam built on the Tennessee River by TVA in 1934 was named Norris Dam. Like all midwestern Progressives he was an isolationist in foreign affairs.

Nye, Gerald P. (1892–1971): Born in Wisconsin, Gerald P. Nye began his career as a journalist in Iowa, but between 1924 and 1940 was one of the most influential Progressives in the Senate. He certainly maintained a high profile. A Republican elected from North Dakota, he led the Progressives within the party after making his name aged only 32 as chairman of the Senate committee which investigated the Teapot Dome affair, the most notorious political scandal of the 1920s. An eloquent spokesman for midwestern isolationism, he chaired the Senate committee which in 1933–34 investigated the part the US munitions industry had played in bringing America into war in 1917. The Nye committee failed to find much damaging evidence that pressure from arms dealers was responsible for US declaration of war in April 1917 and he lost influence after Pearl Harbor, leaving the Senate in 1945.

O'Neill, Eugene (1888–1953): The only American playwright to win the Nobel prize for literature, Eugene O'Neill wrote tragedies, often in classical mode. He had tasted the bitterness of life before he was 30. Born into an unhappy New York stage family, he left Princeton after one term and quickly became a jobless alcoholic who tried suicide and caught TB. While in hospital he started to write a play and found the occupation which was his salvation. After four years producing for Provincetown Players, his first Broadway play won him a Pulitzer prize in 1920, and the dozen plays he wrote before 1930 made his reputation. Thereafter he lived the life of a recluse in California and Georgia with his third wife Carlotta Monterey and wrote his only comedy (and most performed play) *Ah, Wilderness!* The Nobel prize came in 1936 and, despite suffering a degenerative nervous disorder, he completed his most acclaimed work, the tragedy *Long Day's Journey Into Night,* between 1935 and 1943. 'I love life,' he explained, 'But I don't love life because it is pretty . . . There is beauty to me even in its ugliness.'

Palmer, A. Mitchell (1872–1936): A Quaker born in Pennsylvania, Alexander Mitchell Palmer studied law on graduating from Swarthmore in 1892 and was elected as a Democratic congressman from 1909 until 1912, running unsuccessfully for the Senate in 1916. Appointed attorney general by Woodrow Wilson in 1919, he attacked price fixing and the trusts because he believed they caused wartime and postwar profiteering. He became notorious for the 'Palmer raids' of 1919–20, when some 10,000 anarchists, socialists and communists were arrested and hundreds jailed or deported, essentially for their political views. He also helped break the 1919 steel strike by vigorous use of injunctions. When he failed to win his party's nomination for president in 1920 he retired from public life and returned to practising law.

Peek, George M. (1873–1943): A midwestern agricultural expert, George Peek made his name between 1917 and 1918 as a member of the war industries board headed by Bernard Baruch. He then moved to Illinois as head of an agricultural implements corporation named Moline Plow. Throughout the 1920s he was closely associated with the farm bloc, which sought to save agriculture from adverse terms of trade by a mixture of favourable legislation and raising farm prices. Peek helped persuade Congress to pass the McNary-Haugen bill in 1927 and 1928. This would have dumped US farm surpluses abroad to sustain domestic price levels, but commerce secretary Herbert Hoover opposed it and president Calvin Coolidge vetoed it twice. After the agricultural and industrial catastrophe of 1929–33, FDR made Peek head of AAA, where he insisted that dumping surpluses was still the answer, and resisted Tugwell's more radical policy of subsidy to restrict supply. Defeated over policy, he resigned from AAA in 1934 and became adviser to an export–import bank which financed the dumping of US farm surpluses overseas.

Pendergast, Thomas J. (1872–1945): Born into a family which ran the politics of Kansas City, Missouri, Thomas Joseph Pendergast took control of the state's Democratic party machine in 1907 and held it until he was convicted on corruption charges in 1940. Unlike many Democratic party political bosses, he supported Franklin Roosevelt at the 1932 presidential convention. But like other local politicians, he benefited from the federal patronage the New Deal brought through its vast public works programmes.

His family concrete company built all the federally aided public buildings in the city, and his political machine sent Harry Truman to the Senate in 1934. As with other corrupt local political leaders like Curley, Crump and Hague, Roosevelt happily worked with him until 1938 when Pendergast's power began to wane and the president authorized federal investigation of an insurance swindle which had made Pendergast $750,000. Jailed for fifteen months, he died waiting for a presidential pardon which never came.

Perkins, Frances (1880–1965): Born in Boston, Frances Perkins was one of a generation of women active during the Progressive period in the cause of social justice, in particular the control of economic exploitation of child and female labour. Her work took her away from her native Massachusetts to Chicago and New York, where she was angered by the 1911 Triangle Shirtwaist Company fire which claimed the lives of 147 young women sweatshop workers. Her lobbying helped secure a 54-hour work week and her friendship with Al Smith, Robert Wagner and Franklin Roosevelt gave her influential contacts within the Democratic party. As governor of New York, Smith made her industrial commissioner in 1928, a post she retained when Roosevelt succeeded Smith. As president, FDR made her secretary of labor, the first woman to serve in cabinet. She held this post until Roosevelt died, and became one of his most influential and trusted advisers. She insisted that the codes in Title I of the NIRA cover minimum wages, maximum hours and health and safety regulations, and she was active in backing Harry Hopkins in the CCC and FERA. Under her leadership the labor department intervened more effectively to regulate and control working conditions, and she initiated 'contract compliance', whereby employers seeking government contracts had to meet minimum conditions. The 1938 Fair Labor Standards Act outlawed child labour and set enforceable national minimum wages and maximum hours, which she defended through the period of the war economy between 1940 and 1945.

Randolph, A. Philip (1889–1979): Asa Philip Randolph was known as 'the grand old man of the African-American labour movement' while he was still in his fifties because his service to black workers was so significant and unstinting. Born in Florida he went to City College, New York, and while working part time as a porter in 1917 organized a union of elevator operators in the city. With Chandler Owen, Randolph published *The Messenger*, a socialist magazine aimed at the working class, which attracted the attention of socialist labour leaders like Debs and anti-socialist ones like Gompers. An outspoken opponent of segregated unions, he taught at the Rand School and ran several times for mayor as a socialist. His real work began in 1925 when he helped found the United Brotherhood of Sleeping Car Porters, a segregated union for black workers, and spent twelve years struggling to secure recognition from the Pullman Company, which finally signed a collective bargaining agreement in 1937. Even more significant was the 1941 March on Washington by black workers in all industries, which Randolph organized and called off only when president Roosevelt issued Executive Order 8802, which established the Fair Employment Practice Committee as a first step towards ending racial discrimination in war industries. Little progress had been made on this by 1945, or indeed by 1963, when Randolph helped organize another March on Washington to demand real equality for black Americans.

Reuther, Walter (1907–70): Born in Wheeling, West Virginia of a German father, Walter Reuther began as apprentice tool and die maker for Wheeling Steel in 1924 but moved to Ford Motors in Detroit in 1927, becoming foreman in 1931. He studied at Wayne University and with his brother Victor cycled across Europe and into the Soviet Union, where he worked for a Ford subsidiary in 1934. Returning to the US he became a key rank-and-file activist in the upsurge of CIO and UAW unionization which characterized the New Deal, was blacklisted by Ford and beaten up by Ford thugs in 1937. During the war his reputation rose rapidly as the most effective and creative labour leader of his generation, advocating production reform to build 500 planes a day and serving on government war economy boards. When Sidney Hillman died in 1946 Reuther was his obvious long-term successor, and the 113-day strike he led at GM in 1946 raised his profile. That same year he survived an attempt on his life, and by 1947 had taken control of the UAW. As president he played a leading part expelling communists and pioneered long-term binding contracts with Chrysler, GM and Ford which became the basis of US postwar industrial relations.

Robinson, Joe (1872–1937): Born on a farm in Arkansas, Joseph Taylor Robinson went to the state university and Virginia Law School before practising law from 1895 until 1902, when he was elected to Congress. He served in the House until November 1912, when he was elected governor, but went to the US Senate on 28 January 1913 and remained there until his death. Hard-working, aggressive, temperamental, Joe Robinson began as a southern Populist backing W.J. Bryan in 1896, but became a friend of Bernard Baruch, and balanced Al Smith's presidential ticket as a southern conservative in 1928. Senate majority leader when the Democrats took control in 1933, he played a leading part in persuading Congress to pass 16 major laws during the first New

Deal, but instinctively opposed the whole direction of New Deal policy towards deficit finance, more federal and presidential authority, public power projects like TVA and so on. He was especially hostile to Eleanor Roosevelt's political activities on behalf of black Americans. Nevertheless, when FDR tried to reform the Supreme Court in 1937 he worked loyally in a lost cause. His death of a heart attack on 14 July effectively killed the 'court-packing' bill.

Rockefeller, John D. (1839–1937): John Davison Rockefeller did more than anyone to shape the era of finance capitalism which emerged in the US between 1910 and 1945. He organized the US oil industry, after the first rich oil reserves had been discovered in Pennsylvania in 1859, and came to control 90 per cent of it; he created the first trust, Standard Oil; he became easily the richest man in America, accumulating more than $500 million before he died; he endowed millions to education and private foundations. Frugal, gentle and single-minded in private life, he also debauched local and national politics by wholesale bribery and corruption; evaded the law; and used fraud and force to smash powerless people who stood in his way. The 20th April 1914 Ludlow massacre, in which state troops killed 17 women and children of his striking coalminers in tented encampments in Colorado, led to federal government enquiries into industrial relations during the Progressive era and made his name hated by millions of Americans. By then Rockefeller had been retired for two years, and when he died aged 98 laws had been enacted which partially controlled the forces he and capitalists like him had unleashed. By then he had become a legend, the symbol of American free enterprise and the price it exacted.

Rogers, Will (1879–1935): Between 1910 and 1935 Will Rogers was one of the best-known and best-loved public figures in America. Born of wealthy Irish-Cherokee parents in the Indian territory of what became Oklahoma, he went briefly to military academy before joining a circus as a rope and riding artist. East coast audiences laughed at his southwestern accent and patter so that by 1912 he was a vaudeville star. By 1920 his rumpled cowboy clothes and skills had become simply the background to his real talent: homespun aphorisms and sardonic comments on the news, more penetrating and far less wordy than those which had made the newspaper columnist Mr Dooley famous during the Progressive era. For example, 'My ancestors didn't come over on the *Mayflower* – they met the boat'; or, on events in Paris in 1919, 'The US never lost a war or won a peace conference'; or of Coolidge's bull market, 'Two-thirds of the people promote while one-third provide'; or, of the 1932 Pecora investigation, 'A holding company is someone you give your coat to while the police search you'; or 'I don't belong to any organized political party. I'm a Democrat.' In 1932 he won 22 votes at the Democratic presidential convention. He wrote syndicated newspaper columns, broadcast radio talks and made films, dying in his prime in an air crash. Little survives in film or sound of his unique talent, though there is a magnificent statue of the greatest political humorist of his generation in the Capitol building, Washington DC.

Roosevelt, Eleanor A. (1884–1962): Born into one of America's most socially prominent families, miserably unhappy in childhood, married to a cousin who became president and greatest leader of twentieth century democracy, Eleanor Anna Roosevelt is the only first lady in history to have played a significant political role of her own. Her father was an alcoholic and both her parents had died by the time she was 10. Sent to school in Britain, she became a confident adult who followed the paternalistic Roosevelt tradition as a settlement house worker, when she met and married her distant cousin Franklin in 1905. She bore him four sons and two daughters while providing the base for his political career, and then had to relive earlier rejection upon discovery of her husband's serious love affair with Lucy Mercer in 1917. FDR's electoral defeat in 1920 and polio in 1921 were further blows, although she was freer in the 1920s to fulfil a public career supporting women's rights, labour unions and black equality. When Franklin was elected governor of New York in 1928, and president in 1932, she did not abandon her own political career, though it was clear in the 1930s that her opinions on public affairs were far to the left of his. With his usual cleverness, FDR took credit from blacks, liberals and socialists, while assuring conservatives that he could not stop his wife using First Amendment freedoms. She survived him by 17 years, remaining an outspoken champion of women's rights, racial equality and labour unions and a power within the inner circle of Democratic party leadership.

Roosevelt, Franklin D. (1882–1945): Of Dutch landowning descent and a distant cousin of Theodore Roosevelt, Franklin Delano Roosevelt (FDR) went to Groton, Harvard and Columbia Law School before marrying Eleanor, another cousin, and entering politics in 1910. Elected as a Democrat to the New York legislature with Al Smith and Robert F. Wagner, he was Woodrow Wilson's assistant secretary of the navy from 1913 and James M. Cox's running mate on the losing 1920 presidential ticket. Polio struck in 1921 and forced him to use painful leg braces and a wheelchair for the rest of his life. But the onset of polio took him out of public life at a crucial period between 1921 and 1924. With southern bigots and northern machine politicians struggling for control of the party, he was spared the need to take sides until he could return to public life. When Smith lost the 1928 presidential race, FDR won the governorship of New York and the presidency in 1932 as economic catastrophe made Democrats electable again. He promised 'a New Deal' but had little idea what this meant. Mastery of press conference and radio broadcasting helped him restore the nation's morale, but FDR was essentially a pragmatic opportunist. He chose economic salvation through reflation not out of conviction but as the net result of improvisation as 16 major laws passed Congress in three months – the most astonishing burst of legislation in US history. This attempt to plan agriculture, business, finance and industry meant government spending fuelled recovery. Yet Roosevelt had promised to cut the cost of government by 25 per cent. Though the Supreme Court declared much of the early New Deal unconstitutional, Congress passed more careful reforms in 1935 and FDR's re-election in 1936 was the largest popular victory in history. Failing to reform the Supreme Court, Roosevelt redeemed his 1932 pledge in 1937–38 and slashed public spending. Unemployment rose steeply – and this time people called it 'the Roosevelt recession'. Converted to the virtues of deficit finance, FDR presented his 1940 budget in Keynesian context, while after Pearl Harbor in 1941 all restraint on spending went as the US was finally drawn into the world conflict. FDR was as inspired a leader in war as in peace. His 1941 Four Freedoms speech set the agenda for democratic nations, while his government supplied British and Soviet allies, fought in Africa, Europe and the Pacific, and secretly developed the atomic bomb. FDR insisted Germany and Japan surrender unconditionally, and though critics later charged he had been outmanoeuvred by Stalin, the fact was that a nation demoralized when he took power in 1933 dominated the world's economic, financial, military and political affairs when he died on the eve of victory in April 1945. This was the legacy of a great president and key figure in twentieth-century world history.

Roosevelt, Theodore (1858–1919): Theodore Roosevelt (TR) was asthmatic and short-sighted as a child. Much of his life was spent overcompensating for these handicaps in hectic sporting activities and outdoor life. He loved nature, but was also a keen hunter (the 'Teddy bear' is named after him) and voracious reader. Graduating with the coveted Phi Beta Kappa from Harvard in 1880, he combined physical activities with literary ones, writing many books and forming friendships with men of letters like Rudyard Kipling, whose phrase 'take up the white man's burden' was coined with the US and TR in mind. 'Bristling with buck teeth and jingoism', as one observer put it, Roosevelt believed in both imperialism and social reform throughout his vigorous political career. This began in state politics and continued in the US civil service, and later as New York police commissioner, where he was an effective reformer and foe of corruption. Assistant secretary of the navy in 1897, he urged war with Spain and won fame as leader of the 'Rough Riders' in Cuba. Republican party bosses, fearful of his liberalism and national reputation, kicked him upstairs as William McKinley's vice president in 1901. But when within months McKinley was assassinated, 'that damned cowboy', as the Republican party old guard called him, became, at 42, the youngest president in history. He personified the crucial transition from Mugwump reformism to Progressivism, and used the White House as a 'bully pulpit' to attack trusts, expose corrupt political bosses, limit labour unions and generally regulate and control the economy. For helping end the Russo-Japanese war in 1905 he won the Nobel peace prize and left office in 1909 as the most popular president in living memory. He went big-game hunting in Africa ('I trust some lion will do his duty' said one political opponent), but became bored in retirement, and alarmed when the Ballinger-Pinchot affair showed that his successor Taft was letting speculators imperil conservation. He sought his party's nomination in 1912 but, failing to get it, ran as Progressive candidate on the New Nationalism platform, splitting the Republican vote and letting Woodrow Wilson win. Having confirmed his party's fears, he roamed the wings of the political stage, growling against Wilson's policies, before dying in 1919. His is one of four presidential faces carved on Mount Rushmore.

Smith, Alfred E. (1873–1944): Known as 'the hero of the cities' and 'the happy warrior', Al Smith's political career exemplified the emergence of urban America. Born of Catholic parents on the lower east side of New York, he dropped out of high school and ran errands for a saloon keeper and Democratic precinct leader. Tammany Hall votes sent him to represent the city in the Albany state legislature in 1903, where he made his name leading the investigation into the 1911 Triangle Shirtwaist Company fire in which 147 young women died. Its findings transformed Smith from a machine politician into a social reformer, and working-class votes made him New York's governor in 1918. Beaten in the Republican sweep of 1920, Smith was re-elected in 1922, 1924 and 1926. In these years he reorganized government, reformed public housing, parks and welfare, and supported the rights of labour unions to organize and bargain collectively, while cutting the cost of government. No governor in the Union could match his record when he ran for president against Herbert Hoover in 1928. But hatred of him as a Catholic, anti-Prohibitionist and working-class New Yorker, which had ruined his bid to become his party's candidate in 1924, made his national campaign in 1928 an ordeal from which, in a sense, he never recovered. He carried only eight states (and lost in New York), but was the first Democrat to win majorities in the dozen largest cities in the US – the base on which his party built its national dominance between 1933 and 1945. Denied the Democratic presidential nomination in 1932, he fell out with Roosevelt during his campaign, pursued business interests in the 1930s and became a bitter opponent of the New Deal, voting for Alf Landon in 1936 and Wendell Willkie in 1940.

Stimson, Henry L. (1867–1950): Born in New York to a prosperous professional family, Henry Lewis Stimson was part of the east coast conservative establishment which ran public affairs, especially foreign affairs, during his lifetime. After Yale University and Harvard Law School, Stimson became a successful trial lawyer who helped President Theodore Roosevelt prosecute trusts between 1906 and 1909. In 1911 TR's successor Taft made him secretary of war, but he left government service to enlist as an artillery officer in the first world war. He worked as a government lawyer and negotiator in foreign affairs in the 1920s, and was Herbert Hoover's secretary of state between 1929 and 1933, signing the 1930 London naval treaty and responding ineffectively to Japan's annexation of Manchukuo in 1931. Alarmed by the way America's military weakness hindered any effective response to Japanese aggression in China, and alarmed also by the rise of fascism, Nazism and militarism in the 1930s, Stimson recommended rearmament to a nation preoccupied with domestic problems. FDR made him secretary of war in 1940 when he worked with general George C. Marshall organizing victory. He was responsible for the internment of Japanese-Americans in concentration camps after 1941, oversaw the Manhattan Project which developed the atomic bomb and, after reading a special committee report on its use, advised President Truman to drop the bomb on Hiroshima and Nagasaki in August 1945. He then retired and lived in Long Island until his death.

Taft, William H. (1857–1930): Born in Cincinnati, Ohio, William Howard Taft is the only man in history to have been both president and chief justice, a remarkable achievement in itself and even more so for a man who once wrote, 'Politics, when I am in it, makes me sick.' After Yale and Cincinnati Law School he practised law, became active in Republican politics and from 1900 until 1904 was governor of the Philippines which the US had just captured from Spain and made a colony. Taft set those strategically vital islands on the road to self-rule, which they secured in 1945. Theodore Roosevelt made him secretary of war between 1904 and 1909, when Taft succeeded him. Taft was the heaviest president in history, but TR believed he lacked political weight and by 1910 had become so bitterly opposed to his conduct in office, especially over the Ballinger-Pinchot affair, that he ran against him in 1912, split the Republican vote and let Wilson win. Yet Taft's was an effective administration, winning more than twice as many anti-trust suits as TR had done, creating the parcel post and overseeing passage of the 16th and 17th Amendments for federal income tax and direct election of senators. Warren Harding made him chief justice in 1921, the only appointment he had ever really craved, and he led the Court during its most conservative phase this century.

Taylor, Frederick Winslow (1856–1915): Though dead by 1915, Frederick Winslow Taylor's influence on US industrial production methods between 1910 and 1945 was profoundly important. The son of a lawyer, he was born in Philadelphia. Educated partly in France, he spent 18 months travelling in Europe before entering Harvard law school, graduating in 1874. Poor eyesight made him abandon further study, and by 1878 he was labouring in a Philadelphia steel mill. With Clarence M. Clark he was US doubles champion at lawn tennis in 1881 while studying for an engineering degree at night school. He became his firm's chief engineer in 1884, after which he evolved his doctrine of scientific work study, which measured the time, cost and efficiency of every production task. This became the theory behind US methods of mass production, and as consultant to Bethlehem Steel he devoted the rest of his working life to publishing the many papers in scientific and technical journals which made both his name and the doctrine which became known as Taylorism. This took on the force of secular religion with many great industrialists and manufacturers, and guided the approach of Henry Ford and others. Taylor's special field was machine tools and concrete manufacture and the Society to Promote the Science of Management, established in 1911, was renamed the Taylor Society after his death.

Thomas, Elbert D. (1883–1953): Classically educated and a Mormon missionary to Japan between 1907 and 1912, Elbert Duncan Thomas was professor of political science at the University of Utah, when he was elected to the Senate as a Democrat from Utah in 1932. He is notable for the amendment he introduced to the Agricultural Adjustment Act which the Roosevelt administration was trying to rush through Congress in 1933 to reform American farming in time for the new growing season. The Thomas amendment conferred on the president power to expand the money supply by issuing more greenbacks, remonetizing silver and reducing the gold content of the dollar. This conceded the central belief of the Populist party, which had merged with the Democrats when Thomas was a teenager in 1896. In the 1930s it provided the crucial financial opening for America to choose a reflationary, rather than a deflationary, path out of economic depression and was thus a key decision in the early New Deal.

Thomas, Norman M. (1884–1968): The best-known and most articulate socialist of his generation, Norman Matoon Thomas joined the movement in 1917, the very date when, after an auspicious start, American socialism started into irreversible decline. Born in Ohio, valedictorian at Princeton, he was the third generation of his family to enter the Presbyterian ministry where his work for the Social Gospel movement in the slums of New York revealed 'grotesque inequalities ... exploitation and unnecessary poverty all about me'. This shaped his socialist beliefs, while his pacifism meant opposition to American involvement in the first world war and forced resignation from his ministry. He edited *The World Tomorrow* and *The New Leader*, wrote dozens of books, ran for governor of New York in 1924, and for mayor of the city in 1925. He succeeded Eugene Debs, when he died in 1926, as leader of the Socialist Party of America. An outspoken supporter of public works, shorter hours, unemployment insurance, retirement pensions, the abolition of child labour, slum clearance, public housing, agricultural relief, wealth taxes and the nationalization of basic industries, he fiercely opposed rearmament and racial discrimination. Much of this agenda was seized by the Democrats between 1933 and 1945, but Thomas ran for president every four years between 1932 and 1948. After Pearl Harbor he supported US war aims, though attacking internment of Japanese-Americans, and lived to see the US adopt an American version of the welfare state.

Truman, Harry S. (1884–1972): A fiesty, no-nonsense little man, Truman had the authentic tang of character. His middle initial stood for nothing. Since his paternal grandfather's name was Anderson Shippe Truman, and his maternal grandfather's name was Solomon Young, Harry's parents decided on 'S' – a compromise appropriate to a politician from Missouri, a state created by a political compromise in 1820. There was no thought of politics at first. After high school he started life as a haberdasher, served with distinction in the first world war, then went bankrupt in his late thirties and turned for help to Tom Pendergast, whose family had run the politics of Kansas City, Missouri, since the 1870s. Elected to the US Senate in 1934, Truman made his name investigating government defence spending scandals during the second world war, and when Roosevelt decided to drop Henry Wallace as his running mate in 1944 he picked Truman as a border state politician to win crucial moderate support. Though Truman had resisted civil rights legislation, his support for high wages and welfare was enough to win endorsement from the CIO. Despite the fact that FDR was terminally ill in 1944, no one prepared Truman to take over the presidency when FDR died on 12 April. He knew nothing of the atomic bomb, for example, yet had to take an immediate decision on its use. Equally serious, between 1945 and 1947, the new president had to refashion US foreign policy with the onset of the Cold War, and was much in the hands of the east coast foreign affairs elite, especially George C. Marshall and Dean Acheson. The resulting Truman doctrine, announced in 1947, which pledged resistance to Communist subversion or aggression around the world, became the basis of US foreign policy until the end of the Cold War in 1990.

Tugwell, Rexford G. (1891–1979): Like Raymond Moley and Adolph Berle, Rexford Guy Tugwell was a professor of political economy at Columbia who joined Franklin Roosevelt's staff during his 1932 campaign and became the most influential member of the Brains Trust. Born in New York, he took his Ph.D. at the University of Pennsylvania and made his name with six books on managing twentieth-century economies. He was an expert on agricultural economics and made policy for secretary of agriculture Henry A. Wallace when the AAA was established. Tugwell's crucial contribution was to see that chronic farm surpluses could only be solved when the Western world was in severe economic depression by paying American farmers to produce less through subsidy. This subsidy was raised by levying a tax on those who processed farm products for sale. But in the 1936 *Butler* case the Supreme Court ruled this was unconstitutional. Nevertheless, because farm subsidies clearly worked, and farmers favoured them, Congress found ways round the Court's decision and agricultural subsidy became a permanent part of federal farm policy until 1945, and indeed until the 1990s. In 1935 Tugwell became head of FDR's Resettlement Administration, which dealt with social problems created by the Dust Bowl, flood control, dam building and the collapse of the sharecropping system of agricultural production. Tugwell left Roosevelt's administration in 1937, becoming chairman of the New York planning commission, chancellor of the University of Puerto Rico and in 1941 governor of Puerto Rico, where he remained until 1945. His best-known book, *The Stricken Land*, was published in 1946.

Wallace, Henry A. (1888–1965): Son of Henry C. Wallace (see below) and grandson of the founder of *Wallace's Farmer*, Henry Agard Wallace's reputation as a radical began when, as FDR's secretary of agriculture, he was in charge of the revolution in agricultural planning and spending policy brought about by the New Deal. He managed to work harmoniously with Tugwell, Frank and Davis at the AAA, and to get round the Supreme Court ruling against the AAA in the 1936 *Butler* case. His problems also included rescuing agricultural land literally blown away during the Dust Bowl years of the 1930s. He succeeded Garner as vice president when Roosevelt won a third term in 1940, but was replaced by Truman in 1944. Wallace ran as a Progressive for president in 1948, favouring *rapprochement* with the Soviet Union, and describing his era as 'the century of the common man'.

Wallace, Henry C. (1866–1924): Editor of *Wallace's Farmer*, which his father founded during the years of agricultural unrest after 1873, Henry Cantwell Wallace was secretary of agriculture in the Harding-Coolidge administrations between 1921 and 1923. Though he died in 1924, he tried to tackle the chronic problem of declining land, crop and livestock prices by setting up a bureau of agricultural economics and backing the McNary-Haugen bill (which related farm prices to those between 1910 and 1914, when farming had been prosperous). This concept of parity remained a key feature of agricultural policy and economics until 1945 and beyond.

Washington, Booker T. (1859–1915): Though Booker T. Washington died in 1915 he exercised great influence over the generation of Afro-Americans who flourished between 1910 and 1945. Born a plantation slave, he spent his teenage years working as a labourer, but through enormous effort gave himself an education and rose to become spokesman for black Americans and counsellor to two presidents. Graduating from a Virginian agricultural institute, he taught school, but his commanding presence and speaking voice won the attention of black crowds and leaders alike, and in 1881 he was asked to head Tuskeegee Institute. Under his leadership, Tuskeegee transformed itself from a shanty into the nation's foremost centre of vocational training for black Americans. Washington taught the prudent, *petit bourgeois* virtues of thrift, industry, self-help and accommodation to white supremacy. His creed has been summarized as follows: 'Do not antagonize the white majority. Do not ask for the right to vote. Do not fight for civil liberties, or against segregation. Go to school. Work hard. Some day the other things may come.' The most influential black leader to emerge after the civil war, the last years of his life saw that leadership challenged by younger and more assertive rivals such as W.E.B. Du Bois. Du Bois launched the Niagara Movement to promote 'the talented tenth', an elite group of black activists who helped found the biracial NAACP in 1910 to pursue integrationist goals.

White, Harry Dexter (1892–1948): Born in Boston of Russian parents on 9 October 1892, Harry Dexter White took a Ph.D from Harvard in 1930 and was an influential economist during the New Deal. Appointed assistant director of research at the US treasury in 1934, he became director of monetary research there in 1940, as the economy was being shifted rapidly on to a war basis, special assistant to secretary of the treasury Henry Morgenthau in 1942 and assistant secretary the following year. Each successive step revealed how much the Keynesian economic ideas he shared with Lauchlin Currie at the White House, and Marriner Eccles at the Federal Reserve, were gaining ground over the orthodox budget balancing finance of Morgenthau himself. He was finally assistant secretary of the treasury in 1945–46 and is generally regarded, with Keynes, as architect of the Bretton Woods agreement, establishing the policy and institutions on which the postwar world economy was based. He was director of one of these institutions, the International Monetary Fund, from 1946 until 1947 but, as an influential New Dealer, fell under suspicion of the House Un-American Activities Committee in 1948, and died of a second heart attack as it was beginning its fateful investigation of former state department employee Alger Hiss on 18 August 1948.

White, Walter Francis (1893–1955): Born in Atlanta, Georgia, of a postman father one-fourth African-American and schoolteacher mother one-sixteenth, Walter White was blue-eyed, blond and so pale skinned he could have passed for white. But when a white mob terrorized his home in the 1906 Atlanta race riot, he knew that his destiny was to fight for equality and justice for black Americans. His Congregational background was intensely religious, and though denied access to Georgia's segregated high schools he went to Atlanta College prep school, taking his BA at the college in 1916. He then led a protest which stopped plans to pay for a new white high school by eliminating seventh grade from Atlanta's black schools and founded a city branch of the National Association for the Advancement of Colored People. This attracted the attention of NAACP national leaders, and by 1918 he was working in the New York office. Race relations were very bad in the 1920s, and White investigated more than 40 lynchings and eight race riots, publishing *Rope and Faggot: A Biography of Judge Lynch* in 1929. By then he had become acting secretary of the NAACP and in 1931 was appointed executive secretary. He played a key role in sustaining the NAACP through a period when civil rights played second fiddle to wider economic questions and war. His great aim was to make lynching a federal crime, but though two such bills passed the House, the Senate rejected them and president Roosevelt, fearful of losing crucial southern support, refused to back them. However, with A. Philip Randolph, the black railwaymen's leader, White did force FDR to issue the landmark 1941 executive order prohibiting racial discrimination in defence industries and creating the influential Fair Employment Practice Committee. His efforts to establish civil rights and end school segregation through the courts in the 1940s bore fruit later. He was also deeply interested in race relations in India and the West Indies, attended in 1921 the Pan-African Congress and advised the US delegation at San Francisco when the United Nations was founded in 1945. Despite deep differences with W.E.B. Du Bois, who became an advocate of separate black development in the 1930s, he rehired Du Bois for the NAACP in 1944 when Atlanta University fired him. Acknowledged as 'one of the ablest lobbyists in the Capital' and 'the most potent leader of his race in the US' he was a prolific journalist and author of many books.

White, William Allen (1868–1944): Born in Emporia, Kansas, William Allen White became the most influential midwestern journalist of his generation. He studied at the state university and by 1895 was owner and editor of the *Emporia Gazette.* He made his name in 1896 with an article denouncing Populism headed 'What's the matter with Kansas?' but supported Theodore Roosevelt's brand of Progressivism and through syndicated columns was by 1920 an important local and national opinion former. His biography of Woodrow Wilson and the two he wrote of Calvin Coolidge sold well: the latter in particular, entitled *A Puritan in Babylon,* is still the best study of the thirtieth president. A Progressive Republican in the 1930s, White supported much New Deal legislation, especially social security, the Wagner Act, banking and stock market regulation, and liked Roosevelt personally. But he endorsed Alf Landon in 1936 and was highly critical of FDR's abortive bill to 'pack' the Supreme Court in 1937. By then, as war beckoned, his columns increasingly criticized Republican isolationism and he chaired a national committee to aid Britain and France in 1940.

Willkie, Wendell (1892–1944): Born in a small town in Indiana, Wendell Willkie graduated from the state university in 1913, studied at Oberlin College in 1916 and was admitted to the Indiana bar the same year. He practised law in Indiana until 1920, and in New York until 1930, when he became president of Commonwealth and Southern, an electric power utility corporation. When the Roosevelt administration created the Tennessee Valley Authority in 1933, Willkie became the most persistent and resourceful opponent of the federal government's policy of building dams to generate hydro-electric power and sell it at rates private utilities could not match. David Lilienthal, also from Indiana, was more than a match for Willkie, and by 1938 had won the political struggle over public power. Nevertheless, his opposition to a key New Deal programme won the support of rank-and-file Republicans, who nominated him on the sixth ballot at the party's Philadelphia convention in 1940. The last of the 'dark horse' presidential candidates, Willkie won more votes than any Republican before and more states than Hoover in 1932. After defeat Willkie went on a 59-day world tour and returned to write *One World*, a book about what the US must do after winning the war. It sold a million copies in the year its author died.

Wilson, Thomas Woodrow (1856–1924): Son of a Presbyterian minister, Woodrow Wilson was born in Virginia, grew up in the south and read history at Princeton and law at the University of Virginia. He took his Ph.D. at Johns Hopkins and taught history there and at Princeton, writing several standard works on history, government and politics. As president of Princeton from 1902 until 1910 he transformed a snobbish, second-rate university into one with a world reputation, and was elected Democratic governor of New Jersey in 1910, where he was an effective Progressive reformer. He won his party's nomination for US president in 1912 on the forty-sixth ballot and, with the Republicans hopelessly split, went to the White House in 1913. His campaigning about the New Freedom promised to break private monopolies and restore free competition, and his first term crowned the Progressive reform movement, reducing the tariff for the first time since the civil war, establishing the Federal Reserve Board, initiating federal income tax and reforming and regulating trade and commerce. The outbreak of war in Europe in 1914 cut short his domestic programme and increasingly came to dominate the rest of his public life. His formidable intellect was combined with pious Christian morality and idealism, and he wished America to stay out of war but impose peace afterwards. Yet his lifelong pro-British sympathies were clear. When Germany repeatedly violated this one-sided neutrality, he reluctantly asked Congress to declare war on 6 April 1917. US intervention helped stop German victory on the western front in March–September 1918, but though Germany capitulated on 11 November 1918 on the basis of Wilson's Fourteen Points, he was outmanoeuvred at the Paris peace conference by Clemenceau and Lloyd George, and signed a punitive treaty which was the negation of his ideals. Worse was to follow. The Senate refused to ratify the treaty or join the League of Nations, Wilson suffered a serious stroke in 1919–20 and left office a broken man, despite having won the Nobel peace prize in 1920.

Wright, Frank Lloyd (1867–1959): The twentieth century's most celebrated American architect, Frank Lloyd Wright was born in

Wisconsin, son of a travelling preacher and musician. He studied at the state university, though without gaining a degree in architecture, and aged 26 became an associate of the established architect Louis Sullivan in Chicago. Wright's 'prairie school' began the trend towards open living, in which one room flows into another, so characteristic of US homes; and he then developed the concept of 'organic architecture', where a building seemed to grow out of its environment. He built his home, school and studio at Taliesin in Wisconsin, holding court there each year for his many admirers. Wright's many public buildings include the Imperial Hotel in Tokyo, which survived the 1923 earthquake, the Unitarian Church in Madison, Wisconsin and the Guggenheim Museum in New York, completed after his death.

Wright, Orville (1871–1948): and Wilbur (1867–1912): Two Ohio brothers achieved mankind's eternal dream of heavier-than-air powered flight at Kitty Hawk, North Carolina, on 17 December 1903. Self-educated sons of a Christian minister, they personified good, old-fashioned American know-how. As young men, they hand-built a large press to enter the printing industry, then opened a bicycle factory and shop. As the race to powered flight quickened after 1900 the Wright brothers saw that all previous attempts had been based on conceptual error. The central problem was not how to 'ride the air' but one of control. By building dozens of large kites and unmanned gliders in their cycle workshop, testing them in what were effectively the world's first wind tunnels, and finally flying them extensively, they developed a three-dimensional system of control around lateral, vertical and horizontal axes which still operates in all winged aircraft today. Adding their own four-cylinder engine, they took the Flyer overland to Kitty Hawk sand dunes and tossed the coin which gave Orville the honour of flying 835 feet in 59 seconds before five witnesses and a camera. They were aviation designers, builders and promoters as air power grew to dominate geopolitics between 1910 and 1945, and though Wilbur died of typhoid in 1912, Orville lived to see jet propulsion and rockets.

SECTION VII

Maps

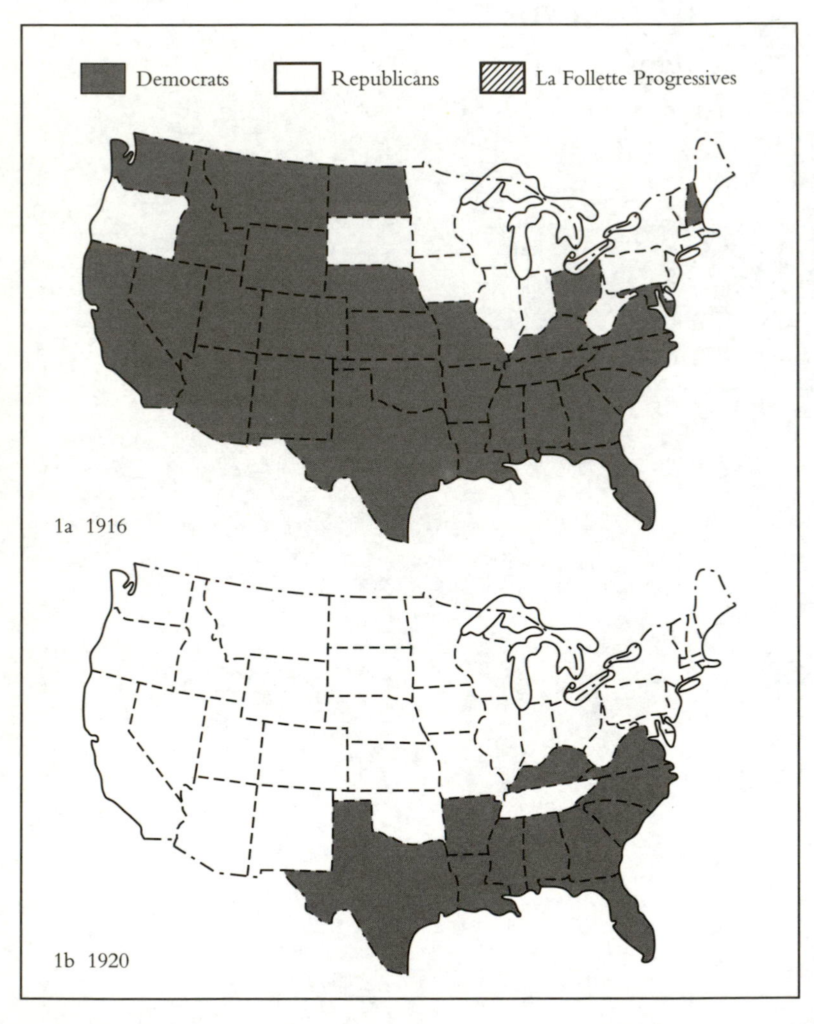

1 The Presidential Elections, 1916–44
Source: Samuel Lubell, *The Future of American Politics* (Harper & Row Publishers, 1965)

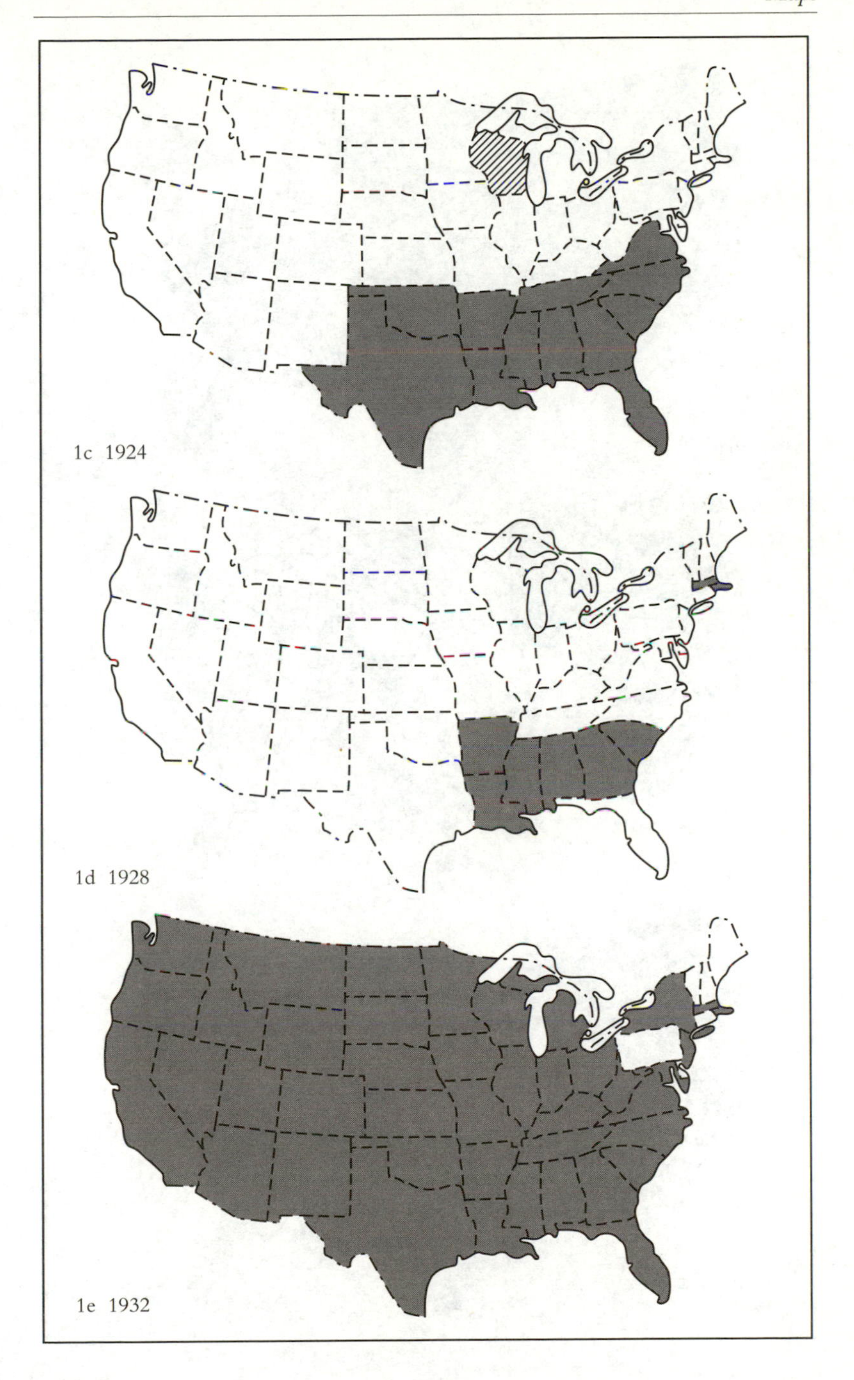
1c 1924
1d 1928
1e 1932

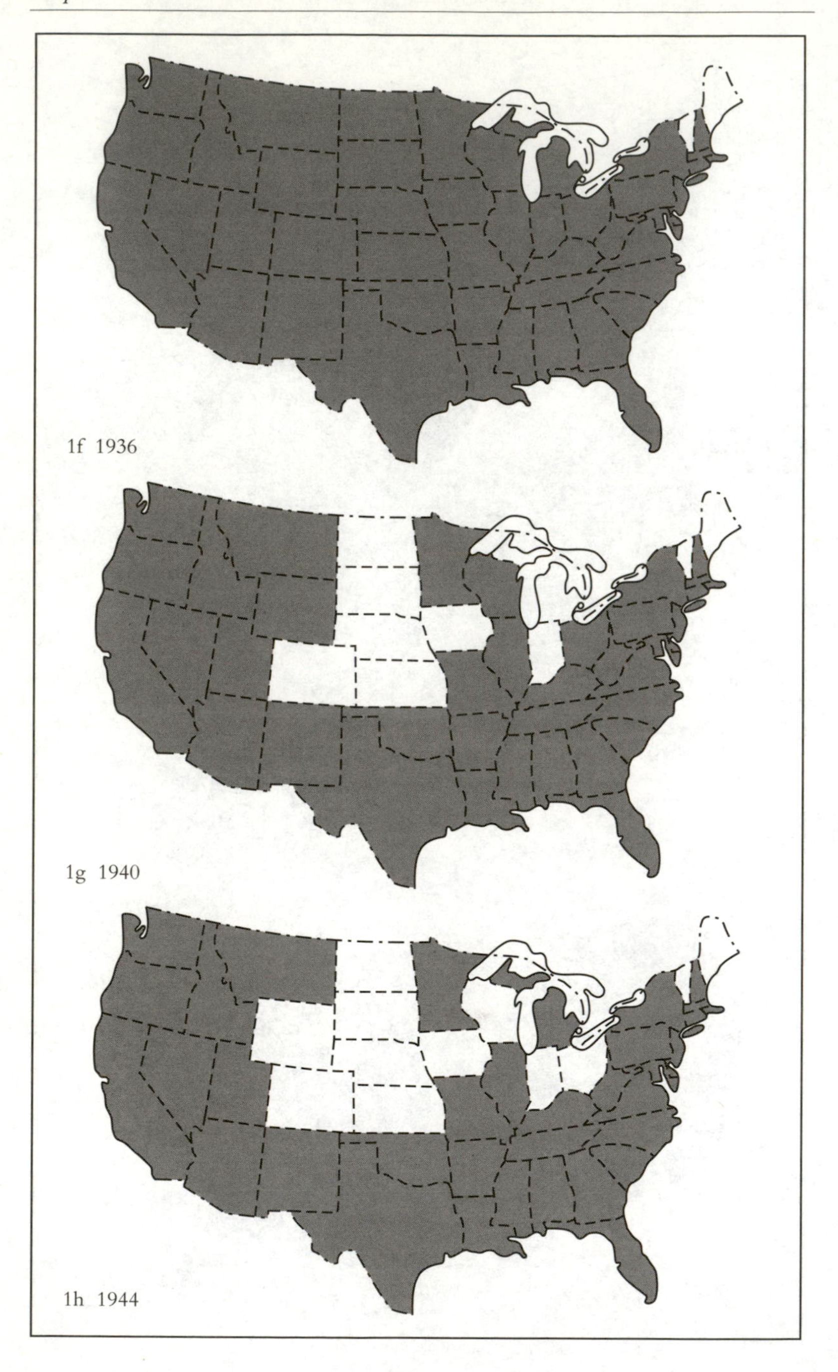
1f 1936
1g 1940
1h 1944

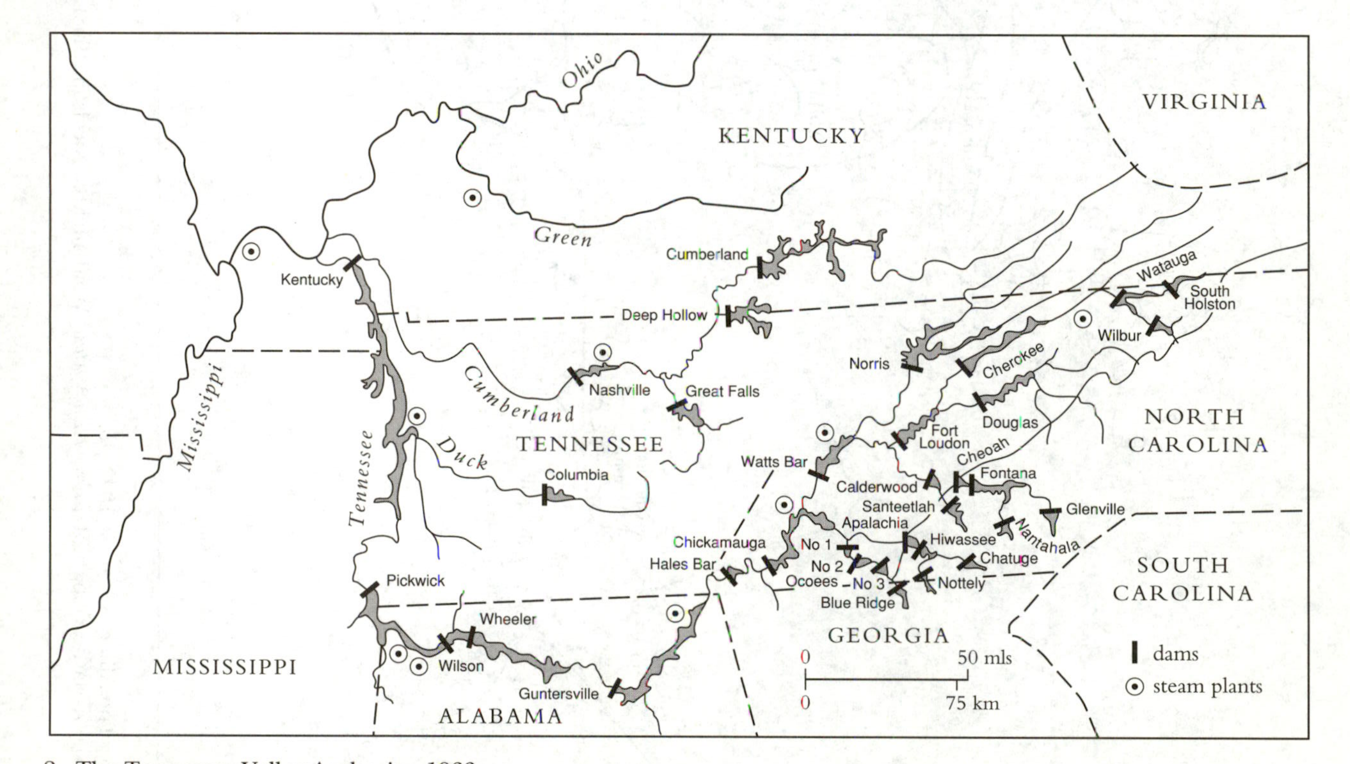

2 The Tennessee Valley Authority, 1933
Source: Martin Gilbert, *American History Atlas* (Weidenfeld & Nicolson, 1968)

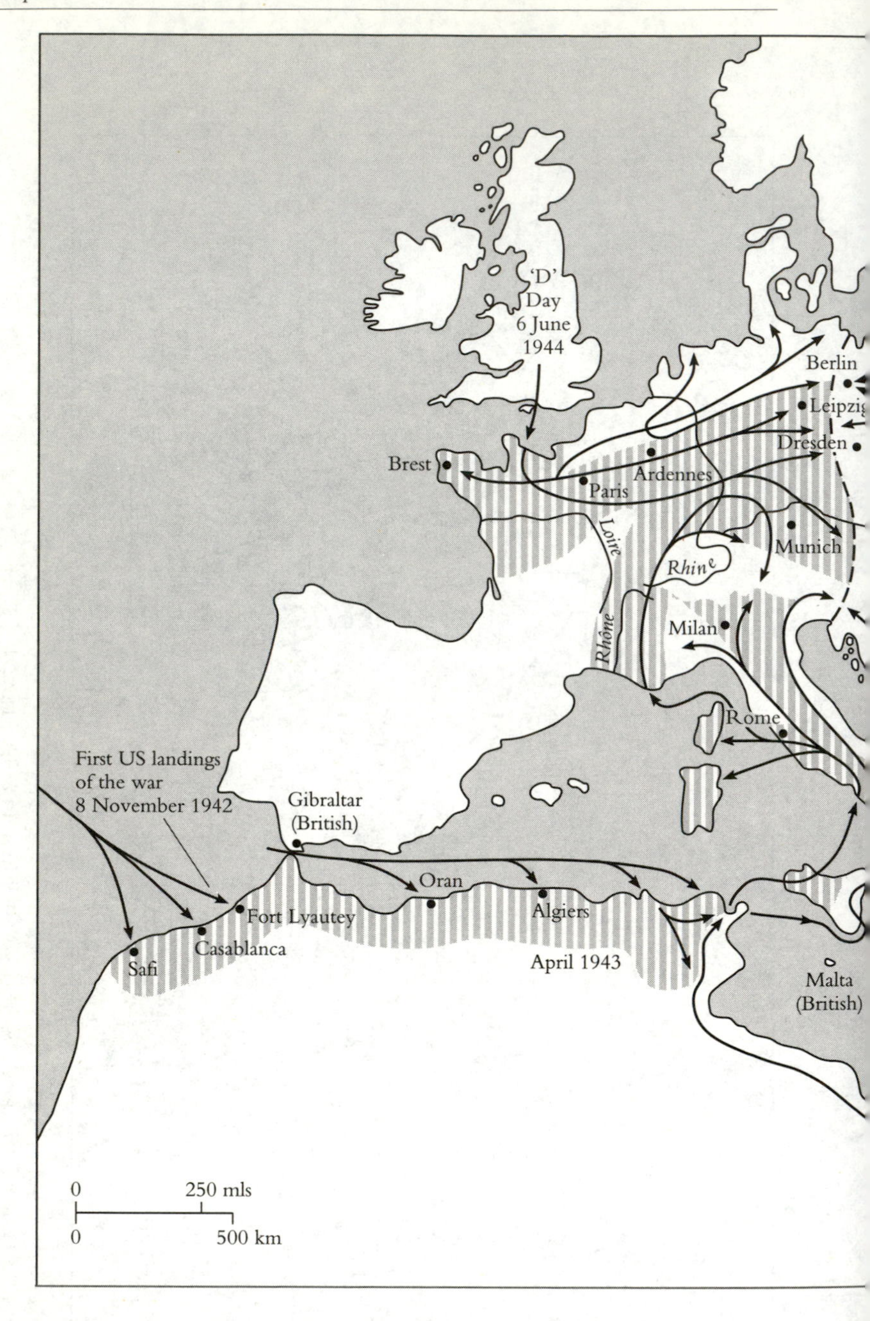

3 The Allied Advance, 1942–45
Source: Martin Gilbert, *American History Atlas* (Weidenfeld & Nicolson, 1968)

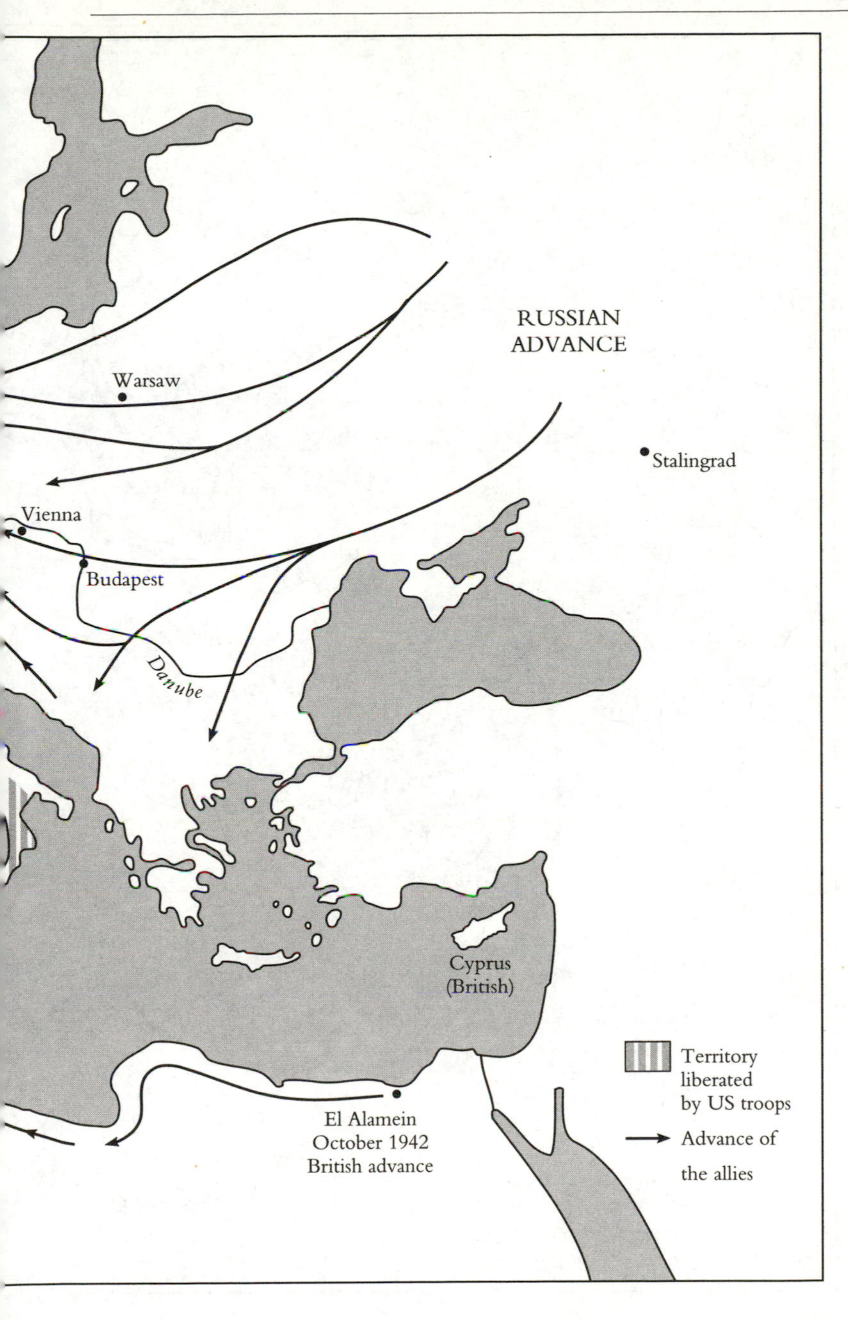
RUSSIAN
ADVANCE
Warsaw
Stalingrad
Vienna
Budapest
Danube
Cyprus
(British)
El Alamein
October 1942
British advance
Territory
liberated
by US troops
Advance of
the allies

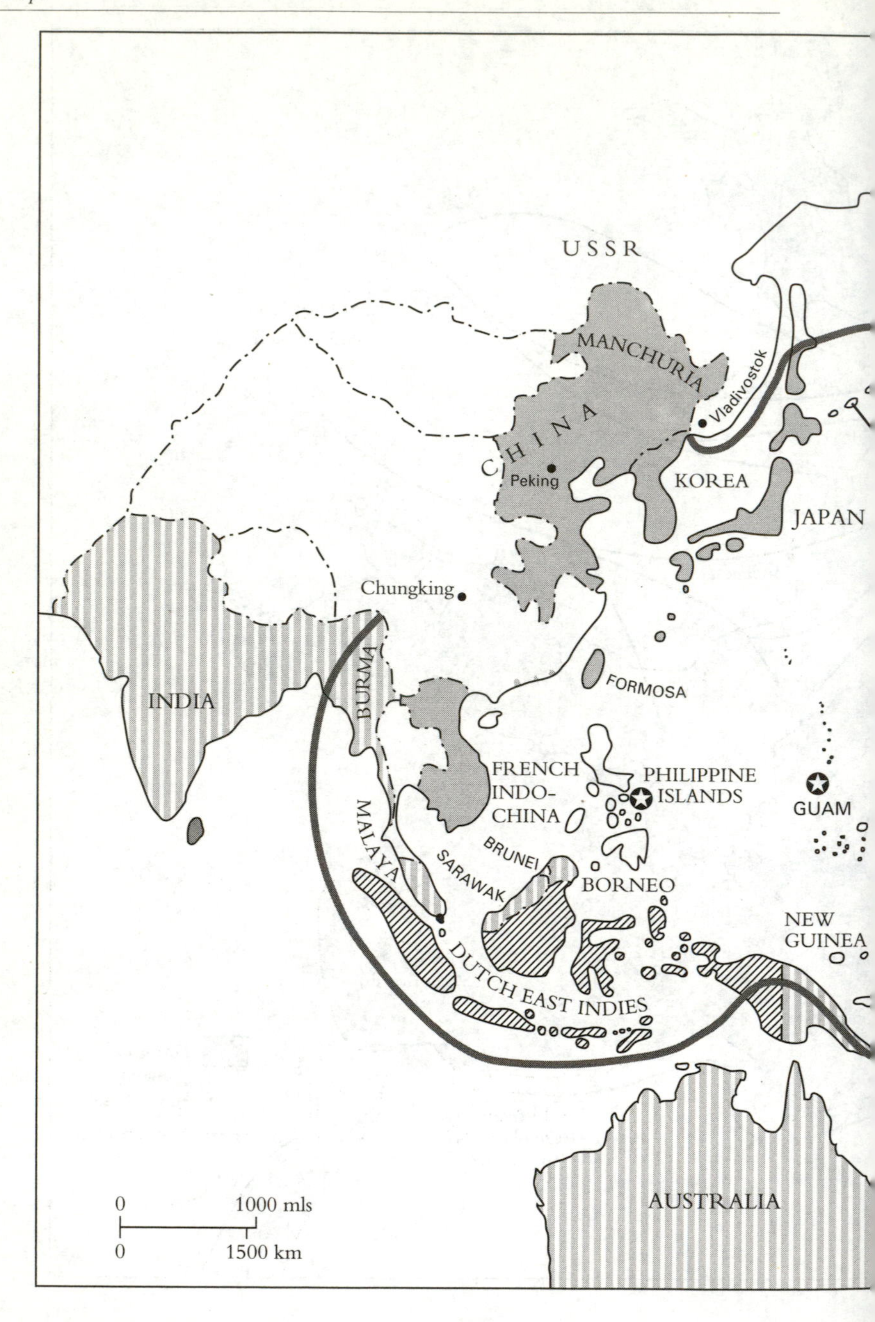

4 The War in Asia, 1941–42
After: Martin Gilbert, *American History Atlas* (Weidenfeld & Nicolson, 1968)

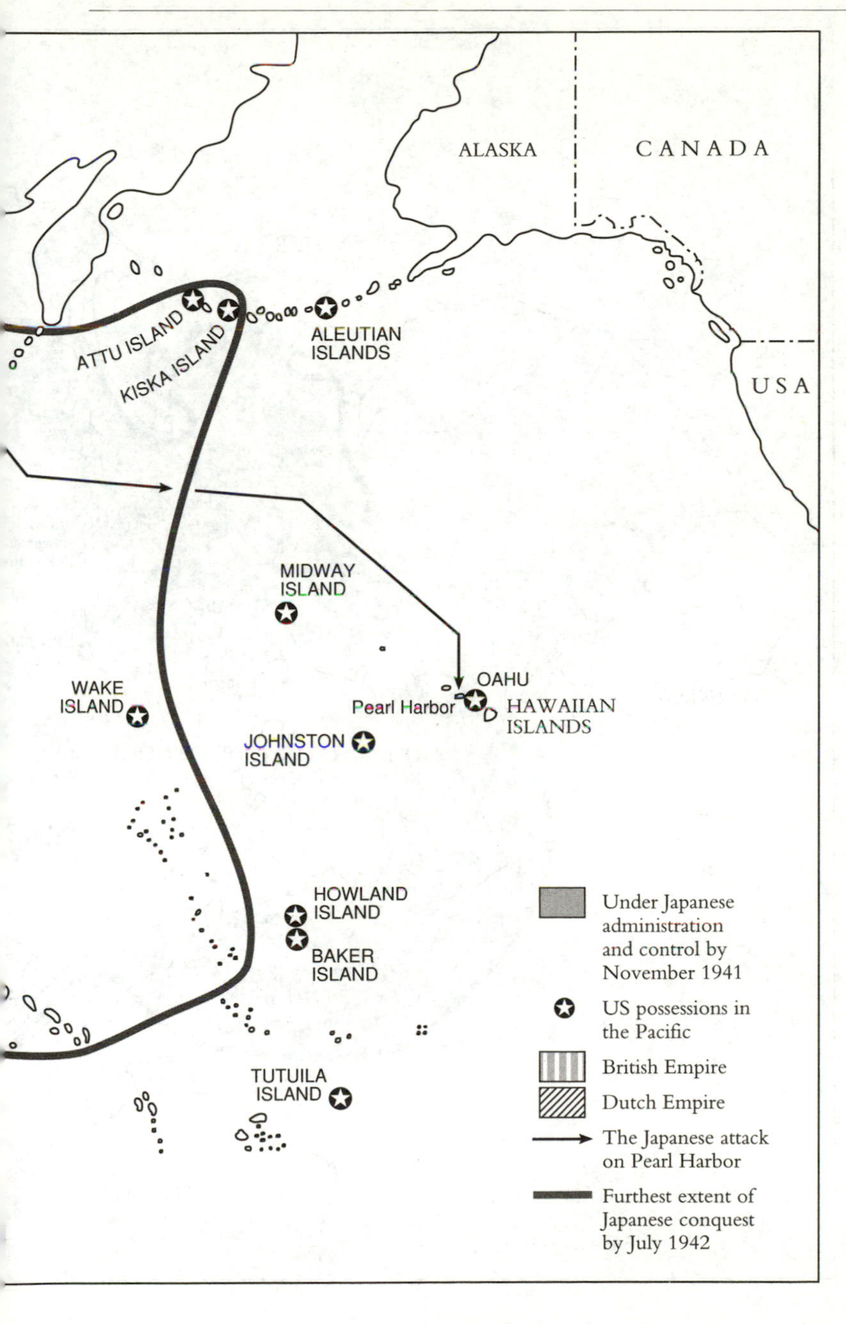
ALASKA
CANADA
USA
ATTU ISLAND
KISKA ISLAND
ALEUTIAN ISLANDS
MIDWAY ISLAND
WAKE ISLAND
OAHU
Pearl Harbor
HAWAIIAN ISLANDS
JOHNSTON ISLAND
HOWLAND ISLAND
BAKER ISLAND
TUTUILA ISLAND
Under Japanese administration and control by November 1941
US possessions in the Pacific
British Empire
Dutch Empire
The Japanese attack on Pearl Harbor
Furthest extent of Japanese conquest by July 1942

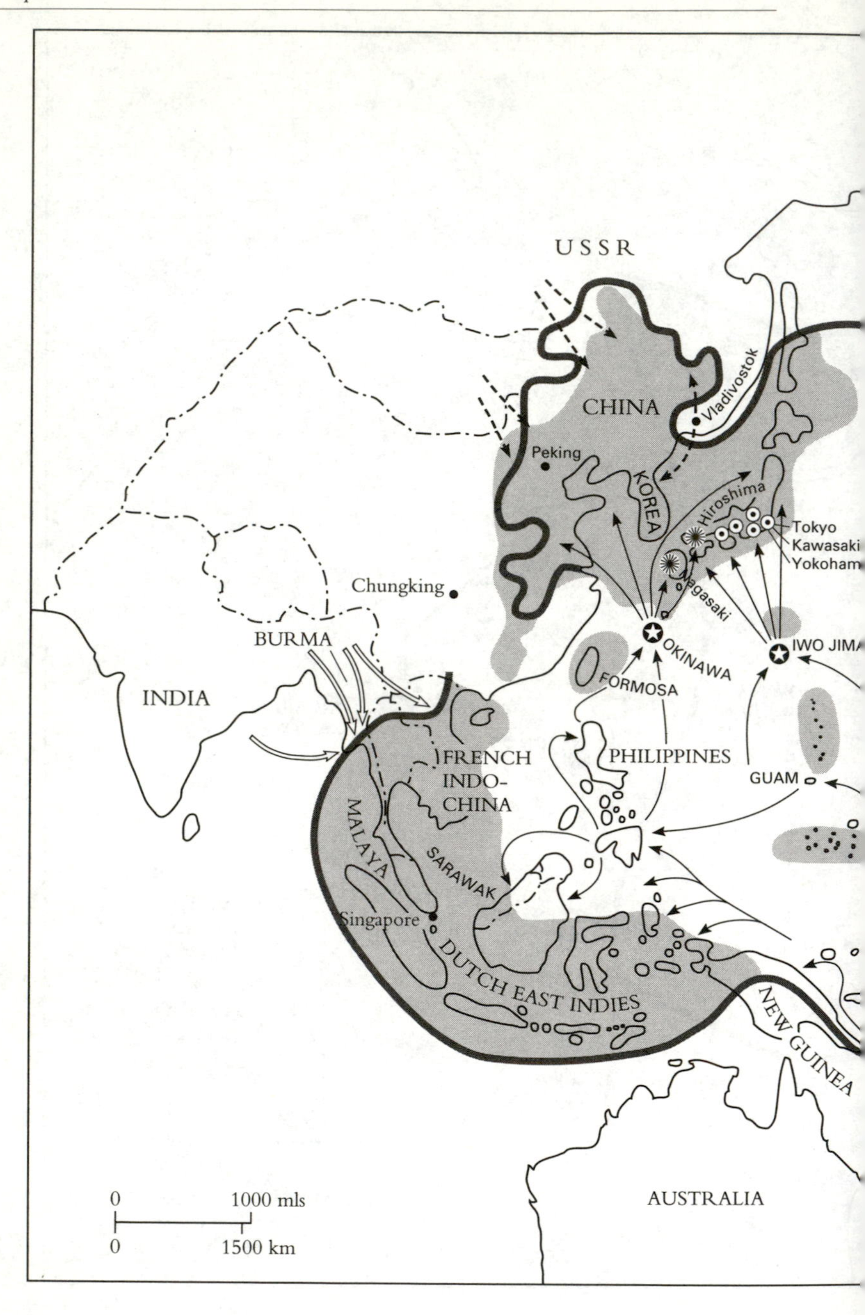

5 The Defeat of Japan, 1942–45
After: Martin Gilbert, *American History Atlas* (Weidenfeld & Nicolson, 1968)

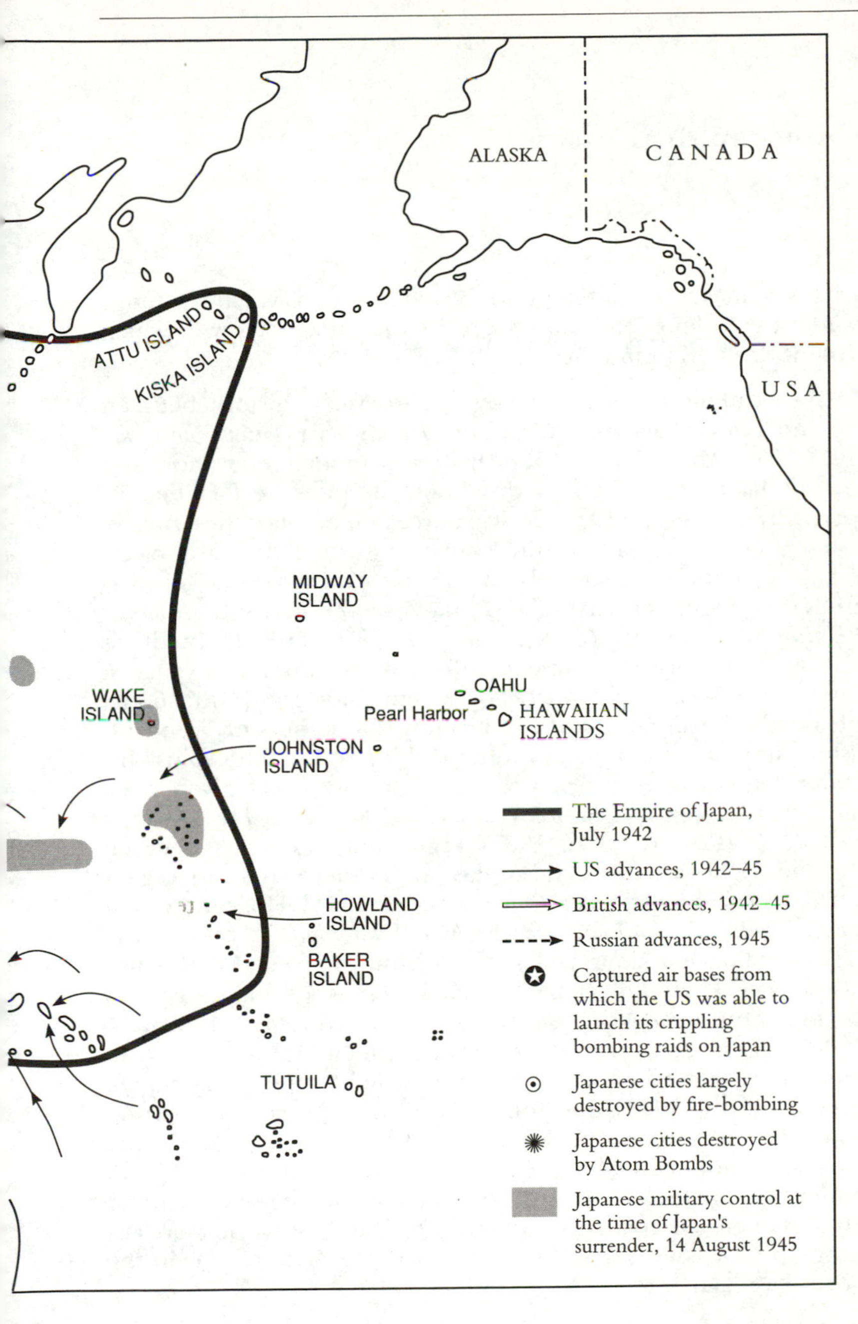
ALASKA
CANADA
ATTU ISLAND
KISKA ISLAND
USA
MIDWAY ISLAND
OAHU
Pearl Harbor
HAWAIIAN ISLANDS
WAKE ISLAND
JOHNSTON ISLAND
HOWLAND ISLAND
BAKER ISLAND
TUTUILA
The Empire of Japan, July 1942
US advances, 1942–45
British advances, 1942–45
Russian advances, 1945
Captured air bases from which the US was able to launch its crippling bombing raids on Japan
Japanese cities largely destroyed by fire-bombing
Japanese cities destroyed by Atom Bombs
Japanese military control at the time of Japan's surrender, 14 August 1945

Bibliographical essay

This essay makes no attempt to be comprehensive, but merely includes about 75 of the most useful books and essays with which to follow this period in more detail.

The most influential single study of American history between 1910 and 1945 is Richard Hofstadter, *The Age of Reform: from Bryan to FDR* (New York, 1955). Every historian of my generation and after has been influenced by this book, despite the fact that its approach now seems dated and its sources literary and descriptive. Though the argument is still convincing its limits are clear: African-Americans appear only in passing, American socialism is confined to footnotes. Arthur S. Link, *American Epoch: a History of the United States since the 1890s* (New York, 1956) lacks Hofstadter's intuition but balances factual information admirably against analysis, and was a major source for the chronologies in this book. Professor Link's lifetime work publishing the papers of Woodrow Wilson and writing a multi-volume biography underpins his *Woodrow Wilson and the Progressive Era* (New York, 1954); Robert H. Wiebe, *Businessmen and Reform* (Chicago, 1968) and *The Search for Order, 1877–1920* (London, 1967) argue that the years between 1910 and 1920 saw the middle class fight successfully to regain control of the political economy; while Richard Hofstadter, *The American Political Tradition and the Men Who Made It* (New York, 1948) contains sparkling essays on Wilson, Hoover and the two Roosevelts. J. J. Huthmacher, 'Urban Liberalism and the Age of Reform', *Mississippi Valley Historical Review*, vol. 49 (1962–63), 231–42 is a seminal article contrasting the middle-class reform agenda with that of organized labour, which came to dominate legislation in the 1930s, and John Thompson, *Progressivism* (BAAS Pamphlets in American Studies, 1979) suggests that the Progressive movement was not united at all but was simply a coalition of single-interest groups which came together around 1910 and then fell apart during and after the first world war. His bibliographical essay is a useful summary of the state of play in the historical debate.

Urban politics became increasingly important between 1910 and 1945 and, of the many studies published, Melvin G. Holli, *Reform in Detroit: Hazen S. Pingree and Urban Politics* (New York, 1969),

Zane L. Miller, *Boss Cox's Cincinnati: Urban Politics in the Progressive Era* (Chicago, 1980) and Lyle W. Dorsett, *The Pendergast Machine* (New York, 1968) are all useful. Allen Davis, *Spearheads for Reform: The Social Settlement Movement* (New York, 1968) is the best book about the legacy of Jane Addams and Hull House, while J.J. Huthmacher, *Robert F. Wagner and Urban Liberalism* (New York, 1970) reveals the symbiotic relationship which developed between machine politicians and reformers during and after the Progressive era.

For the first world war, apart from Arthur S. Link's many books, see Robert H. Ferrell, *Woodrow Wilson and World War One* (London, 1985) on diplomacy and David Kennedy; *Over Here: the First World War and American Society* (Oxford, 1982) on the substantial domestic repercussions. For the domestic impact of the peace, see Ralph A. Stone, *The Irreconcilables: the Fight Against the League of Nations* (New York, 1973). J.M. Keynes, *The Economic Consequences of the Peace* (London, 1920 and 1979) is a classic account by an eye-witness which makes compelling reading. Organized labour becomes important in national politics after 1910, and the best general study of this is Foster Rhea Dulles and Melvyn Dubofsky, *Labor in America: a History* (Arlington Heights, 1984). Patrick Renshaw, *The Wobblies: the Story of Syndicalism in the United States* (London, 1967) discusses the colourful IWW, while the best narrative history of labour unions and the working class down to the New Deal, scholarly yet dramatic, is Irving Bernstein, *The Lean Years: A History of the American Worker*, vol. 1, 1920–1933 (Boston 1960).

For the 1920s the most readable starting point is William E. Leuchtenberg, *The Perils of Prosperity 1914–32* (Chicago, 1958), but more political detail can be found in A.M. Schlesinger, *The Crisis of the Old Order: The Age of Roosevelt*, vol. 1 (Boston, 1957) and David Burner, *The Politics of Provincialism: the Democratic Party in Transition* (New York, 1968). Ray Ginger, *Six Days or Forever?* (Oxford, 1974) is a superb study of the Scopes 'monkey' trial which illuminates the whole subject of small-town America in the 1920s; while for the causes of the Wall Street crash and the Great Depression, the most influential account is John Kenneth Galbraith, *The Great Crash, 1929* (Harmondsworth, 1975). Jim Potter, *The American Economy between the World Wars* (London, 1985) is excellent on the economic side, while Samuel Lubell, *The Future of American Politics* (New York, 1965) explains that the true significance of the 1928 presidential election was that for the first time the Democrats won a majority of the votes in the dozen largest cities in America, so anticipating the landslide victories they won in the 1930s.

Prohibition and the Ku Klux Klan were both actively at work during the 1920s, and to find out more about them see Andrew Sinclair, *Prohibition: the Era of Excess* (London, 1962); Kenneth Allsop, *The Bootleggers: the Story of Chicago's Prohibition Era* (London, 1968); David Chalmers, *Hooded Americanism: the History of the Ku Klux Klan* (Duke, 1987); and Kenneth T. Jackson, *The Ku Klux Klan in the City* (London, 1962), a fascinating study of the urban importance of the Klan during its second manifestation after 1915. This was in part stimulated by the Great Migration of black Americans seeking work in the urban North. Gilbert Osofsky, *Harlem: the Making of a Ghetto* (London, 1971), Allan Spear, *Black Chicago* (Chicago, 1967) and August Meier and Elliott Rudwick, *From Plantation to Ghetto* (New York, 1962) analyse this story; while two landmark accounts are Gunnar Myrdal, ed., *An American Dilemma* (2 vols, New York, 1944), with which the modern study of race relations can be said to have begun, and St Clair Drake and Horace Cayton, *Black Metropolis* (2 vols, New York, 1962). Some stimulating essays on black history are contained in Nathan Huggins, Martin Kilson and Daniel Fox, eds, *Key Issues in the Afro-American Experience*, vol. 2 (New York, 1971); and the subject is further discussed in Patrick Renshaw, 'The Black Ghetto 1890–1940', *Journal of American Studies*, vol. 8 (1974), 41–59. Three useful essays on different aspects of the 1920s are: Henry F. May, 'Shifting Perspectives on the 1920s', *Journal of American History*, vol. 43 (1956–57), 405–28; Burl Noggle, 'The Twenties: a New Historiographical Frontier', *Journal of American History*, vol. 53 (1966–67), 299–315; and Paul W. Glad, 'Progressives and the Business Culture of the 1920s', *Journal of American History*, vol. 53 (1966–67), 75–90.

The historiography of the New Deal is voluminous, but William E. Leuchtenburg, *Franklin Roosevelt and the New Deal* (New York, 1963) and Anthony Badger, *The New Deal: the Depression Years* (Basingstoke, 1989) are invaluable introductions. Richard Hofstadter, *The American Political Tradition and The Men Who Made It* (New York, 1948) contains an essay on FDR which (given its date), is written with remarkable perspective (there is another equally good essay on Herbert Hoover). But the great indispensable narrative history is still A.M. Schlesinger, *The Age of Roosevelt* in 3 volumes: *The Crisis of the Old Order, The Coming of the New Deal* and *The Politics of Upheaval* (Boston, 1957, 1960, 1961). For a critical view of Roosevelt by his former chief of staff Raymond Moley, *After Seven Years* (New York, 1939) is particularly informative on the Hundred Days, while Harold Ickes, *The Secret Diary of Harold L. Ickes, 1933–41*, 3 volumes (New York, 1953, 1954, 1955) and David E. Lilienthal *The Journals of David E. Lilienthal*, vol. 1, 1939–45 (New York, 1972) provide contemporary comment by two key New Dealers. Frances Perkins, *The Roosevelt I Knew* (New York, 1964) is a memoir by FDR's secretary of labor.

The crucial role of unions in this period is best approached via the detail and drama of Irving Bernstein, *Turbulent Years: A History of the American Worker*, vol. 2, 1933–41 (Boston, 1970) and Melvyn Dubofsky and Warren van Tine, *John L. Lewis: a Biography* (Chicago, 1977), a magnificent life of the key figure in labour's 1930s renaissance. Walter Galenson, *The CIO Challenge to the AFL* (Harvard, 1960) and Sidney Fine, *Sit Down: the General Motors Strike of 1936–37* (Ann Arbor, 1969) are both meticulous recreations of central episodes. Robert Lekachman, *The Age of Keynes* (New York, 1975) shows how new ideas revolutionized economic policy during the New Deal, while Patrick Renshaw, *American Labour and Consensus Capitalism, 1935–1990* (Basingstoke, 1991) argues that this in turn transformed labour's role from the New Deal onwards. The function of TVA is eloquently defended in David Lilienthal, *Democracy on the March* (New York, 1953) and the role of the PWA in Harold Ickes, *Back to Work* (New York, 1975). For the political crisis over the Supreme Court, see Robert Jackson, *The Struggle for Judicial Supremacy* (New York, 1941) and John W. Chambers, 'The Big Switch: Justice Roberts and the Minimum Wage Cases', *Labor History*, vol. 10 (1969) 44–73, while FDR's most dangerous political opponent is painted in T. Harry Williams, *Huey Long* (London, 1970). The following are invaluable articles on key areas of 1930s history: C.G. Wye, 'The New Deal and the Negro Community', *Journal of American History*, vol. 59 (1972–73), 621–39; J.R. Moore, 'Sources of New Deal Economic Policy', *Journal of American History*, vol. 61 (1974–75), 728–44; T. Saloutos, 'New Deal Agricultural Policy', *Journal of American History*, vol. 61 (1974–75), 394–416; and David Brody, 'Labor and the Great Depression: the Interpretative Prospects', *Labor History*, vol. 13 (1972), 231–44, and 'Radical Labor History and Rank-and-File Militancy', *Labor History*, vol. 16 (1975), 117–26.

The second world war can be approached via Herbert Feis, *The Road to Pearl Harbor* (Princeton, 1950), which was for long the standard indictment of Roosevelt's responsibility, but has been substantially modified by Roberta Wohlsletter, *Pearl Harbor: Warning and Decision* (Stanford, 1963). A Iriye, *The Origins of the Second World War in Asia and the Pacific* (London, 1987) is a more recent account, partly based on Japanese sources, while Robert Dallek, *Franklin Roosevelt and American Foreign Policy, 1932–1945* (New York, 1979) covers the whole of the crucial period of depression and war. W.F. Kimball, ed., *Churchill and Roosevelt: the Complete Correspondence* (London, 1975) contains a wealth of primary material on the complexities of wartime diplomacy, while Herbert Feis, *Churchill, Roosevelt and Stalin: the War They Waged, the*

Peace they Sought (Princeton, 1974), itself based largely on correspondence, shows that the seeds of the Cold War were planted during the wartime alliance.

The domestic history of the war has, until recently, been comparatively neglected, but can now be studied in Richard Polenberg, *War and Society: the United States, 1941–45*, (Westport, 1980); John M. Blum, *V Was for Victory* (New York, 1976); and in two books by A.M. Winkler, *Home Front USA* (Arlington Heights, 1986) and *The Politics of Propaganda: the Office of War Information, 1942–1945* (Yale, 1978). For industrial relations in the war economy, Nelson Lichtenstein, *Labour's War at Home: the CIO in World War II* (Cambridge, 1982) and Howell Harris, *The Right to Manage: Industrial Relations Policies of American Business* (Madison, 1982) show how shopfloor relations were transformed between 1941 and 1945, while Patrick Renshaw, *American Labour and Consensus Capitalism, 1935–1990* (Basingstoke, 1991) argues that war significantly modified the great gains labour had made during the New Deal. Neil Wynn, *The Afro-American and the Second World War* (London, 1976), Karen Anderson, *Wartime Women* (Westport, 1994), David Wyman, *The Abandonment of the Jews: America and the Holocaust, 1941–47* (New York, 1986) and Roger Daniels, *Concentration Camp USA: Japanese Americans during World War II* (Berkeley, 1962) examine important individual examples of social history.

For the military history of the war, Ronald H. Spector, *Eagle Against the Sun: the American War with Japan* (Harmondsworth, 1987) is useful for the Pacific theatre, while Chester Wilmot, *The Struggle for Europe* (London, 1954) is a vivid war correspondent's account of the dispute between the Allies over strategy after D-Day 1944, which should be compared with the superb Stephen Ambrose, *Eisenhower*, vol. 1, 1890–1952 (London, 1984).

Few issues have received more sustained attention than the onset of the Cold War, with which my book concludes. George F. Kennan was long seen as the father of America's diplomatic policy of containment, because he wrote both the famous 'long telegram' from Moscow, warning about postwar Soviet objectives, and as ' "X" The Sources of Soviet Conduct' *Foreign Affairs* (1947), which was vastly influential. For later analysis by historians, see John L. Gaddis, *The United States and the Origins of the Cold War, 1941–1947* (New York, 1972); Walter La Feber, *America, Russia and the Cold War* (New York, 1993); Daniel Yergin, *A Shattered Peace: the Origins of the Cold War and the National Security State* (Harmondsworth, 1980); and Stephen Ambrose, *The Rise to Globalism: American Foreign Policy, 1938–1980* (New York, 1993) – all excellent discussions of a controversial subject, which is handily summarized by Richard

Crockett, *The United States and the Origins of the Cold War 1941–53* (BAAS Pamphlets in American Studies, 1990).

Index

References in **bold** type indicate main entries.